DIGITAL LIBRARIES - METHODS AND APPLICATIONS

Edited by **Kuo Hung Huang**

Digital Libraries - Methods and Applications
Edited by Kuo Hung Huang

Published by InTech
Janeza Trdine 9, 51000 Rijeka, Croatia

Publishing Process Manager Ivana Lorkovic

Technical Editor Teodora Smiljanic

Cover Designer InTech Design Team

Additional hard copies can be obtained from orders@intechopen.com

Digital Libraries - Methods and Applications, Edited by Kuo Hung Huang
p. cm.
ISBN 978-953-307-203-6

For EU product safety concerns:
IN TECH d.o.o., Prolaz Marije Krucifikse Kozulić 3, 51000 Rijeka, Croatia,
info@intechopen.com or visit our website at intechopen.com.

Meet the editor

Kuo Hung Huang is associate professor and chairman in the Department of E-learning Design and Management at National Chiayi University, Taiwan. His current research interests are in the areas of GIS in education, digital library, distance learning, and computer education. For years, he has been participating in the Taiwan e-Learning and Digital Archives Program for promoting the digital library resources in schools. In addition, he distributes animations of the digitized resources to the general public for further disseminating knowledge and culture. Since 2011, he is conducting collaborative projects with a foreign university for integrating digital libraries in classrooms.

Contents

Preface

The invention of paper and printing technology resulted in the widespread circulation of culture, knowledge, and religion. However, rapid information transmission on computer network facilitates the global sharing of the rich cultural heritage and local collections through digital archives. When most people think of digital library, their idea of the term is limited to archives of digital documents. Without a doubt, a digital library is a library in which collections are stored in digital formats, as opposed to print materials, and accessible by computers. The popularized use of the term digital library may have been in the NSF/DARPA/NASA Digital Libraries Initiative to the Corporation for National Research Initiatives in 1994. Nowadays, the term is primarily used for a type of information retrieval system which stores and accesses digital content remotely via computer networks. As aggregating distributed content for distribution, the vision of libraries is not limited to technology or management, but user experience. Therefore, a digital library is more like the definition by the DELOS Digital Library Reference Model (Candela et al., 2008) as: "An organization, which might be virtual, that comprehensively collects, manages and preserves for the long term rich digital content, and offers to its user communities specialized functionality on that content, of measurable quality and according to codified policies."

The contributors to this book are not of the same discipline, nor do they necessarily possess a unified view of "digital library". In this sense, this book is an attempt to share the practical experiences of solutions to the operation of digital libraries. The chapters in this book explore the implication of digital libraries from the perspectives of design, operation, and promotion. In the section of "Framework and Application", four chapters examine the application of digital libraries and then propose framework or design architectures accordingly. In the next four chapters, the authors focus on the issues of operation and provide technical solutions. The functionality of digital libraries varies greatly. For this reason alone, the issues of operation include interactive accessibility of supported information resources, support for collections of information resources, important role of metadata, various services related to their operation, distributed architecture, and network user access. The authors contribute their expertise and experiences to improve information retrieval. In the final part, Promotion and Evaluation, four chapters bring the research focus to the promotion and evaluation of digital libraries. Evaluating digital libraries is a challenging activity, as digital libraries are complex, dynamic and flexible. Because of the gap between the perspectives of digital library researchers and professionals (Borgman, 1999), communities from diverse fields have different viewpoints and approaches on evaluation. Even though no unified evaluation model exists, more efforts are still needed to evaluate digital libraries in accepted approaches.

In this book, we indicate interdisciplinary routes towards a broadly accepted model of digital libraries. Although there is no common agreement on how to proceed to a successful digital library, the scholars and practitioners seek to develop theories and empirical investigations that will advance our understanding of digital libraries. Our hope is that this book will help readers to become aware of the very wide range of methods, to understand the framework behind the approaches, to appreciate the wealth of applications, and to find more methodologies for assessment research.

References

Candela, L. *et al.* (2008). *The DELOS Digital Library Reference Model. Foundations for Digital Libraries*, Version 0.98, Project no. 507618, DELOS, < **http://www.delos.info/files/pdf/ReferenceModel/DELOS_DLReferenceModel_0.98.pdf>.**

Borgman, C. L. (1999). What are digital libraries? *Competing visions, Information Processing and Management*, 35(3), 227–243.

Kuo Hung Huang
National Chiayi University
Taiwan

Part 1

Framework and Application

1

Convergence and Divergence Among Digital Libraries and the Publishing Industry

Terence K. Huwe
Institute for Research on Labor and Employment Library
University of California, Berkeley
United States of America

1. Introduction

The Internet's dynamic impact on society, industries and individuals has been studied intensively across a broad number of academic disciplines. Digital media are spurring both creativity and dislocation in every field of study, as well as the workplace. These forces have also triggered sweeping changes in how traditional players in the creation of knowledge and scholarship operate and interact with each other. "Digital convergence," as it is widely known, invites not only creativity and enterprise, but also new and energetic competition in nearly every line of work (Yoffie, 1996).

The evolving roles of the traditional publisher and the research library in the United States are particularly illuminating as indicators of the ferment that the digital era is producing. These two groups have long enjoyed ties of mutual benefit, but now face radical forces of change, and find themselves in competition with each other—as digital publishers. Indeed, it is now possible for each agent to assume the characteristics of the other: librarians can act as digital publishers, and publishers can add new roles as preservationists and guarantors of long term access to content. Innovators in each group are already experimenting with expanded services in large and small ways. Ventures may involve wholly new services, or more basic experiments that gauge their audience's interest.

The opportunity to assume much-enlarged professional roles and offer services with good prospects for success places publishers and digital librarians in a new relationship, and is causing fundamental shifts in each field. Can digital libraries act as full-service publishers? If so, should they undertake such a path? Likewise, when the lifespan of a work of literature or scholarship is measured in its entirety, publishers can scarcely miss synergistic opportunities that add new functions and skills to their historical areas of expertise. Indeed, other "content creators" of every stripe frequently assume custodial and interpretive roles—much like library services—acting as repository managers, purveyors of social media and online conversationalists. Should publishers assume any of these roles? These questions go to the heart of both the library and the publishing professions. How each group decides to answer them will have a significant impact on the future of scholarship, education and entertainment, as well as the form and function of digital libraries themselves.

This article will explore the recent history and pivotal experiences of U.S. publishers and research libraries, and the prospects for competition or collaboration between the two groups. The crux of this analysis will lie not on industry studies, but rather on an evaluation of the "professional cultures" of publishing and digital libraries. Although commercial publishers and digital libraries are not identical types of organizations, they share many values and their necessary skills hold many similarities. Indeed, the underpinnings of their respective skill sets are closely related. Therefore even though outright competition is a viable strategy, so also is a future based on strategic alliances of mutual benefit. Whatever course history takes, the outcome will have an important impact on both of these information-handling groups as well as the social and technological architectures of knowledge resources.

Sociology provides us with solid theories that evaluate the dynamics of competition and strategic collaboration, and such theories have grown in importance during the digital era. Andrew Abbott (1988, 1991) has argued persuasively that professions that handle related areas of expertise will take advantage of new opportunities to advance their status, whether by adding skills into existing portfolios or by forming new levels of licensure, standards, or international oversight. At the same time, there is also a growing perception that all kinds of digital production occur on a continuum of activity, involving many phases and a diversity of players, reinforcing the need for traditional players such as publishers and digital librarians to look beyond traditional spheres of authority for new opportunities. What is more, theories about competitive motives and their interplay with digital convergence are not limited to sociology; similar theories now appear in business literature, as well cultural debates about the future of scholarship (Ellison, J & Eatman, T, 2008; Tian, et al, 2009; Banks, 2006).

This is little doubt that the technological hurdles to assuming the role of digital publisher have never been lower; the remaining barriers are of an organizational nature, such as the urge to hold onto prevailing beliefs about functional roles and workflows, not to mention pre-conceived notions of how markets or services "should" operate. The present turmoil is both energizing and destabilizing for all established players in the information professions, and conditions are so dynamic that 2011 may bring a host of new challenges for both groups. With these factors in mind, the following review of the cultures and recent histories of these two crucial players in knowledge creation may provoke insights about the future strategies—and prospects—of both groups, whether they may compete or collaborate, and what impact their choices may have on the future development of digital libraries.

2. Competing professions: the new landscape

Digital technology has been rewriting professional roles for many years. This process is dynamic and stressful for the affected groups. Understanding how professions compete for dominance has gained new importance in the digital era, because each affected group must come to terms with the possibility that their own native area of expertise—whether it is publishing, distributing or archiving, for example—may be taken over by a competing group with a better idea.

The current ferment in all professional groups that manage information is one of the best examples of competition for new roles in the digital era. For a long time, publishers and libraries in particular have enjoyed stable perceptions of their roles, but those days are gone and not likely to return. Instead, these two groups (and many others, to be sure) are deeply involved not only in re-imagining what their core services are, but also what roles they may be able to "poach" from others in the overall process of knowledge creation.

Abbott's (1988) broad analysis of the U.S. system of professions sheds considerable light on the relationship between expert labor, technology and organizational design, and offers some explanations for patterns of competition between different professions. Professionals have standing in society to evaluate the important matters of our lives, ranging from medicine through law; they "diagnose" and "treat" conditions and are regulated by organized bodies of their peers. Expert status depends upon sound and irrefutable "abstract knowledge": a set of skills that is controlled by the profession and applied to practical problems. The use of specialized language is one example of how abstract knowledge retains power; engineers or doctors utilize sophisticated terminologies to retain authority over their practice areas. Also with respect to medicine, physician associations aggressively protect the meaning and definition of "practicing medicine," fending off efforts by other practitioners such as acupuncturists to gain higher levels of recognition for their treatments. Professions that lose control of their system of abstract knowledge risk the loss of prestige and status. The height of professional power is determined by licensure by state- or national-level licensing bodies, which confer the official status to practice a profession. This is the case with accountancy, law, medicine and other fields. Professions and occupations that are not universally licensed by government—such as publishing and libraries—are at greater risk of competition from others who may seek to offer their own expert solutions.

2.1 Treatment substitution

Digital technology has created numerous opportunities for the expansion (or reduction) of prestige. Competing groups, such as librarians, publishers or technology managers, may attempt to take over new areas of responsibility, in essence by offering a better treatment than their competitors. As technology influences working life, professional status may rise or fall depending on the vitality of abstract knowledge. New types of abstract knowledge, such as the ability to understand how people use technology and information resources, or how to structure metadata for a digital future, are potential sources of new professional power (Abbott, 1988).

Treatment substitution holds three important lessons for the information professions. First, power, or the standing to diagnose and treat, is best maintained by the strategic preservation of abstract knowledge. Second, constant self-evaluation publicly exposes weaknesses in the abstract underpinnings of professional expertise, which can invite competition. Third, digital media offer new groups the chance to expand their zones of influence, if their practitioner skills provide them with new abstract knowledge. Because of these factors, all of the information professions are using digital technology to gain political leverage and to take new roles in knowledge creation.

2.2 The knowledge creation continuum

Abbott's study of the professions was originally conducted before the most explosive years of Internet growth began rewriting the rules for scholarly activity and publishing. Subsequent research about the impact of new technologies on the creative and intellectual processes of scholarship strengthens his theories about competition among the professions.

During the early days of the Internet era, the Getty Information Institute established useful models for understanding what was happening to the traditional information industries (Fink, 1999). Researchers at the Getty Information Institute identified the "knowledge creation continuum" as a means for understanding scholarly communications. Under this model, all of the various players in the creation of knowledge operate upon this continuum, bumping into each other as they find new opportunities during the digital era. Each player dominates a "zone of progressive release" of knowledge, as creative work finds its way from author to reader. This dynamic process defines much of the action underway at the present time, as authors, publishers, media outlets and repositories such as digital libraries redefine their roles.

Organization studies researchers, university leaders, and information professionals have also found the metaphor of the continuum to be useful. Tian et al (2009) recast the continuum as a "data-information-knowledge spiral," lending the visual image of upward movement. Ellison & Eatman (2008), who wrote a major policy document about the American tenure system, identify a "continuum of scholarship" that encompasses not only the faculty but every contributor to the knowledge creation process. Fister (2001) undertook a study of trade publishing to explore the changing roles of all of the industry's contributors on a continuum of actions, seen with an information professional's perspective.

As the continuum (or spiral) evolves, zones of added value may collapse into one another. This trend is also widely studied, and is well described by Marcus Banks (2006), in his analysis of the shifting distinctions between (and potential disappearance of) "grey" and "non-grey" literature. The application of abstract knowledge governs strategic action; therefore an assessment of the comparative robustness of abstract knowledge among various groups may provide a useful indicator of future success. It may also reveal who is most likely to compete with each other, and which zones of progressive release they will move into.

2.3 Publishers and libraries face blurring boundaries

The abstract knowledge bases of publishers and digital librarians contain many similarities, but they are also distinct in how they perceive special skill. For publishers, the skills of discovering, editing, preparing and selling books for consumers or for academics is a well-understood chain of actions; as a result publishers historically have viewed themselves as indispensable players on the knowledge creation continuum. For librarians, collection, categorization, interpretation and preservation of vast repositories of literature likewise define the core expertise of the profession.

However, digital technology has blurred the distinct boundaries for just where each zone of expertise begins and ends. New technologies, beginning with desktop publishing programs and moving onward through an avalanche of electronic devices and networked information, now make it possible for other skilful groups to offer competing publishing solutions. For example, digital librarians may choose to enter the publishing zone, or publishers may launch new programs as archivists or preservationists of the knowledge they create. The "open source" movement is another example, with universities offering a full-scale publishing alternative to commercial journals. Open source journals are free of charge and compete directly with expensive and respected scholarly journals—a classic example of treatment substitution. Likewise, much of the struggle between publishers and libraries over the past 20 years has focused on price control or access to markets, with publishers advocating for greater pricing authority over knowledge resources and librarians advocating for expansive access, within the reasonable constraints of the "first sale" principle that underlies the book market (Lessig, 2003.)

If information can be managed in new and flexible ways, traditional perceptions of both publishers and digital libraries are also more fluid than they once were in the eyes of other groups (Koenig, 1988). For example, information technologists have competed with numerous strategies to manage information, including search engines, database services, large-scale archiving and records management. These forays into the traditional role of publisher or librarian have been sustained for as long as computers have been in existence.

2.4 New media, new competition

The digital era presents many opportunities for enterprising individuals to reinvent publishing practices. As a result, most information-handling professionals are evaluating their options, using models such as the knowledge creation continuum to understand what moves to make. It is a dangerous and exciting time to be in the publishing industry, and also in the library field; virtually all of a sudden, new agents that range from software developers to authors are able to style themselves as a publisher to varying degrees, or as managers of repositories of information (Regazzi & Caliquiri, 2006). In such a tumultuous environment, success comes from possession of abstract knowledge that can make sense of the new and unknown. In this regard, the creation and evolution of digital libraries is much influenced by what goes on in the publishing sector, as well as in the library sphere.

As publishers and digital librarians confront competition from new agents on the knowledge creation continuum, their responses to the turmoil are instructive for assessing how digital libraries will grow. As conditions change, the traditional beliefs of entrenched players such as publishers and librarians can either help or hinder efforts to protect their traditional roles. With that in mind, an overview of recent history and the professional dialogues of publishing and librarianship follows below, as a preface to analyzing each group's challenges and their prospects for collaborating or competing with each other.

3. Dystopia and distress: publishing's professional dialogue

As the disruptive power of technology creates a diversity of opinion about what will come next, established players typically respond to new challenges by drawing on their known areas of expertise. For example, publishers have responded to the digital era by analyzing the shifting terrain through the lens of market analysis and the benchmarking of sales goals. This approach made good sense, as it served the industry well prior to the digital era. Indeed, as recently as 2003, the U.S. publishing industry's total revenue was in excess of 100 billion dollars, with a substantial percentage of revenue generated by book publishing. Reporting on the book industry in that same year, Datamonitor, a market analysis firm, opined that the "online publishing industry" had not yet materialized, and forecast even higher revenue in 2010 (Datamonitor, 2003). Yet by 2009, the U.S. publishing industry had revenue of slightly more than 50 billion dollars, e-books and e-readers had gained wider acceptance, and industry analysts lowered their revenue forecasts (Datamonitor, 2010).

In the face of such alarming figures, the publishing industry interpreted the emergence of a digital marketplace as a threat to revenue. This initial perception influenced much of the industry's professional dialogue about what would follow. Notably, a market-based system of perception and strategic thinking is based on viewing readers as consumers who purchase books; certainly this is a valid assessment, but as a paradigm, it excludes viewing readers as members of "community" who have many interests in addition to purchasing books, such as social interaction with publishers and authors. The general tendency to view readers as consumers has been a strategic "Achilles heel" for publishing and has persisted for years, but is beginning to break down (Cader, 2008).

3.1 A history of embattlement

Publishers have perceived their industry as embattled for decades, due to a series of destabilizing events that predated the emergence of the Internet. It is important to understand the impact of this long-running and alarmist professional dialogue, decades old as it is, on the current strategic thinking of publishers.

Throughout the 1970s and 1980s, the dominance of the mass-market paperback threatened the profitability of trade publishers. Thomas Whiteside (1981) describes this threat as part of the "blockbuster complex": new rules pushed ever-increasing resources to the production of high-volume bestsellers at the expense of "mid-list" books of interest and value. The mass-market crisis period was quickly followed by bookseller consolidation, as Barnes and Noble and the now-defunct Waldenbooks expanded and began exerting heavy influence through their buying patterns. (Overdorf and Barragree, 2001).

As the Internet and the World Wide Web made all-digital publishing a serious option, Web-based reading alternatives began to grow very rapidly, causing consternation and even panic for publishers. High-powered online distribution services such as Amazon seemed to gain even more influence than their predecessors of the print-only era over what readers would choose to buy. The invention of "digital ink" and the e-book seemed to pose further threats to publisher profits. With sales and market development as analytical paradigms, publishers entered the digital era without adequate strategic preparation for technological change. Consequently, they retained a sense of embattlement, as new agents who possessed innovative abstract knowledge began to emerge—once again demonstrating the process of treatment substitution (Abbott, 1988).

With much narrower margins and downward pressure on budgets, traditional publishing's internal dialogue reached new rhetorical heights of anxiety after the turn of the century. *The New Yorker* magazine launched a Weblog called "Publisher Death Watch," which kept track of downsizing businesses, including individual posts from demoralized staff (La Force, 2008). Jason Epstein, long-time Publisher at Random House and a major thinker of the publishing profession, responded to the growing anxiety with a variety of new business models, including on-demand print publishing, as well as passionate philosophical manifestos meant to renew and uplift (Epstein, 2008). Epstein has been joined by other prominent figures such as Peter Jovanovich, offering a series of roadmaps for survival, focusing on adaptation to new technology and digital rights management (Epstein, 2010; Jovanovich, 2009; Nawotka, 2008). Yet even as new ideas began to flow, publishing staff morale reached new lows. Debate at publisher association meetings often reflected the grim business environment. At the 2008 Association of American University Presses meeting in Montreal, incoming president Alex Holzman declared that "We meet under darkening clouds," referring to lightning-fast technological change, the open access publishing movement, new competitors, economic downturns and more (Howard, 2008).

At the same time, independent booksellers—key partners to the publishing industry—had also suffered severe losses in market share, complicating traditional revenue streams. Booksellers have long enjoyed close (though sometimes fractious) relationships with publishers, and therefore publishers possessed keen understanding of bookstores as their key sales outlet. However since 1985, independent booksellers have been shrinking in number, although some robust bookstores (such as Powell's in Portland, Oregon) continue to thrive. New super-stores such as Borders and Barnes and Noble entered the vacuum left by disappearing independents, bringing different business patterns for sales and returns of merchandise with them. With fewer and larger retailers, the unique process of returning unsold books to publishers for credit has had far greater impact on sales cycles and profits. Under such conditions, reverberations of distress flowing from the bookselling industry carry heavy impact for publishers. When Barnes and Noble, which dominates U.S. bookselling, announced that it may put itself up for sale in 2010 or 2011, the announcement created fresh alarm for publishers (Bosman, 2010, 2010a).

3.2 Core competencies face new realities

The sheer drama of the publishing industry's waves of consolidation, downsizing and new ventures helped to focus the profession's attention on the meaning and value of its core skills and roles. These skills and roles are typically boiled down to four principal functions, although they can vary in name. These roles are Agents; Editors; Design and Marketing; and Sales staff (Fister, 2001). Publishing work begins with authors via agency, and proceeds to add value by editing and preparing an author's work for sale. Each of the functions along this path to market is labor-intensive, requiring large investments of time and resources, and each is also widely held to be an essential, value-added service that no other group can offer at a higher standard. Of the four roles, editing is held as the most durable service that publishers offer (Schatzkin, 2010, La Force, 2008).

The curricula of graduate programs that grant degrees or certificates in publishing reflect several of the trends underway in the marketplace. For example, the *New York Times* Knowledge Network co-hosts an ePublishing certificate program with Rosemont College, and the introductory description for the program is telling as a gauge of uncertainty. It states: "*The world of publishing is changing rapidly, due to one little letter: "e." The advent of ePublishing has launched an era of rapid change, growth and turmoil in the publishing industry. What are these new technologies and how do they work? How will they continue to develop and be used? What will the industry look like in five years, in six months, next week? And what skills are needed to survive and succeed in the publishing workplace?*" (*New York Times* Knowledge Network, 2010).

Just as this description articulates the widespread uncertainty, a closer review of the 36 unit master's degree at Rosemont College illustrates how transferrable the core skills of publishing have become. Over the course of study students learn the principles of editing, marketing, production and more; yet the same curriculum could easily appear as coursework for a career in Web administration, journalism or information science. The ease with which digital publishing skills may transfer to other fields accentuates how publishing expertise is much more widespread than it was just 15 years ago, and that other groups can now learn these skills and experiment with publishing strategies (Rosemont College, 2010).

3.3 Tipping toward innovation

The professional dialogue of publishers is intriguing, given the industry's continued existence despite its many challenges. The blockbuster mentality produced much alarm, but also yielded impressive revenue streams for publishers who could respond with strong bestselling lists. It has also made many authors into multi-millionaires. Mass-market books did not "kill" publishers; instead, they revolutionized marketing strategies. The success of mass market paperbacks spawned the larger-format, higher-profit "trade paperback," which was conceived as a business builder and a permanent artifact for library collections (Epstein, 2010). Big distributors during the print-only era and the print-plus-digital era (as evidenced by Amazon) have also contributed some positive impacts on sales, by creating unexpected top selling titles. E-books, while they are growing in use, still constitute just a few percentage points of total book sales—and book sales, although they have been shrinking since 2004, nonetheless generated more than 25 billion dollars in 2009 (Datamonitor, 2003, 2010). Moreover, 2010 appears to be the year that acceptance of e-book devices and electronic text reading will accelerate in popularity. By the end of 2010, 10.3 million people are forecast to own an e-reader, and will buy as many as 100 million e-books (Richtel & Miller, 2010). With such rapid trends underway, the influential Book Industry Study Group has devoted considerable energy and resources to study the whole of the industry, with a close focus on electronic products (Healy, 2008). Publishers have also have released content in aggregated and topical "libraries" such as Wiley Custom Select, which offers a course-reader solution to professors (WileyPLUS, 2010). In short, the business environment, though fraught with challenges, continues to be functional, and publisher strategies have been evolving at a faster pace (Brown & Boulderstone, 2008).

Although new ideas are being actively studied, staff morale continues to suffer. Attention to the publisher "death watch" and a "rallying the troops" rhetorical style continue to dominate the tenor of publishing's professional dialogue. In 2010, the Book Industry Study Group conducted an important survey of publishing staff, to gauge their perspectives and sentiments regarding new media and e-books. When asked when they expected to see fundamental change in their own functional work area, 31 percent of respondents replied that it had "already happened", and 45 percent said it was "happening now" (Schatzkin, 2010). At the same time, enterprising digital publishers such as O'Reilly Media have countered with comprehensive business models that draw on the full array of social media, creating interactive user experiences that go beyond the book format (Hane, 2010). By 2008, the full force of experimentation and pursuit of innovation had gripped the publishing industry, creating a sense of making up for lost time.

4. Digital librarians: preserving the past, looking forward

Throughout the same eras of upheaval and change, librarians faced similarly daunting challenges. Clarion calls heralding the imminent demise of a proud profession crowded the professional literature of every specialized sector of librarianship for decades (White, 1989, Lowry, 2001). In response, various innovators have explored a mulitiplicity of strategies. Nancy Lemon (1996) argues that rethinking traditional roles enables librarians to climb organizational "value chains;" James Matarazzo and Toby Pearlstein (2010) review the plight of news media libraries and see a history of cyclical renewal, in which existing jobs give way to new opportunities in new locations. Among corporate libraries, a wide variety of bare-knuckle strategies have been put forward, urging librarians to find a competitive edge by offering services that can be demonstrated to boost profits (Chandler & Carroll, 2002). In the public libary sphere, despite straitened civic budgets and the shock of new media, libraries have achieved a degree of success in staying relevant. Circulation, library card membership and on-site use of services are at an all-time high, countering the idea that community libraries are outdated during the digital era. On the contrary, they are more popular than ever (Nolte, 2010). Therefore even as pessimism about the future became a standard feature in the professional literature, a parallel stream of daring and innovative thinking has run concurrently among a wide spectrum of library specialists.

The resulting intellectual ferment has produced new paradigms and new energy for rethinking library goals in light of the emergence of digital technology. Rather than wait to see what would happen, librarians repeatedly took initiative with new media. They staked an early claim on the crucial issue of intellectual property and copyright, working both with and against publishers as needed to preserve the library's public service mission. As part of this process, librarians became more deeply aware of the publishing industry's travails with digital media. This awareness led to greater strategic knowledge about the marketplace. (Fister, 2001; Katz, 2010; Hane, 2010; Howard, 2008).

4.1 Spanning "online" eras

Librarians were shaken by the rapid emergence of Web-based information resources, because they had been important players in the previous "online" economy that was dominated by firms like LEXIS/NEXIS and Dialog Information Services. This first "online" era gave librarians the opportunity to cast themselves as experts who conducted mediated searches on behalf of users such as attorneys, scientists and business leaders. As the initial "online" era faded and the Internet exploded into growth, librarians joined the first wave of Internet e-mail "conversationalists", Web content users, Web site producers, and aggregators of high quality information. They also grasped the importance of creating stable and robust Web portals, which organized and "branded" library-hosted aggregations of databases; such activist strategies stretched scarce budgets while formalizing a Web-based library presence (Howard, 2009). Similarly, the economic upheaval caused by the skyrocketing price of scholarly journals generated energetic responses on the part of research libraries, including formation of the Scholarly Publishing and Academic Resources Coalition (SPARC), as well as active congressional lobbying to protect copyright and "fair use" principles from a runaway marketplace. The same upheaval also sparked a sustained outreach to faculty, in search of much stronger partnerships with the academy's principle content creators. In general, digital librarians have been agents for innovation over the past 15 years, and have participated in the sweeping process of rethinking scholarly communications (SPARC, 2010; Berkeley Research Impact Initiative, 2009).

This lengthy process of trial and error has transformed digital librarians' self-perception. Rather than viewing digital media as a force of dislocation that would bring ruin to the profession, digital librarians have instead embraced it. Likewise, constant downward pressure on budgets forced innovative survival plans to the forefront, emphasizing new technologies (Howard, 2009, McKenzie, 2009).

4.2 Metadata as enhanced competency

Perhaps the most significant advance on the part of digital librarians has been the profession's embrace of structured metadata and taxonomy as a reinvigorated core competency. Even as they faced the twin challenges of integrating new technologies and shrinking budgets, digital librarians participated in the formation of international metadata standards such as the Dublin Core (Dublin Core Metadata Intiative, 2010). Libraries became key institutional members of new groups such as the Coalition for Networked Information and the National Digital Library Federation. Academic librarians experimented with diverse forms of preservation, including digital repositories, e-journals, and increasingly, full-scale publishing initiatives that originate within the library (Furlough, 2009).

Many metadata platforms and languages have been explored, but Extensible Markup Language (XML) has become a dominant tool for managing digital assets (OASIS, 2010). XML is a "meta-language of languages," enabling developers to create taxonomies and metadata schema that are customizable, portable and attached to the "digital objects" they describe. The emergence of national and international standards for metadata, the ascendance of digital objects which are transferrable among collections, and a strong focus on systems interoperability have elevated the library profession to a technical status considerably higher than it enjoyed before the advent of the digital era (Johnson, 2010). Although digital librarians are not the only XML developers—many computing firms and other academics are heavily involved—they have left an imprint on the development stream of XML.

XML-based systems have become accepted across many industries beyond the academy, and now play a crucial role in information management and data warehousing by large corporate firms. XML-based information architectures are essential tools for managing text, images and other artifacts, creating new workflows that are based on the principle of "one text, multiple outputs". This kind of workflow would transfer very effectively to the publishing world, yet the publishing industry has been slower to adopt XML workflows at a universal level. The opportunity to manage digital assets using XML is an important leap forward that publishers have not yet fully embraced, and forward-looking commentators have recognized this shortfall (Ganesan, 2010; Young & Madans, 2009).

4.3 From online repository to publishing platform

The turmoil of the Internet's early years also produced solid initiatives to understand the digital library as a publisher in its own right. Thomas (2006) provides an early and comprehensive road map that offers large research libraries a template for launching high quality publishing services. She also describes the early emergence of online repositories as a new form of curated information resources. Online repositories grew quickly throughout the early years of the twenty-first century, taking much inspiration from the digital archiving efforts of the computer science and engineering fields (Furlough, 2010). Library-managed repositories also grew up with a strong bias for interoperability, which has led to more dialogue about the need for large-scale "federations" of digital libraries, even at the international level (Van de Sompel, 2006, et al).

As these repositories became more accepted, use skyrocted. The University of California's eScholarship repository experienced more than one million downloads in its first two years of operation. "Post prints" and research reports are now also collected in online repositories, and are frequently overseen by digital librarians, or at least coordinated by them. In late 2009, eScholarship recast itself as a full-scale "publishing platform," which drew strength from the reputation of its source—the University of California system. Although this is not the only example of a library-sponsored publishing service with university imprimatur, it is certainly one of the most high profile experiments (SPARC, 2006).

The evolution of library-based online repositories and their current transformation into full-scale publishing platforms is a prime example of how contributors can expand their role and move into new "zones of progressive release" (Abbott, 1988, 1991). Digital librarians' publishing solutions are guided by two objectives: first, to empower authors, and second, to create robust, collaborative blocs of institutions that share expertise and improve access. These are new "treatments" that address the changing needs of academic publishing (Van de Sompel, et al, 2006). Publishers are rushing to reinvigorate their relationships with authors, but to some degree they are playing a game of catch-up.

5. Convergence and divergence: strategies and examples

Recent events in these two fields reveal several interesting trends, not only in strategic planning but also in the underlying thinking of leading commentators. Although there is considerable ferment and thus many trends underway, there are four areas where publishers and digital librarians face similar challenges. The strategic decisions that each group makes in the coming years will have significant impact on their long-term futures.

First, the hurdles to publishing a well-packaged text artifact are dropping rapidly. The result has been that authors, both in the academic and popular literature spheres, now have the option of creating their own digital artifacts without publishers' assistance. Many already manage online presences and engage in dialogue with readers. In response publishers and digital librarians are testing strategies that reinforce their own roles.

Second, the disruptive nature of digital media has forced publishers and digital librarians to evaluate their own native skill sets in a new light. The library profession's core competencies—collection development, information counselling, interpretation and preservation—involve in-depth analysis of information resources. Yet librarians already format, revise, copy-edit and even print bibliographies, scholarly e-journals, festschrift, and full-scale books in many cases. As these content-intensive roles become more important, research libraries have responded by creating senior management positions with titles such as director of digital scholarly publishing, director of digital publishing, or director of built content. These positions carry responsibility for assessing new opportunities to publish, as well as assisting research faculty in doing so themselves.

Publishers also have the opportunity to review what they do well, re-evaluating existing functions to include new services such content aggregation, developing much-enlarged Web presences, taking on custodial roles and offering services for long-term preservation of their own built content. The technological hurdles to adding new services of this nature are just as low for publishers as they are for librarians who are involved in digital publishing. Both groups are limited chiefly by imagination, by perceived commitments to doing "business as usual," and by the high cost of retraining their already-well-trained work forces to take on new tasks in addition to their existing workflows.

Third, both publishers and digital librarians are looking beyond the boundaries of their own fields of expertise for new ideas and strategies. For example, new social media have carried a heavy impact on the news industry, and both librarians and publishers have studied newspapers as a cautionary tale. News media were one of the first zones where readers began "talking back" to the press and contributing substantive new content (as well as trivial or satirical interactions). The Blogosphere has also attracted interest, although it increasingly produces voluminous and cyclical "blooms" of creative work that are followed by inactivity and the formation of "dead zones." This pattern suggests that new media are only as vibrant as the minds that are driving them forward (The Economist, 2010). However, over time the Blogosphere has become firmly established as an effective platform for commentary, news, cultural critique and debate. The Blogosphere's experience implies that longer-term value takes time to emerge as a new technology matures.

Fourth, both groups have come to realize that as digital convergence has accelerated, bold action is required. As a consequence, the pace of intellectual thought that is devoted to innovation has also accelerated. There is also greater acceptance that bold actions may succeed or fail, yet they must be attempted to gain new knowledge and expertise. Both groups show evidence of complex responses to the necessity of taking bold action, because both groups believe that they must protect legacy print programs, whether as book sales or print collections, even as they step into new digital futures. This is a difficult balancing act, because reader and user community loyalty may be challenged as risks are taken.

These four trends illustrate the turmoil, and indeed, the excitement of the times for both publishers and librarians. They also illustrate how each group is operating on the knowledge creation continuum, and how they might choose convergent or divergent strategies when compared to each other.

5.1 Convergent strategies

With respect to convergent strategies, publishers and digital librarians are aware that their core competencies must now include a robust and dynamic "conversation" with their readers, collaborators and user communities. Although this may seem obvious during the Internet era, it nonetheless symbolizes a major challenge for established players on the knowledge creation continuum. New ideas and new technologies, commonly known as "Web 2.0", currently emphasize ubiquitous interaction in a wide variety of locations and via a long list of tools, ranging from desktop computers to "smartphones."

Among publishers, this interactive paradigm and the tools it has spawned have caused a seismic shift in thinking. A book's usefulness is no longer limited to the experience of reading it; it now has a lifespan that can take many forms, involve communities in addition to solo readers, and last for years (Norrington, 2010). In response publishers have launched serious attempts to enter the Web 2.0 sphere. Likewise, digital librarians have seen their print-based mission expand exponentially to include not only the finished works of scholarship and literature, but also the artifacts created by the overall process of creating scholarship, from start to finish. Library responses also include innovative combinations of digital collections and community-building features, such as allowing commentary, running newsfeeds, and adding Wikis to facilitate dialogue.

Publishers continue to focus on sales and profits, and they are experimenting with social media to increase revenue. Two strategies dominate the landscape: narrowcasting and community-subscriber services (Kist, 2008). Narrowcasting refers to the strategy of discovering discrete markets or user communities who share strong interest in very specific literature, and then offering them targeted products that are based on market analysis (Shaver and Shaver, 2009). This approach is greatly assisted by "viral marketing," a common term in the Internet era, which describes how news of events or products can travel very quickly, even circumnavigating the globe in a matter of hours in some instances. Narrowcasting would be paired with general marketing strategies, just as print sales would be complemented by e-book sales, still a small (but growing) revenue stream.

Community-subscriber based strategies also make explicit publishers' new role as their own distribution outlets, joining bookstores, libraries and online firms such as Amazon in direct consumer outreach. Direct outreach is another example of treatment substitution, as it establishes a new zone of service on the knowledge creation continuum for publishers, shifting them further into the zone of distribution and perhaps even preservation.

Recent developments in textbook publishing provide evidence of innovative approaches by publishers and digital librarians, who are exploring classroom teaching aids. It is now possible to print textbooks or sections of them on demand, use e-readers to read them, or purchase printed readers, and the entire idea of how textbooks support teaching is rapidly evolving. Publishers are now perfecting "portal" style learning zones on the Web, which are based on textbooks but include many added features, including unbundled chapters, added teaching aids and accompanying training modules. Interestingly, 55 percent of students still prefer to buy the textbook in print as part of their study plan (Vance, 2010; WileyPLUS,

2010). Meanwhile, digital librarians are also involved in teaching portals, and they have been perfecting e-reserve systems and new formats for class e-readers (bSpace, 2010).

Finally, publishers are beginning to show interest in managing their backlists more along the lines of a repository or collection of resources. However, whether publishers will take up archiving and preserving content remains uncertain. Once again, networked information technologies have lowered the hurdles to creating online archives. But in practical terms, taking on an archival role would require publishing staff to learn new skills, or recruit new talent to join the firm. Early evidence suggests that publishers have not fully embraced the link between the process of acquiring, editing and selling books and the long-term value of archiving the material (Schatzkin, 2010). This further suggests that publishers continue to regard themselves as facilitators of the early stages of a book's lifespan, but not as the custodians of its entire lifespan.

5.2 Divergent strategies

There is a large common ground of shared strategies among publishers and digital librarians, derived primarily from the interactive nature of social media, and how it may be adapted for research or to enhance popular literature. However, the points of divergence between the two groups are pronounced. Divergent strategies flow directly from the history of each group.

Digital librarians are working very hard to preserve and advance the role of managed knowledge resources, branded by the library, as part of the teaching process. In addition to experimentation with e-reserves and e-readers, they are now staking a large claim on the full-service teaching Web "portals." Open-source instructional portals now include a variety of added functions, including the ability at attach related files, images and simulations (bSpace, 2010). They also operate as eportfolios for students that follow them throughout their academic careers, and as information management tools for the faculty. Academic librarians perceive important new roles for information services in these learning spaces.

Academic librarians are also brainstorming about ways to enhance "built" content that is created by the faculty—a key zone of knowledge creation where libraries may assume the role of digital publishers. The opportunities are vast, as pre-publication content creation encompasses the supporting information, texts and data sets that lead to finished work. Strategies to preserve this knowledge base are rapidly taking shape, and they are evidence of innovative thinking about librarian core competencies (Abels et al, 2003).

What is more, the library profession's original core competencies—particularly collection development and classification—gain new relevance and importance as digital publishing moves to the forefront. Metadata schemes are vital tools for managing vast amounts of digital assets. The prevailing scheme, the Metadata Enhanced Technical Standard (METS), has seen heavy involvement by digital librarians; it ensures that metadata are portable and stay attached to a digital artifact, allowing the metadata and the object they describe to migrate over time (Library of Congress, 2010). In contrast, publishers are in the early stages of harnessing XML to manage content more flexibly (Ganesan, 2010).

The most significant divergent characteristic between publishers and digital librarians has been librarians' willingness to enter into collaborative alliances, launching aggressive outreach to faculty authors, building political lobbying groups, and forming consortia that negotiate for better prices. They also have become software developers at their host universities, emphasizing open-source computing (Van de Sompel,2006). Ming-xing Huang (2010) envisions even more broad alliances, called "Digital Library Alliances"—which would enable academic libraries and their partners to enhance digitization initiatives and search capabilities in ways that mimic large commercial firms such as Google. Digital librarians have also sought explicit partnerships with publishers themselves, when a shared goal could be seen. For example, the California Digital Library (CDL) entered into an early agreement with the Berkeley Electronic Press (BePress)—a full service journal publishing solution (BePress, 2010, eScholarship, 2010).

Conversely, publishers' efforts to form large-scale collaborations have taken more measured steps. With respect to libraries, collaborative efforts most often take the shape of advisory committees, which meet with editors and publishers once or twice per year. This has been a useful process, contributing to several significant joint efforts, such as the Wiley Online Library (Wiley Online Library, 2010). Wiley's new "learning space" includes extensive links to library services for training and other assistance in using the aggregation of content.

Digital librarians could afford to choose a collaborative stance, because they have been able to draw on strong relationships with their user communities. Historically, library patrons would visit a library in person, creating opportunities for a direct, personal relationship with well-trained professional staff. Armed with very good metrics on what library patrons actually need and how they prefer to gain access to resources, digital librarians are exploring how to create "user experiences" that reinforce a bond between the library and the user.

Just as important, the library profession conceptualized the digital library as a matrix of content, services and human interactions from the earliest planning process. In essence they have argued that a digital library is far more than a content platform; it is an entire community (Lyman, 1996). For example, facilitating and teaching how to use of information services, whether print or online, is a measurable core competency for librarians. They have argued that technology should enhance human connectivity, rather than replace it, and they have backed up this claim with solid e-metrics showing how people are using libraries.

This assertion of the digital library as community is not nearly as evident in the professional literature of publishing. However, publishers are beginning to reach similar realizations about digital media, and are examining different approaches. As online publishing creates new synergies between print and electronic artifacts, the book gains a broader venue for discovery: the Web itself. Publishers continue to evaluate reader responses to books and related Web sites; and while print books will continue to exist, new zones are opening up for books to grow via Web sites, as e-books, and as subjects of reader forums. If indeed these trends follow their current course, the digital or Web version of a given book may eventually become the "master copy of record." (Kist, 2008).

6. Collaborate, compete, or both?

Digital librarians possess all of the tools and expertise needed to compete directly with publishers. As universities accelerate their plans to create open-source journals and lend their imprimatur to them, digital librarians may take key leadership roles in managing the new archives and repositories, perhaps even the most central role of content owner. If so, they will be building upon existing relationships with the faculty; the two groups work in close proximity and in many cases share research interests.

Digital libraries also share the advantage of their host institution's imprimatur. This prestige enables them to expand their initiatives and to gain institutional support in doing so. This trend is already underway; if it accelerates, the trend would carry multiple benefits for digital librarians (Hahn, 2008, 2008a). First, it would cement and formalize their new role as a digital publisher within the academy. Second, the new status conferred by the role of digital publisher will provide digital librarians with a fresh opportunity to argue the value points of their longstanding core competencies. Third, recognition of editorial work as a library skill will advance the professional status of digital librarians in the eyes of the research faculty and within the university administration.

All of these enhancements to the status of digital librarians within the academy are excellent examples of "treatment substitution" as described by Abbott (1988). Not only is the publisher role being offered by a competing group—digital librarians—it is also being used as a springboard to advance the status of the library profession as a whole.

6.1 Impetus for collaboration

Even though digital libraries' enhanced imprimatur strengthens their chances of becoming effective digital publishers, evidence indicates that they remain quite receptive to collaboration, often proposing complimentary services in dialogue with publishers (Hahn, 2008, 2008a). This suggests that digital librarians could become partners in more ambitious alliances with publishers, structuring them to preserve revenue streams while advancing user access. Such a strategy would serve as a means for using digital media to find solutions to the longstanding problems of the former print-only era, with advantages for both parties.

At present, digital librarians are exploring strategies to manage the entire lifespan of knowledge creation and the materials that lead to a finished work. These include data sets, simulations, and non-text artifacts of every sort. It is also increasingly common for research libraries to manage their own data functions and image collections, and work closely with other campus organizations that are involved in similar work (Whalley, 2010). The role of data manager is being assumed by many innovators, not only at colleges and universities but also at the Library of Congress and other national-level collections.

The digital librarian-as-data manager could be a very powerful ally for publishers who seek to transform their books into extended "dialogues" with readers, including related data resources and coherent and portable metadata management tools.

6.2 Collaboration as revenue protection

Much is made of the "scholarly journals crisis" and the imbroglios, both legal and rhetorical, that it has engendered; yet the crisis has also revealed how the best minds in both the publishing world and library profession view the economics associated with their mission. As the difficult issues of pricing academic journals have been addressed, publishers have also learned more about how digital librarians view the future, and digital librarians have gained a much deeper understanding of the travails of publishing. This could lead to shared understandings and strategic alliances that bring both groups together, as they confront changing markets for academic and consumer-oriented publishing.

Publisher-librarian collaborations will stimulate fresh perspectives about where value is being generated for both partners. Revenue protection is vital for publishers, and need not come at the cost of fair use and related user benefits, which digital librarians seek to protect. Pricing models for electronic publishing vary dramatically, and have been the site of much tinkering over the years. It is unclear at this time which pricing models are going to be the most effective for publishers, as scholarly communications evolve, and consumer behavior changes (Kist, 2008). A digital library perspective on value and pricing could be crucial for publishers as they attempt to create new markets and new revenue streams.

Finally, evolving perceptions of how markets work in the digital era may encourage knowledge creators and providers to work together. Longstanding beliefs about how to sell any type of consumer product are in flux, creating new opportunities to reframe markets for particular advantage to particular players. As a result, many thinkers who study organizations and markets are now exploring new models for understanding business practices. The metaphor of the "supply chain"—which guides how goods or services move forward, from creation to the market—has limited ability to explain how business can operate in a networked and digital environment (Yoffie, 1996). In response, researchers are re-imagining the supply chain as a "web" of relationships, which spreads in many directions, and can create new revenue streams even as established revenue streams fade (Shaver & Shaver, 2009; Yoffie, 1996; Institute for the Future, 1996). The print publishing process is quite linear and so publishers continue to find the supply chain paradigm useful, but at the same time, the web of relationships is a useful means for studying the impact of new media. These competing paradigms may influence how each group forms strategies and views collaboration as opposed to competition.

6.3 Competition and its consequences

There are compelling arguments for publishers and digital librarians to join forces in response to the digital era. But at the same time, modern society thrives on competition and the evolution of the Internet has been heavily influenced by innovation, as well as anticipation for the "next big thing." On one side, a long-term, deeply rooted publisher-library coalition could save both parties considerable time and resources; yet on the other side, if either group devises a matrix of strategies for fully assuming the other's role while preserving its own, that group would gain a whole new level of prestige. The shape and makeup of digital libraries would be heavily affected by such an outcome, no matter which group were to prevail.

Library education provides an example of how core competencies can be repurposed to gain strategic advantage. A career in libraries requires an accredited master's degree, often accompanied by a second subject-area degree. This level of education is comparable to that of most editorial staff. Publishing practices are widely known, further easing the assumption of a publishing role. Digital librarians who work in large institutions already edit newsletters, bibliographies and even book series. Moreover, digital librarians can partner with academics and administrators who have resources to underwrite publishing programs at research universities; as discussed above, this trend is well underway (Hahn, 2008).

Publishers also may see advantage in taking on roles currently found in the sphere of libraries, for many of the same reasons. The rigors of publishing require outreach, interpretation of markets, and management of large backlists. With low barriers to the creation of repositories and value-added "collections" of knowledge, it is reasonable to argue that digital librarians' role in collection development could shift to publishers, along with enhanced public service functions via the Internet. Since publishers understand market dynamics and sales strategies, the arsenal of strategy at their disposal is significant.

7. Conclusions

Publishers and libraries have enjoyed strong links over the years, marked by moments of collaboration as well as competition. The urge to compete has accelerated due to the impact of digital media, and the increased ease of launching digital publishing initiatives. Moreover, both groups have skills within each other's core functions. Publishers are exploring how to manage content over time, and to find new value in their backlists. Digital librarians have overseen well-established publishing programs, often linked to special collections, and this provides them with skills for launching digital publishing programs. Against this backdrop, both groups are evaluating whether their core skills should expand to include roles that encompass the full lifespan of creative and scholarly works.

This process has been driven by technological evolution, and the forces of digital convergence. The processes that govern competition, collaboration or a combination of both have been well-studied by sociologists such as Andrew Abbott (1988, 1991), whose theories suggest that ongoing competition between these two knowledge-creating groups is quite likely. Even though the process of publishing is distinct from the practice of librarianship, the workflows and intellectual activities of both of groups are closely connected. Taken together, they encompass a large zone of influence on the knowledge creation continuum.

Digital media make explicit the linkages between the processes of publishing, and the library-centric processes of information counselling, interpretation and preservation. These linkages are increasingly apparent to both groups, inviting serious study of their future options, as commercial, educational and entertainment markets continue to evolve. The rewards for success in creating expanded information management roles are also apparent, both from profit perspectives and as a means of increasing prestige. The forum of competition has increased beyond the well-known debate about journal-pricing and open source publishing programs, and now includes opportunities for attracting user and reader "attention" with Web 2.0 technologies. All of these factors suggest that publishers—both trade and professional—will find themselves looking at the library field for fresh ideas, and that the reverse will occur among librarians.

With the reduction of the technological barriers, the remaining obstacles are fundamentally organizational or cultural. The temptation to perpetuate known ways of managing workflows may obscure new opportunities for either group to make bold moves and take on new roles. Likewise the personnel expense of adding new functions—such as repository management for publishers, or greatly-increased editorial roles for digital librarians—is another hurdle. If organizational or cultural factors hinder strategic thinking, it is possible that collaboration between the two groups may increase as they struggle to innovate.

Even though Abbott's theory of treatment substitution augurs long-term competition in many forms, the outcomes are far from certain. Strategic planning among both publishers and digital librarians is crucial for creating advantage and reformulating their professional visions for the future. There are three areas to monitor as early indicators of how competition will play out. These include the direction of digital textbook and e-book design and function, since technical innovations may originate from either group; the advance of interactive repositories that increase the value of original creative works; and the formation of new workflow strategies to repurpose existing skills and add new functions. The strategic choices of each group will carry wide impact on the design of digital libraries, and therefore the processes of convergence and divergence among the two groups are worthy indicators for study by all stakeholders in digital library development.

8. References

Abbott, A. (1988). *The System of Professions.* University of Chicago Press, 978--2260-00695, Chicago

Abbott, A. (1991). The order of professionalization: An empirical analysis. *Work and Occupations,* Vol. 18, No. 4 (November 1991) 355-384, 0730-8884

Abels, E; Jones, R; Latham, J; Magnoni, D.; Marshall, J (2003). *Competencies for InformationProfessionals of the 21st Century.* SLA, Inc, retrieved from http://www.sla.org/competencies1997 on July 21, 2010

Banks, M. (2006). Towards a continuum of scholarship: The eventual collapse of the distinction between gray and non-grey literature. *Publishing Research Quarterly*, Vol. 22, No. 1 (March 2006) 1-11, 1053-8801

Berkeley Research Impact Initiative (2010). Retrieved on August 1, 2010 from http://www.lib.berkeley.edu/scholarlycommunication/

BePress (2010). The Berkeley Electronic Press: see http://www.bepress.com

Bosman, J. (2010). Biggest U.S. book chain weighs sale. *The New York Times*, August 4, 2010, p. B4, 0362-4331

Bosman, J. (2010a). Quick change in strategy for a bookseller. *The New York Times*, August 12, 2010, p. B1, 0362-4331

Brown, D. & Boulderstone, R. (2008). *The Impact of Electronic Publishing: The future for publishers and librarians*, Saur, 978-3-598-11515-8, Munich

bSpace (2010). Retrieved on September 2, 2010 from http://ets.berkeley.edu/bspace

Cader, M. (2008). Innovation is iteration: Thinking next to the box. *Publisher Research Quarterly*, Vol. 24, No. 4 (December 2008) 240-250, 1053-8801

Chandler, Y., & Carroll, C. (2002). Libraries and librarians: The key to growth and survival? The relationship between corporate productivity and information services. *INSPEL*, Vol. 36, No. 4 (December, 2002) 223-254, 0019-0217

Datamonitor (2003). *Publishing in the United States*. Retrieved from http://www.datamonitor.com

Datamonitor (2010). *Publishing in the United States*. Retrieved from http://www.datamonitor.com

Dublin Core Metadata Initiative (2010). See http://www.dublincore.org, retrieved on July 26, 2010

The Economist (2010). The empire slips away. *The Economist*, Vol. 395, No. 8688 (June 24-July 2, 2010) 62, 0013-0613

Ellison, J and Eatman, T. (2008). *Scholarship in Public: Knowledge Creation and Tenure Policy in the Engaged University*. Syracuse, NY, Imagining America, retrieved on August 3, 2010 from http://www.imaginingamerica.org/TTI/TTI_FINAL.pdf

Epstein, J. (2008). The end of the Gutenberg era. *Library Trends*, Vol. 57, No. 1 (Summer 2008) 8-16, 0024-2594

Epstein, J. (2010). Publishing: The revolutionary future. *New York Review of Books*, Vol. 57,No. 4 (March 11, 2010) 1-2, 0028-7504

eScholarship (2010). See http://escholarship.org/uc/ucias, retrieved on July 28, 2010

Furlough, M. (2009). What we talk about when we talk about repositories. *Reference & User Services Quarterly*, Vol. 49, No. 1 (Fall 2009) 18-32, 1094-9054

Fink, E. (1999). The Getty Information Institute: A retrospective. *D-Lib Magazine*, Vol. 5, No.3, (March 1999), 1082-9873. Retrieved from http://www.dlib.org/dlib/march99/fink/03fink.html on July 21, 2010

Fister, B. (2001). Trade publishing: A view from the front. *portal: Libraries and the Academy*, Vol. 1, No. 4 (2001) 509-523, 1530-7131

Ganesan, D. (2010). The best reason for re-engineering book publishing—the need for XML. *TeleRead* (2010). Retrieved from http://teleread.com/2010/01/20

Hahn, K. (2008). Publishing services: An emerging role for libraries. *Educause Review*, Vol. 43, No. 6 (November/December 2008), 1527-6619

Hahn, K. (2008a). *Research library publishing services: New options for university publishing*. Association of Research Libraries, Washington, DC. Retrieved from http://www.arl.org/bm~doc/research-library-publishing-services.pdf

Hane, P. (2010). Eye on O'Reilly, OpenCourseWare, Ebooks, Blio and More. *Information Today,* Vol 27, No. 5 (May 2010) 7-11, 8755-5286

Healy, M. (2008). Experimentation and innovation in U.S. publishing today: Findings from the Book Industry Study Group. *Publisher Research Quarterly,* Vol. 24, No. 4 (December 2008) 233-239, 1053-8801

Howard, J. (2008). Scholarly presses discuss how they're adapting to a brave new e-world. *Chronicle of Higher Education,* Vol. 54, No. 44 (July 11, 2008), 0009-5982

Howard, J. (2009). Libraries explore big ideas to overcome small budgets. *Chronicle of Higher Education,* November 22, 2009, retrieved on July 30 from http://chronicle.com/article/Libraries-Explore-Big-Ideas/49227/, 0009-5982

Huang, M., Xing, C., & Zhang, y. (2010) Supply chain management model for digital libraries. *The Electronic Library,* Vol. 28, No. 1 (2010) 29-37, 0264-0473

Institute for the Future (1996). *Twenty-First Century Organizations: Reconciling Control and Empowerment.* Institute for the Future, Menlo Park, CA.

Johnson, M (2010). *The Book is Overdue: How Librarians and Cybrarians Can Save Us All.* Harper, 978-0061431609, New York

Jovanovich, Peter. (2009). Publishing in hard times. *Publisher Research Quarterly,* Vol. 25, No. 2 (June 2009) 67-72, 1053-8801

Katz, R. (2010). Scholars, scholarship, and the scholarly enterprise in the digital age. *Educause Review,* Vol. 45, No. 2 (March/April 2010) 44-56. 1527-6619

Kist, J. (2008) *New Thinking for 21st-century Publishers: Emerging Patterns and Evolving Strategems.* Chandos, 978-1-84334 445-2, Oxford, UK

La Force, T. (2008). Publishing death watch. *The Book Bench: Loose Leafs from the New Yorker Book Department,* December 5, 2008. Retrieved on July 21, 2010 from http://www.newyorker.com/online/blogs/books/2008/12/publishing-titl.html

Lemon, N. (2006). Climbing the value chain: A case study in rethinking the corporate library. *ONLINE,* Vol. 50, No. 10 (November-December, 2006) 50-55, 0146-5422

Lessig, L. (2005). The people own ideas! *Technology Review* Vol. 108, No. 6 (Winter, 2005) 46-53, 0040-1692

Library of Congress (2010). Metadata Encoding and Transmission Standard: Primer. http://www.loc.gov/standards/mets/METSPrimerRevised.pdf

Lowry, C. (2001). "The more things change…" *portal: Libraries and the academy,* Vol. 1, No. 4 (2001) 7-9, 1530-7131

Lyman, P. (1996). What is a Digital Library? Technology, Intellectual Property and the Public Interest." *Daedalus, Journal of the American Academy of Arts and Sciences,* Vol. 125, No. 4 (Fall 1996) 1-33, 0011-5266

MacDonald, S & Uribe, L. (2008). Libraries in the converging worlds of open data, e-research, and Web 2.0. *Online,* Vol. 32, No. 2 (March 2008), PAGES, 0146-5422

McKenzie, J, Dekker, H., Ford, G., Hurley, B., de Lorenzo, D., Ogden, B., Phillips, M., Stanton, T., Xue, S. (2009). Digital Collection Development Task Force: Final Report. Retrieved on July 28, 2010 from http://lib.berkeley.edu/Collections/pdfs/ digital_collection_development_plan.pdf

Matarazzo, J. & Pearlstein, T. (2010). Survival lessons for libraries: Staying afloat in turbulent times. *Searcher,* Vol. 18, No. 4 (May, 2010) 48-53, 1070-4795

Nash, R. (2010). Publishing 2020. *Publisher Research Quarterly,* Vol. 26, No. 2 (June 2010) 114-118, 1053-8801

New York Times Knowledge Network (2010). Retrieved from http://www.nytimes knowhow.com.index.php/epublishing-certificate-program on August 30, 2010

Nolte, C. Print is not dead. *San Francisco Chronicle,* August 15, 2010, p. A2. 1932-8672

Nowatka, E. (2008). Our digital future. *Publisher Research Quarterly*, Vol 24, No. 3 (September 2008) 124-128, 1053-8801

Norrington, A. (2010). Harnessing 'e' in Storyworlds: Engage, enhance, experience, entertain. *Publisher Research Quarterly*, Vol. 26, No. 2 (June 2010) 96-105, 1053-8801

OASIS: Organization for the Advancement of Structured Information Standards (2010). See http://www.oasis-open.org/who/

Overdorf, M & Barragree, A. (2001). The impending disruption of the publishing industry. *Publishing Research Quarterly*, Vol. 17, No. 3 (Fall 2001) 3-18, 1053-8801

Regazzi, J & Caliguiri, N. (2006). Publisher and author partnerships: A changing landscape. *Learned Publishing*, Vol. 19, No. 3 (July 2006), 183-192, 0953-1513

Richtel, M, & Miller, C.M. Of two minds about books. *The New York Times*, September 2, 2010, p. B1, 0362-4331

Rosemont College (2010). Graduate Publishing Program. Retrieved on August 30, 2010 from http://www.rosemont.edu/gps2/graduate/academics/publishing/study.php

Shatzkin, M. (2010). BISG's Making Information Pay 2010: Selected Survey Results. Retrieved on July 27, 2010 from http://ww.bisg.org/contentweb/papers mip2010

Shaver D. & Shaver, A.S. (2009). Books and digital technology: A new industry model. *Journal of Media Economics*, Vol. 16, No. 2 (November 2009) 71-86, 0899-7764

SPARC (2006). *SPARC Innovator: University of California (July 2006.* Scholarly Publishing and Academic Resource Coalition, retrieved on August 3, 2010 from http://www.arl.org/sparc/innovator/uc.shtml

SPARC (2010). Scholarly Publishing and Academic Resource Coalition. Retrieved from http://www.arl.org/sparc/about/index.shtml

Thomas, S. (2006). Publishing solutions for contemporary scholars: The library as innovator and partner. *Publishing Research Quarterly*, Vol. 22, No. 2 (Summer 2006) 27-37, 1053-8801

Tian, J., Nakamori, Y., & Wierzbicki, A. (2009). Knowledge management and creation in academia: A study based on surveys in a Japanese research university. *Journal of Knowledge Management*, Vol. 13, No. 2 (March 2009) 76-92, 1367-3270

Vance, A (2010). $200 text vs. free. *The New York Times*, August 1, 2010, B3, 0362-4331

Van de Sompel, H., Lagoze, C., Bekaert, J., Liu, X., Payette, S., & Warner, S. (2006). An interoperable fabric for scholarly value chains. *D-Lib Magazine*, Vol. 12, No. 10 (October, 2006), 1082-9873. Retrieved from http://www.dlib.org/back2006.html

Whalley, B. (2010). E-Books and E-Content 2010: Data as Content. *Ariadne*, Vol. 64 (July 2010). 1361-3200. Retrieved on August 20, 2010 from http://www.ariadne.ac.uk/issue64/ebooks-uci-2010-rpt

White, H. (1989). The quiet revolution: A profession at the crossroads. *Special Libraries*, Vol. 80 (Winter 1989) 24-30, 0038-6723

Whiteside, T. (1981). *The Blockbuster Complex: Conglomerates, Show Business, and Book Publishing.* Wesleyan University Press, Middletown, CT, 0819550574

Wiley Online Library (2010). Retrieved on August 30, 2010 from http://olabout.wiley.com/WileyCDA/Section/id-390001.html

WileyPLUS (2010). John Wiley and Sons, Inc. Retrieved from http://www. http://catalog.wileyplus.com/Section/id-402217.html on July 29, 2010

Yoffie, D. (1996). Competing in the age of digital convergence. *California Management Review*, Vol. 38, No. 4 (Summer 1996) 31-53, 0008-1256

Young, D & Madans, P. (2008). XML: Why bother? *Publishing Research Quarterly*, Vol. 25, No. 5 (September 2008) 147-153, 1053-8801

2

Integrated Information Access Technology for Digital Libraries: Access across Languages, Periods, and Cultures

Biligsaikhan Batjargal,[1] Garmaabazar Khaltarkhuu,[2]
Fuminori Kimura[1] and Akira Maeda[1]
[1]*Ritsumeikan University*
[2]*Mongolia-Japan Center for Human Resources Development*
[1]*Japan*
[2]*Mongolia*

1. Introduction

Physical libraries store materials written in various languages, at various periods in history, and dealing with various cultures. As a result, large digital library projects such as Europeana, World Digital Library, HathiTrust, and Google Book Search have collections spanning different languages, periods, and cultures. This diversity complicates information access, in part because the grammars, vocabularies, and scripts of languages usually change significantly over time.

This chapter presents our approach to providing cross-language access that accounts for this evolution of languages over periods ranging from ancient to modern and even considers cultural differences. It also presents our method for providing integrated access to multiple digital libraries, archives, and museums by automatically mapping between different metadata schemas. In section 2, we present the traditional Mongolian script digital library. Our proposed method for Cross-period information retrieval from ancient Japanese historical Materials is discussed in section 3. Later, in section 4, we introduce the federated searching system for humanities databases using automatic metadata mapping.

2. Traditional Mongolian script digital library

In recent years the importance of digital cultural heritage preservation has been increasing in the Asia-Pacific region as well as worldwide. This section provides a summary of the recent achievements of the Traditional Mongolian Script Digital Library (TMSDL) (Khaltarkhuu et al, 2007; Khaltarkhuu et al, 2008), which aims to preserve over 800 years of historical records written in traditional Mongolian for future use and to make them available for public viewing. There are over 50,000 registered manuscripts and historical records written in traditional Mongolian script stored in the National Library of Mongolia. About 21,100 of them are handwritten documents and over 9400 of those are related to the history of Mongolia (Tungalag, 2005). Despite the importance of keeping old historical materials in good conditions, the Mongolian environment for material storage is not suitable for keeping historical records for a long time (Tungalag, 2005). An efficient and effective way to preserve and protect materials of historical importance while making them publicly available is to digitize them and create a digital library.

Mongolian is spoken by most of the Mongolian population as well as by Inner Mongolians and other groups of people who live in several provinces of China and the Russian Federation. It is one of the many languages of the Mongol-Altaic family.

Mongolians have used numerous writing systems, and traditional Mongolian script is the longest surviving script. Although the Mongolian language has also been written in Chinese characters, Phags-pa script, Soyombo script, Horizontal square script, Latin, and Cyrillic script (Shagdarsuren, 2001), by the end of the 20th century the traditional Mongolian script had made an official, government-decreed return. At the result, modern Mongolian language has two distinct writing systems: Cyrillic and traditional Mongolian.

The sounds of words changed as the Mongolian language evolved, but the spelling remained unchanged. Thus was created a difference between written Mongolian and spoken Mongolian. However, in 1946 in Mongolia the Cyrillic script was adopted with two additional characters. At that time the spelling of modern Mongolian in the Cyrillic alphabet was based on the pronunciation of the dialect spoken by the Khalkha, a subgroup of the Mongols. This was a radical change and alienated the Mongolian people from their culture and historical archives written in traditional Mongolian script. Traditional Mongolian script preserves a more ancient language and reflects the Mongolian language spoken in the ancient period, while modern Mongolian reflects pronunciation differences in modern dialects. Traditional Mongolian is a distinct dialect with grammar different from that of modern Mongolian. The traditional Mongolian script is written vertically, from top to bottom, in columns advancing from left to right. This script is the writing system for the Mongolian language and has four derivative scripts: Todo, Manchu, Vaghintara, and Sibe (Xibe). The Todo script was used by the Oirats and Kalmyks, and the Manchu script was a writing system in the Qing dynasty. The Sibe script is used in Xinjiang, in the northwest of China. The Vaghintara script was used by the Buryats. Like Arabic, traditional Mongolian is a contextual script where letters are cursively joined and have initial, medial, and final presentation forms for the same letter. In most cases the letters join together along a vertical stem, but in the case of certain consonants that lack a trailing vertical stem they may form a single ligature with a following vowel. In addition to these cursive and positional forms, many letters also have variant forms used in accordance with spelling and grammatical rules.

Using modern Mongolian to retrieve information from traditional Mongolian documents is not a simple task because the Mongolian language has changed substantially over time. The traditional Mongolian script digital library (TMSDL) (Khaltarkhuu et al, 2007; Khaltarkhuu et al, 2008), which is based on Greenstone Digital Library Software (GSDL) and accepts modern Mongolian query input, will help the user access materials written in traditional Mongolian.

2.1 Ancient-to-modern information retrieval

Thanks to advances in innovative information technologies and to the popularity of the Internet, many ancient historical documents are being digitized and made publicly available. We therefore want to offer an "ancient-to-modern information retrieval" method (Batjargal et al., 2010a; Batjargal et al., 2010b) that considers language differences over time. We aimed to develop a retrieval system with which a user can access cross-period and cross-script ancient document databases by using a query in a modern language.

There has been little research on information retrieval techniques for historical documents, and almost none of the breakthroughs in research on information retrieval and information access have aimed at retrieving information in the native language from ancient, cross-period and/or cross-script foreign language documents.

Few approaches that could be considered a cross-period information retrieval have been proposed (Ernst-Gerlach & Fuhr, 2007; Koolen et al., 2006; Gotscharek et al., 2009; Hauser et al.,2007; Pilz et al., 2008), and there has been little research on information retrieval techniques for historical documents. (Ernst-Gerlach & Fuhr, 2007) focused on modern and archaic German and developed a retrieval method that considers the spelling differences and variations over time. (Koolen et al., 2006) considered the spelling and pronunciation differences between ancient and modern Dutch, while (Gotscharek et al., 2009) and (Hauser et al., 2007) considered the spelling differences and variations between modern and archaic German. (Pilz et al., 2008) considered spelling variations of English and German historical texts. In general, the main challenge for historical European languages like Dutch, English, and German is the spelling variants.

We applied an "ancient-to-modern information retrieval" method to ancient Mongolian historical collections written in traditional Mongolian script. Some ancient historical documents in traditional Mongolian script have recently been digitized and made publicly available, and text-display support for traditional Mongolian script and the input locale is enabled in Windows Vista and Windows 7. The Uniscribe–Unicode Scripts Processor driver was updated to support OpenType advanced typographic functionality of complex text layouts, such as traditional Mongolian script.

The situation for an ancient Mongolian language is a bit different because the Mongols have changed their writing systems several times and more than once have made language reforms that eliminate a difference between written and spoken language (Shagdarsuren, 2001).

2.2 Proposed approach

To cope with cross-period and cross-script Mongolian documents, we propose a simple model that retrieves traditional Mongolian documents using modern Mongolian query. The structure of the TMSDL (Khaltarkhuu et al, 2007; Khaltarkhuu et al, 2008), with the proposed "ancient-to-modern information retrieval" approach (Batjargal et al., 2010a; Batjargal et al., 2010b) is shown in Fig. 1. We utilized the existing approach (Kimura et al., 2009) and improved the "retrieval technique with the modern Mongolian query on traditional Mongolian text" (Khaltarkhuu et al, 2006) by integrating a dictionary. A prototype of the TMSDL (Batjargal et al., 2010a; Batjargal et al., 2010b), which could be considered a cross-period information retrieval system, has been developed. The retrieval method of the TMSDL considers cross-period differences in the writing systems of the ancient and modern Mongolian languages. Adding a dictionary-based query translation approach to the translation module was a major improvement that takes into account age differences in the writing systems of the ancient and modern Mongolian languages. We utilized the developing online version of Tsevel's concise Mongolian dictionary (Tsevel, 1966) under the Creative Commons Attribution-Noncommercial-Share Alike 3.0 Unported license. Tsevel's dictionary was printed in 1966 and is one of two Mongolian dictionaries with definitions written in modern and traditional Mongolian available on the market. It includes over 30,000 words in Cyrillic and traditional Mongolian script.

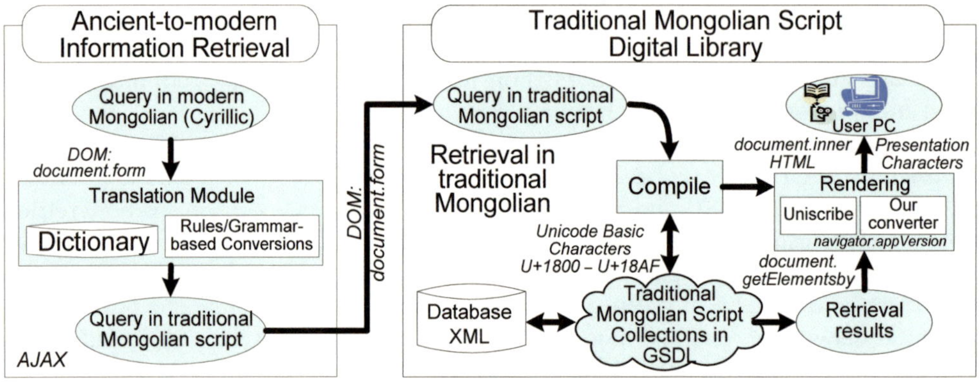

Fig. 1. Ancient-to-modern information retrieval in the TMSDL.

To boost the quality of the translation, the "ancient-to-modern information retrieval" approach (Batjargal et al., 2010a; Batjargal et al., 2010b) matches query terms to words in Tsevel's dictionary. If no exact match is found, the "retrieval technique with the modern Mongolian query on traditional Mongolian text" (Khaltarkhuu et al, 2006), which is based on grammatical rules, is used. The proposed model allows the users to access documents written in an ancient language (traditional Mongolian) with a query input in a modern language (modern Mongolian - Cyrillic). As shown in Fig. 1, the query in modern Mongolian (Cyrillic) is translated into a query in traditional Mongolian script. The query in traditional Mongolian (Unicode characters in the range U+1800 - U+18AF) is then submitted as a retrieval query for traditional Mongolian script collections. Chronological books of ancient Mongolian kings, Genghis Khan, and the Mongol Empire (the largest contiguous empire in history) such as the Altan Tobci (year 1604, 164 pp) and the Story of Asragch (year 1677, 130 pp) etc, are available in the TMSDL with a modern Mongolian input interface. A database of such historical records with a modern language query input will help someone conducting research on the history of the High Middle Ages understand 13th–14th century history of Asia. The modern Mongolian (Cyrillic) input in the TMSDL is illustrated in Fig. 2.

2.3 Experimental evaluation

In an experiment we conducted in order to check the correctness of translations from the modern language to the ancient one, we retrieved traditional Mongolian documents when using modern Mongolian query input in Cyrillic. Because of the large number of unfamiliar ancient proper nouns, terms, and their variants in ancient historical documents, we faced the challenge of measuring recall and precision as well as the challenge of defining relevant documents. To check whether a queries in modern Mongolian (Cyrillic) were translated correctly, we selected queries the most frequently appearing words that are pronounced or written differently in modern and traditional Mongolian and compared their word counts in the search results with the corresponding word counts in "Qad-un űndűsűn quriyangγui altan tobči -Textological Study" (Choimaa & Shagdarsuren, 2002). This textological study contains a detailed analysis of traditional Mongolian word frequencies in the Altan Tobci.

We compared the word count in the search results for two cases: one using only grammatical-rule-based translation, and the other additionally using a dictionary. The version with dictionary integration translated and retrieved 86% of the input queries, whereas the grammatical-rule-based version retrieved only 61% of the input queries. Even

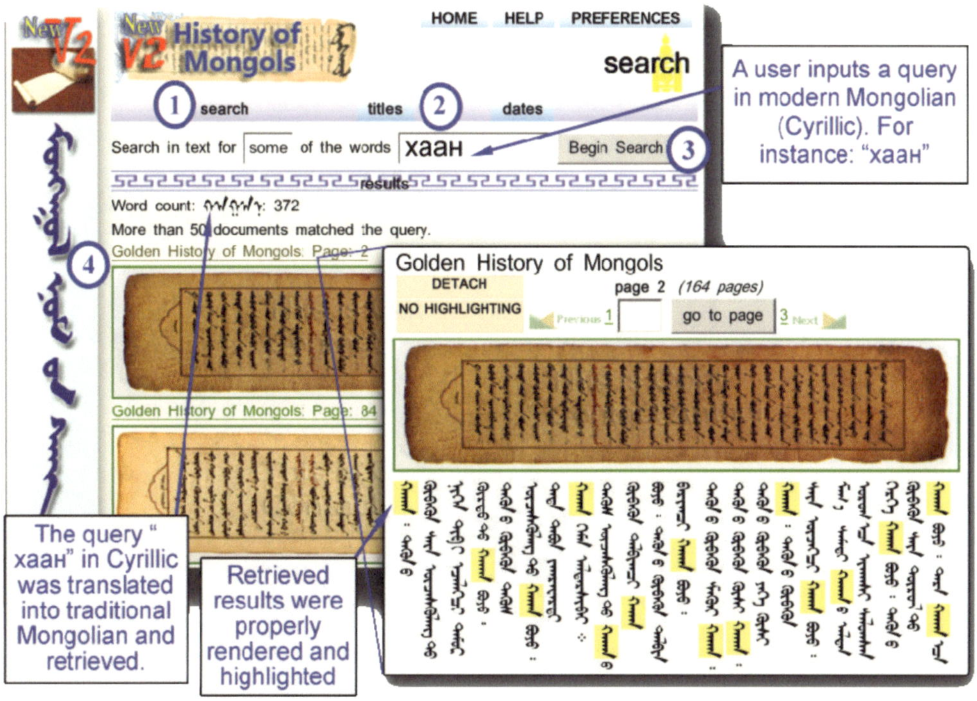

Fig. 2. TMSDL Cyrillic input and retrieval results.

with the dictionary, however, 64% of the input queries in modern Mongolian did not match with a word count that was less than or greater than the actual number (frequency) because of possible errors of translation, grammatical inflection, and text digitization, or limitations of the indexer and retrieval function. Comparisons of the retrieval results are illustrated in Fig. 3, and detailed retrieval results for sample query terms are shown in Table 1 along with modern and ancient forms, their meanings, and the word counts. A retrieval result with the query word highlighted is shown in Fig. 2.

The TMSDL integrated with a dictionary translated and retrieved 86% of the input queries, but only 22% were retrieved without error.

2.4 Summary and future directions

In this section we introduced the TMSDL that utilizes cross-period and cross-script digital collections and that enables historical documents written in an ancient language to be accessed using a query in a modern language. The proposed system is suitable for full text searches on databases containing cross-period and cross-script documents. Such research would involve extensive research in an ancient language that users and humanities researchers may or may not understand. It could apply to humanities researchers who are conducting research on ancient culture and looking for relevant historical materials written in that ancient language. The proposed model will enable users and humanities researchers to search for such materials easily in a modern language. We still, however, need improvements dealing with such problems as a total failure to translate 14% of input queries. Improvements in translation and retrieval techniques also need to be considered.

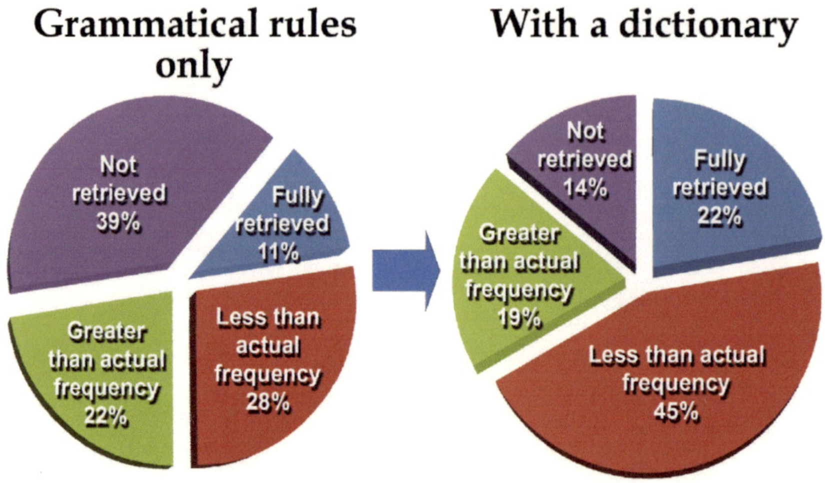

Fig. 3. TMSDL retrieval results obtained using different translation methods.

Word in Modern Mongolian (Cyrillic)	Pronunciation		Word in traditional Mongolian	English translation	Word count in retrieval results		Actual word count	Retrieval state
	Modern	Ancient			Grammatical rules only	With a dictionary		
хүн	hűn	kűműn	ᠬᠦᠮᠦᠨ	man, person, human	0	135	135	Fully retrieved
хаан	qaan	qaγan	ᠬᠠᠭᠠᠨ	king	0	372	372	
даян	dayan	dayan	ᠳᠠᠶᠠᠨ	all, whole	0	0	32	Not retrieved
сайн	sain	sayin	ᠰᠠᠶᠢᠨ	good, well, fine, nice, pretty	0	0	75	
гэр	ger	ger	ᠭᠡᠷ	home, residence	0	51	47	Greater than actual frequency
төр	tör	törü	ᠲᠥᠷᠥ	law, kingdom	0	50	47	
эзэн	ezen	eĵen	ᠡᠵᠡᠨ	lord	0	144	146	Less than actual frequency
богд	bogd	boγda	ᠪᠣᠭᠳᠠ	holy, sacred, divine	0	39	40	

Table 1. Examples of retrieval performance obtained using different translation methods.

Two interesting subjects for future research are the retrieval of information from two distinct ancient languages and using a single query input in a modern language for retrieval from multiple sources in multiple ancient languages.

The next section discusses the our another achievement - cross-period information retrieval method for ancient Japanese historical materials

3. Cross-period information retrieval from ancient Japanese historical materials

Libraries, governments, and major internet providers have recently begun forming consortiums to preserve historical documents stored in libraries. This means that more and more old-text content will soon be accessible on the Internet. The huge amount of knowledge in old documents is obviously as important as that in the recently created digital documents typically available on the web because old documents contain the wisdom of our ancestors.

Retrieving important information from old documents is not always easy, however, because languages and cultures change substantially over time. To access documents written in ancient Japanese by using a query in modern Japanese, for example, we need a cross-period information retrieval system based on a cross-period (ancient-modern) Japanese dictionary.

3.1 Construction of ancient-modern dictionary

Ancient documents in text form are being digitized, and the prevalence of search engines has made the retrieval of information from digital documents a familiar procedure. Current search engines, however, may be not able to acquire proper retrieval results for ancient Japanese documents because there is no ancient-modern Japanese dictionary with sufficient entries.

One reason for this is that the Japanese writing system has no term separation. That is, neither current nor ancient Japanese writing uses space or punctuation to separate words. A morphological analyzer like ChaSen or MeCab, both of which need a modern term dictionary, is usually used to do term separation for modern Japanese, but there is no ancient-modern word dictionary with enough entries and there are no morphological analyzers for ancient Japanese. This makes it difficult to do term separation for ancient Japanese.

We propose a method for constructing an ancient-modern Japanese dictionary by using a parallel corpus of ancient writings and their translations in modern Japanese. The parallel corpus thus consists of pairs of documents in the same language but in ancient and modern versions of that language. From this corpus we try to acquire pairs of equivalent archaic and modern words by analyzing the frequencies of word occurrences in a sentence in ancient Japanese and its corresponding modern Japanese translation.

3.1.1 Related work

Two methods for extracting pairs of equivalent words from a bilingual corpus in modern languages (English and Japanese, for example) have already been proposed, one using a parallel corpus and the other using a non-parallel corpus. In the method using a parallel corpus, equivalence is based on statistical correlation determined using co-occurrence frequency, contingency tables, etc. (Kitamura & Matsumoto, 1996). In the method using a non-parallel corpus, equivalence is based on the context similarity of translation candidates (Tanaka, 2002). The method described here, however, identifies pairs of equivalent words not in two modern languages but in modern and archaic Japanese. As there are few modern language translations of ancient writings, it is difficult to collect a parallel corpus of ancient writings and their translations in modern language. Some famous ancient writings, though, have been translated into the modern forms of their languages. We therefore identify pairs of equivalent words in modern and archaic Japanese by using a parallel corpus comprising famous ancient Japanese writings and their translations in modern Japanese.

3.1.2 Proposed method of dictionary construction

Many well-known ancient writings have modern-language translations, and some of these translations are digitized and open to the public. In a parallel corpus comprising writings in an ancient and modern language, one can usually determine which modern-language sentence corresponds to which ancient-language sentence. A modern word equivalent to an archaic word in an ancient-language sentence is likely to appear in the modern-language translation of that sentence, and vice versa. Word pairs with high co-occurrence frequency in ancient and modern sentence pairs are thus likely to be translation equivalents.

In our method we detect similarities in the appearance tendencies of modern and archaic words in each sentence pair and then use these similarities to extract equivalent pairs of ancient and modern words (Fig. 4).

A. Word Extraction from Parallel Corpus

We use morphological analysis to extract words from the modern-language translations of the ancient writings, and because there is no morphological analyzer for ancient Japanese. We divide the archaic sentences into N-grams and treat those N-grams as archaic words.

An N-gram is a sequence of N characters from a given string. We first extract the first N characters from the target string and then shift one character and extract N characters from the target string. We repeat this shifting-and-extracting process until the Nth character in the N-gram is the last character of the target string. For example, the string "corpus" would be divided into the following four 3-grams: cor, orp, rpu, and pus.

One of the drawbacks of the N-gram approach is that there will be many overlaps. On the other hand, an advantage of the N-gram approach is that it can divide the strings even if the language of the string, like ancient Japanese, does not have explicit delimiters between words. This is why we divide the archaic sentences into N-grams and treat those N-grams as words.

B. Calculation of the Co-occurence of Modern and Archaic Words

In this process, we calculate co-occurrence frequencies of archaic terms and modern terms that are extracted in section 3.1.2.A. This process is conducted for archaic and modern term pairs to appear in the equivalent sentences. In other words, the term pairs appearing in the equivalent sentences are considered as the co-occurring terms.

In each sentence pair, the archaic and modern term pairs are created for every possible pairs of extracted modern terms and archaic N-grams. We count the occurrence frequency of each term pairs. This frequency is the co-occurrence frequency of archaic and modern term pairs.

C. Calculation of Similarity about Appearance of Tendency between Modern Term and Archaic Term

For parallel corpus composed two different languages documents such as Japanese and English, "mutual information" is proposed to use for the similarity between each two terms (Kitamura & Matsumoto, 1996). Our method also adopts "mutual information" in order to calculate similarities about appearance of tendency between modern term and archaic term.

The archaic and modern term pairs that have higher value of their mutual information is considered that appearance of tendency between modern term and archaic term is similar. These term pairs have higher possibility that the modern term is relation in translation for the archaic term. We extract term pairs that have higher similarities than some threshold, and consider that these pairs have relation in translation.

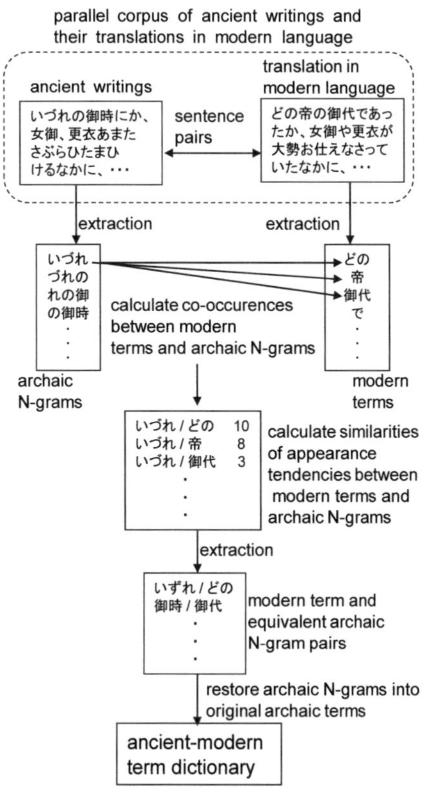

Fig. 4. Flow of the construction of an ancient-modern dictionary.

The mutual information MI of a modern term t and an archaic N-gram g is given by the following formula.

$$\mathrm{MI}(t,g) = \log \frac{P(t,g)}{P(t)P(g)} \tag{1}$$

Probability P(t, g) is the probability that the modern term t appears in the translation of the archaic sentence in which the archaic N-gram g appears, and it can be calculated from the co-occurrence frequency of archaic N-gram g and modern term t. Probabilities P(t) means the probability in the case that the modern term t appears in modern sentence. Probabilities P(g) means the probability in the case that the archaic N-gram g appears in archaic sentence. Probabilities P(g) is able to be acquired from the term frequency of archaic N-gram g as mentioned in section 3.1.2.A.
The archaic and modern term pairs that have higher value of their mutual information are considered that appearance of tendency between modern term and archaic term is similar.

D. Extraction of Translation Pairs of Modern and Archaic Words

In section 3.1.2.C, we extract archaic and modern term pairs that have higher possibilities of relation in translation. However, as the archaic terms of extracted pairs are represented by N-gram, these archaic terms are not always complete archaic term. Some archaic N-gram may be part of archaic term. Another may be combined parts of some archaic terms. In these cases, we have to restore the archaic N-grams to original archaic terms. These archaic N-grams are restored to original archaic terms by comparing spellings, term frequency and co-occurrence frequency between another archaic N-gram. We consider that restored archaic and modern term pairs are related in translation. Finally, we collect these term pairs and construct ancient-modern term dictionary.

3.1.2 Future directions

We proposed a method for constructing an ancient-modern Japanese dictionary by using a parallel corpus of ancient writings and their translations in modern Japanese. If an ancient-modern Japanese dictionary with sufficient entries is constructed by the proposed method, we think that the techniques of natural language processing, for example morphological analysis, could be applied for ancient documents digitized in text form.

We need to improve the term extracting process in order to reduce the number of unnecessary word pairs, to improve the calculation of similarities of the appearance tendencies of modern and archaic words, and to construct a practical ancient-modern Japanese dictionary.

3.2 Cross-period information retrieval system

There has been a lot of research on cross-language information retrieval in the last decade. Various approaches—including query translation, document translation, and the use of an intermediate language—has been studied, and adequate retrieval effectiveness has been achieved for some pairs of languages (e.g., certain European languages).

There has, in contrast, been very little research on information retrieval methods for historical documents, and most of those methods are based on simple keyword matching. Some recently proposed approaches to accessing historical documents consider the evolution of languages and could be regarded as a kind of cross-age information retrieval (Gerlach & Fuhr, 2007; Khaltarkhuu & Maeda, 2006). Our goal is to establish a more effective and sophisticated retrieval method that considers not only language difference over time but also cultural differences between languages and ages.

The architecture or the cross-period information retrieval system we developed is shown in Fig. 5. This system lets old Japanese documents be retrieved using modern Japanese keywords, so old Japanese documents by users who do not know archaic Japanese.

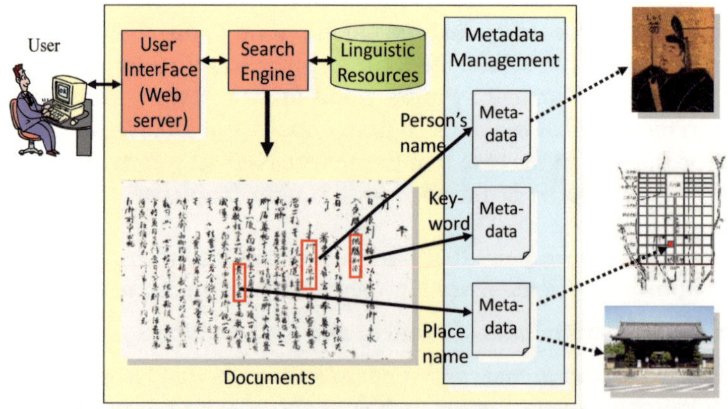

Fig. 5. Architecture of proposed cross-period information retrieval system for ancient Japanese historical materials.

3.2.1 Proposed method for cross-period information retrieval

We use the dictionary-based query translation approach because it is the one most effective for cross-language information retrieval. For dictionary-based methods to be effective we need to use precise and comprehensive dictionaries for both the modern and ancient language. We try to find relations between the entries in those dictionaries and to translate the query terms in the modern language into equivalent terms in the ancient language. For this translation process we propose the following method (Fig. 6).

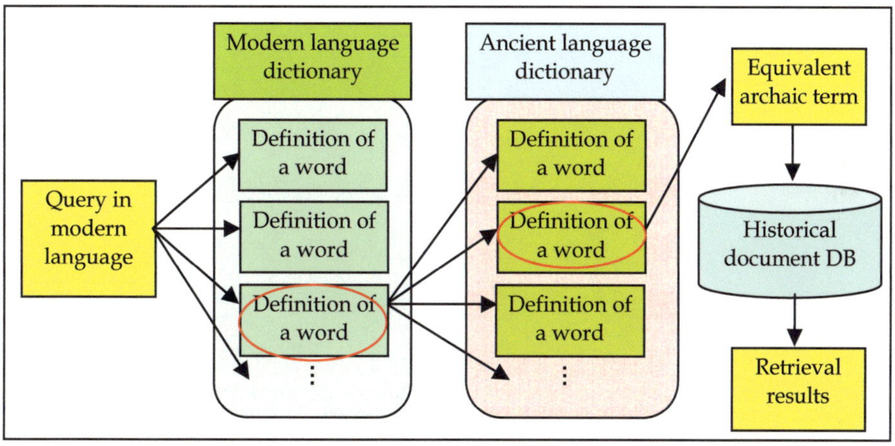

Fig. 6. Overview of proposed method for cross-period information retrieval.

1. For each entry in the modern-language dictionary, we look for an equivalent entry in the ancient language dictionary by calculating the similarities between the definition of the modern word and all the definitions of the archaic words. We can do this using a standard text similarity measure based on the vector space model and the tf-idf term weighting scheme.
2. We then take the most similar definition in the ancient language dictionary and regard the dictionary entry (headword) containing that definition as an equivalent of the modern word.
3. If there is more than one equivalent entry, we find the one most nearly equivalent to the modern word by using a term association measure such as mutual information to disambiguate the candidate translations.

3.2.2 Implementation

We implemented a cross-period information retrieval system for the Japanese historical document called the *Hyohanki* diary. Written in late Heian era (12th century), it is a valuable resource for research on Japanese culture of that time. An example of its original copy is shown in Fig. 7. Part of the *Hyohanki* has deteriorated and is missing, but all of the existing pages (comprising 2,488 diary entries) have been digitized into text format.

As described in Section 3.2.1, we need dictionaries in order to translate modern language query words into archaic words. In the case of the *Hyohanki* diary we can use some existing electronic dictionaries available on CD-ROMs. For modern Japanese we use *Kojien*, one of the most famous and comprehensive Japanese language dictionaries. For ancient Japanese we use *Kokugo-Daijiten*, which covers not only modern words but also archaic words.

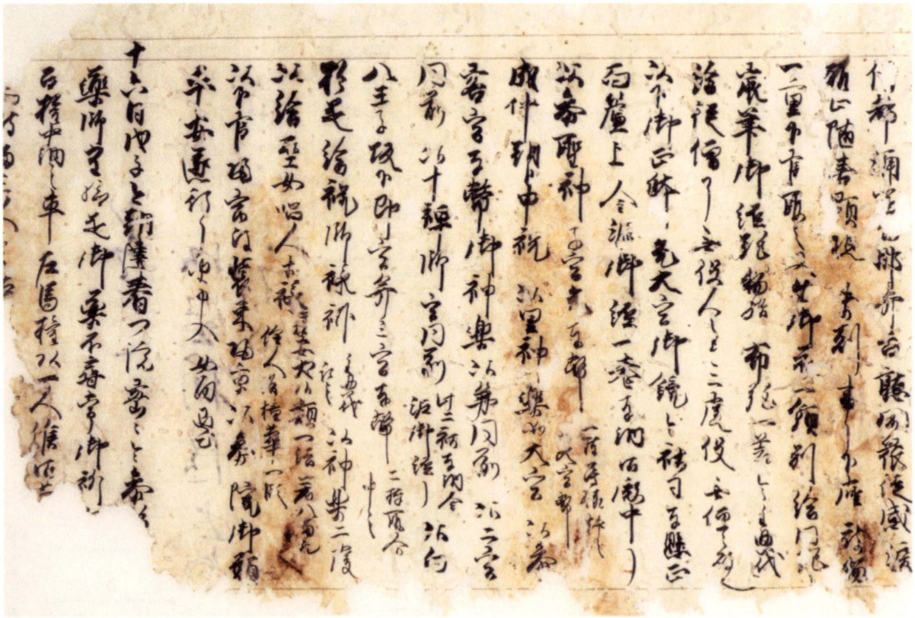

Fig. 7. Part of the original copy of the historical Japanese document *Hyohanki*.

3.2.3 Experiment

We conducted a preliminary experiment to test the precision of cross-period retrieval by our proposed method. We used *Hyohanki* diary entries of as the ancient Japanese document collection and prepared three modern Japanese queries: 戦争 (war), 法要 (Buddhist service), and 裸足 (bare foot). Since the archaic equivalent of each query differs from the query itself, no relevant documents can be retrieved if we use these modern term queries. Note that we consider one diary entry as one document.

Table 2 shows the original modern Japanese query, the ancient Japanese equivalents (translations) obtained by the proposed method, and the precision of retrieval using the translations. For the queries 法要 (Buddhist service) and 裸足 (bare foot), the proposed method worked quite well: 99–100% precision (the ratio of relevant documents in retrieved documents). The query 戦争 (war), however, resulted in very poor precision (27%) because the proposed method returned two translation candidates for this query: 戦 and 軍. If we use only 戦 as the translated query we obtain 100% precision, but if we use only 軍 we obtain only 3.6% precision. This is because the archaic term 軍 has not only the meaning *war* but also meanings like *general* (officer) and *army*. The query 死亡 (death) also resulted in

Modern Japanese query	Translations	Relevant / Retrieved
戦争 (war)	軍, 戦	10 / 37 (27%)
法要 (Buddhist service)	仏事	109 / 110 (99%)
裸足 (bare foot)	跣, 裸足, 跣足	27 / 27 (100%)
死亡 (death)	没	2 / 13 (15%)

Table 2. Precision of the retrieval results in cross-period retrieval.

very poor precision (15%) because its translation 没 also means *deprivation* and *sunset*. These results suggest that we could improve the precision if we incorporate a suitable disambiguation method for the translated archaic terms. For that purpose, we could apply existing disambiguation methods used in Cross-language Information Retrieval.

4. Federated searching system for humanities databases using automatic metadata mapping

This section provides a summary of our approach to constructing a federated searching system for Japanese humanities databases using automatic metadata mapping. The goals of our system are (1) to perform metadata mapping automatically for Japanese heterogeneous humanities databases and (2) to let users access multiple humanities digital libraries by using only one query input. This section also addresses the metadata-related challenges facing Japanese humanities databases. Metadata offers library and information science a solution to the problem of describing and managing the massive quantities of explosively increasing digital information (Zeng & Jian, 2008). Various types of resources and humanities digital libraries coexist with heterogeneous metadata schemas nowadays, and many different metadata schemas are standardized by international standards organizations. How to deal with the diverse forms of metadata and interoperate is becoming a complex issue for research. There have been efforts to make heterogeneous standards interoperable and utilize multiple metadata standards. According to (Chan & Zeng, 2006), several different approaches (element mapping, crosswalk, application profile, metadata registry, etc.) were developed. Reliable metadata interoperability has not been achieved yet because of the heterogeneity of metadata standards and because of the structural differences between standards.

On the other hand, the use of metadata schemas and standards for Japanese humanities digital libraries is a bit tricky. Many metadata schemas of Japanese humanities digital libraries have been accepted in terms of their semantics and content but were developed before the international metadata standards or were developed without considering the international metadata standards and specific encoding methods. Most of the metadata schemas of Japanese humanities digital libraries were not derived from existing international metadata standards, and there is no explicit metadata framework, crosswalk, or metadata registry. It is necessary to understand the semantics of Japanese humanities digital libraries—such as elements, syntax, and structure—in order to perform automatic metadata mapping and achieve metadata interoperability. This section therefore addresses the metadata-related challenges to constructing a federated searching system for Japanese humanities databases.

4.1 Metadata schemas for Japanese humanities digital libraries and their challenges

Humanities digital libraries and their metadata schemas are very heterogeneous because the humanities cover a variety of disciplines, such as literature, law, history, philosophy, religion, visual and performing arts (including music), anthropology, cultural studies, and linguistics (including ancient and modern languages). Achieving metadata interoperability of humanities digital libraries is becoming more crucial in the current information environment, especially in the case of metadata schemas which were not derived from well-known international metadata standards.

One of the differences between western and Japanese databases that is relevant to people interested in constructing a federated searching system is the greater heterogeneity of the metadata schemas of Japanese humanities digital libraries. Many Japanese humanities databases developed metadata schemas based on their domain-specific semantics and content rather than adopt international metadata standards. Moreover, names or labels for metadata attributes/elements are written in Japanese, or labels in Japanese are used as the metadata elements. The co-existence of nonstandard and heterogeneous metadata schemas makes automatic metadata mapping for Japanese humanities databases a rather challenging task.

Another relevant difference is the Japanese writing system(s). Japanese is written in a mixture of three writing systems—one using ideographic symbols, or *kanji*, and the other two using the syllabary scripts *hiragana* and *katakana*—and it is written without explicit word boundaries. The absence of word delimiters makes word segmentation (i.e., tokenization) a critical problem in natural language processing for Japanese. Without knowing the boundaries of words in a sentence, any computer system will fail to perform tasks such as automatic metadata mapping. A single kanji can have many pronunciations and be used differently in words comprising two or more kanji. The situation will be much more difficult when collections contain ancient documents because a modern kanji is not always the same as its archaic equivalent. An archaic word written with a single kanji might be equivalent to a modern word written with more than a single modern kanji, or vice versa. Using a modern language query to find information in Japanese documents that are written in modern and archaic Japanese words is a rather challenging task.

4.2 Federated searching system for Japanese humanities databases

The conceptual architecture of our proposed federated searching system is shown in Fig. 8. As illustrated there, if a user wants to find a humanities resource with the query word in the title, our system retrieves resources having the query word in the title or any metadata field that is similar to a title or could be treated as a title and retrieves these resources from heterogeneous humanities digital libraries even if those libraries do not provide metadata

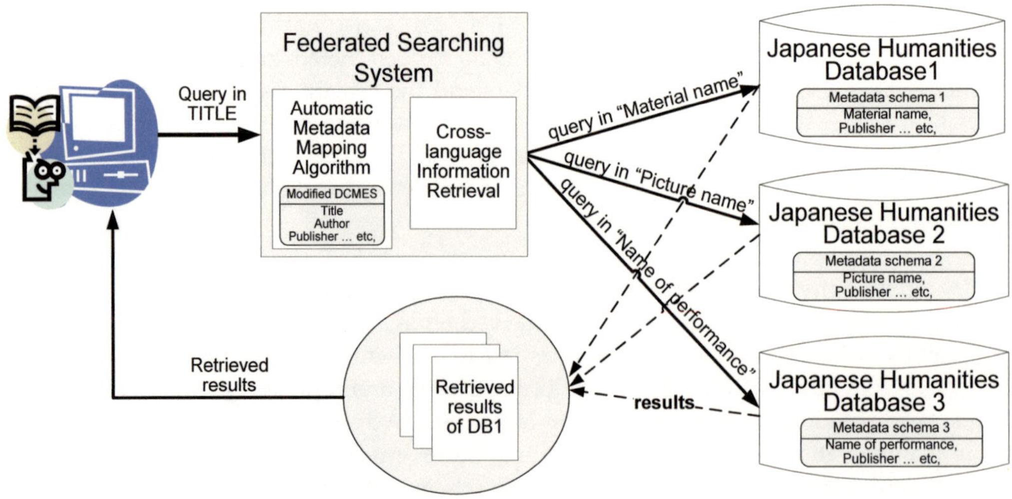

Fig. 8. Conceptual architecture of the proposed federated searching system.

interoperability or crosswalk and do not support Z39.50 protocol, Search/Retrieve Web service (SRW)/Search/Retrieve via URL (SRU), etc.

We are developing a prototype federated searching system of Japanese humanities databases—including the image database of Japanese traditional fine art Ukiyo-e, donated Japanese books database, and old Japanese books database—that are freely accessible in Japanese at the Art Research Center of Ritsumeikan University. We utilized the automatic metadata mapping method of Kimura et al. (2009). This prototype system also has a facility for cross-language searching between English and Japanese, which enables English-speaking users to search Japanese databases available only in Japanese.

4.3 Automatic metadata mapping

In our system the metadata attribute names of heterogeneous Japanese humanities collections in Japanese, the metadata schemas of which are unknown or do not conform to the international standards, are automatically mapped to our modified variant set (hereafter, modified DCMES) of the Dublin Core metadata element set (DCMES) (Dublin Core Metadata Initiative, 2008). Because CREATOR and CONTRIBUTOR are hard to distinguish in Japanese humanities collections, in the modified DCMES they are unified into the new element AUTHOR. When Japanese humanities metadata schemas are successfully mapped to the modified DCMES, our proposed system enables cross-domain metadata harvesting and federated searches as well as the exchange of metadata.

Our automatic metadata mapping method (Fig. 9) consists of two preprocessing phases and four mapping phases.

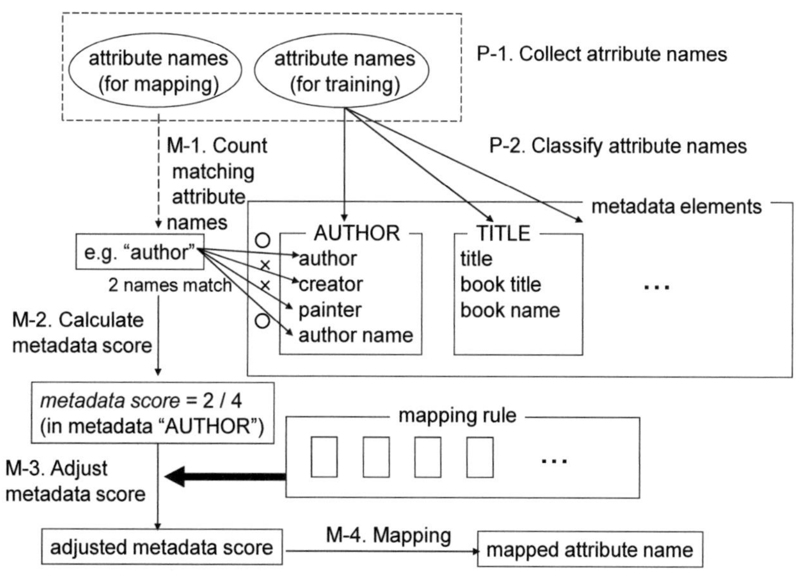

Fig. 9. Flow of automatic metadata mapping.

The preprocessing consists of the following steps:

P-1 Collect attribute names from humanities databases for training and mapping.

P-2 Classify attribute names for training into appropriate metadata elements manually.

The automatic mapping phase consists of the following steps:

M-1 Count the number of partial string matches between the attribute name for mapping and each metadata element.

M-2 Calculate the *metadata score* of each metadata element by dividing the number of partial string matches by the number of attribute names in the metadata element.

M-3 Adjust the metadata score for each metadata element, if the target attribute name matches one or more *mapping rules*, which consist of some kanji characters (or partial words) that are commonly used and known to be relevant to one or more particular metadata elements. (e.g., increase the metadata score for "TEMPORAL" if the attribute name includes "year").

M-4 Map the target attribute name to the metadata element that has the highest metadata score.

If the attribute name is given the metadata score value 0 for all metadata sets, the attribute name is classified into "OTHER" metadata.

Modified DCMES elements mapping	**Metadata elements of Japanese humanities digital libraries**	**Meanings of kanji used in metadata elements of Japanese humanities digital libraries**	**Number of elements**
TITLE	画題等，画題２，役名，外題，外題よみ，所作題，所作題よみ，細目題，細目題よみ，主外題，主外題よみ，系統分類題，演目（統合），演目よみ（統合），画題統合，資料名，資料名よみ，解題	Print title, Picture name, Character names, Official title, Played title, Title of play, Reading of played title, Performed title, Reading of performed title, Detailed title, Reading of detailed title, Main performed title, Reading of the main performed title, Classification title, Name of performance, Reading of the performance, Title of the integrated picture , Material name, Reading of material name, Synopsis	18
PUBLISHER	版元文字，異版，版印1No，版元1No，版元1，版印2No，版元2No，版元2，版元備考，地域版，版元統合	Character publisher, Different edition, Edition stamp #1, Publisher #1, Publisher 1, Edition stamp #2, Publisher #2, Publisher 2, Publisher remarks, Domestic publisher, Joint publisher	11
DATE	西暦，和暦，年月日備考，月日--計算，西暦版，和暦版，月日版，年月日備考版，閏，月，日	Gregorian calendar, Japanese calendar, Edited date, Date calculation, Gregorian calendar edition, Japanese calendar edition, Edition date, Remarked date, intercalary, Month, Day	11
AUTHOR	絵師，編著者等，原所蔵者，彫師等，担当者	Artist, Volume author etc., Original owner, Engravers, etc., Person in charge	5
COVERAGE	地域，位置，続方向，劇場，場立，場名	Performed Place, Location, Spatial, Theater, Place, Place name	6

Table 3. Example of results of the automatic metadata mapping.

Inspecting the data listed in Table 3, one sees that 18 metadata elements (attribute names) of the Ukiyo-e image database, donated books database, and old books database were mapped to the TITLE element in the modified DCMES. Similarly, 11 elements were mapped to DATE, 11 to PUBLISHER, 5 to AUTHOR, and 6 to COVERAGE. These eighteen attribute names were written in various kanji characters that have different meanings, such as "Print title," "Picture name," "Character names," "Official title," "Played title," "Title of play," "Reading of played title," and "Performed title The metadata attribute names used in Japanese humanities digital libraries consist of several words that have combinations of single or several kanji characters, and the meaning of the words depend on the combinations. Our algorithm performs automatic mapping by calculating the overall metadata scores for each metadata element, which are calculated for the words or kanji characters by using training data set and mapping rules. For instance, if the name of a metadata element has the character 名 (name), increase the metadata score for TITLE by 1, for PUBLISHER" by 0.5, and for AUTHOR by 1.

Our study of 334 metadata elements of 50 Japanese humanities digital libraries showed that 65 different elements have a potential to be regarded as TITLE, 46 as AUTHOR, 25 as SUBJECT, 77 as DESCRIPTION, 22 as PUBLISHER, 5 as TYPE, 20 as IDENTIFIER, 5 as SOURCE, 44 as COVERAGE, and 7 as RIGHTS. This shows how heterogeneous metadata schemas of Japanese humanities digital libraries are and that is vital to perform metadata mapping automatically.

Modified DCMES elements	**Average precision (%)**
TITLE	89.9
SUBJECT	100.0
AUTHOR	91.8
PUBLISHER	85.7
IDENTIFIER	100.0

Table 4. Mapping precision of the automatic metadata mapping method.

Metadata Sets	Conditions	Average precision (%)
Standard Dublin Core Metadata Element Set	Without mapping rules	73.8
Standard Dublin Core Metadata Element Set	With mapping rules	79.0
Modified Dublin Core Metadata Element Set	With mapping rules	94.9

Table 5. Comparison of metadata mapping precision.

According to the judgement of a native Japanese speaker experienced in Japanese humanities digital databases who checked the results obtained when our automatic metadata mapping method mapped 334 attribute names of Japanese humanities collections to metadata elements of the modified DCMES, the average mapping precisions ranged from 85.7% to 100% (Table 4).

The average precisions we obtained using standard DCMES without the mapping rules, using standard DCMES with the mapping rules, and using modified DCMES with the mapping rules are listed in Table 5, where one sees that the mapping precision obtained using modified DCMES with the mapping rules is 21.1 percentage points higher than that obtained using standard DCMES without the mapping rules, and this shows that mapping rules improve the metadata mapping considerably. The average precision obtained using modified DCMES with the mapping rules was 15.9 percentage points higher than that obtained using the standard DCMES with mapping rules, and this shows that the modified DCMES also improves the metadata mapping considerably.

4.4 Retrieval in a federated searching system using automatic metadata mapping

To examine the performance of our federated searching system using automatic metadata mapping, we conducted an experiment by inputting a single query to three humanities collections (Ukiyo-e image database, donated Japanese books database, and old Japanese books database). Retrieval results obtained from three collections for the sample query 風流 (elegance) in the TITLE metadata fields are shown in Fig. 10. Retrieval with other sample queries was also successful.

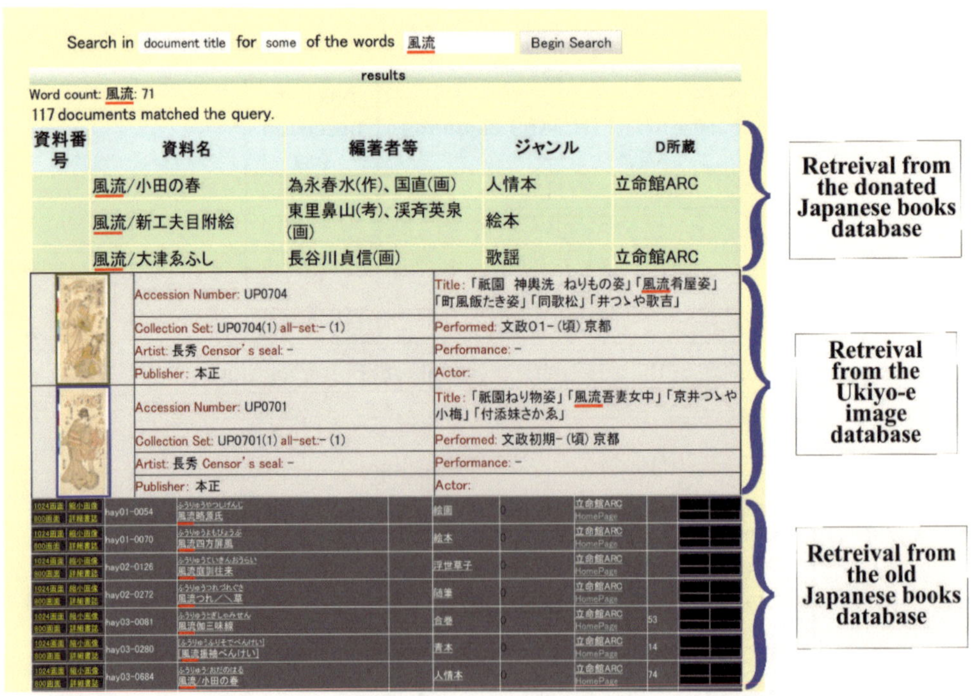

Fig. 10. Retrieval results obtained from three from Japanese humanities digital libraries when using automatic metadata mapping.

4.5 Retrieval in a federated searching system using English queries

Our federated searching system also retrieves resources from Japanese collections when an English query is used. This feature is very useful for users who do not understand Japanese, and it allows searching and browsing Japanese digital libraries in English through a single interface and a single query (Batjargal et al., 2010c). We applied this feature to the Ukiyo-e image database of the Art Research Center of Ritsumeikan University, which is freely accessible in Japanese.

Ukiyo-e, Japanese traditional woodblock printing is known world-wide as one of the fine arts of the Edo period (1603–1868). The texts of Ukiyo-e databases contain archaic Japanese words which reflect the Japanese language of the Edo period. Besides providing information about Ukiyo-e prints, the Ukiyo-e database of the Art Research Center of Ritsumeikan University contains information about the content of the prints. For instance, if the subject of an Ukiyo-e print is Kabuki, the highly stylized classical Japanese dance-drama, the database contains some additional information. Sometimes explanations of cultural and social meaning for the print are also included.

67 metadata elements of the Ukiyo-e database are mapped to the modified DCMES using our automatic metadata mapping method. As shown in Fig. 11, the Ukiyo-e artist name *Kuniyoshi* as an input query was translated as 国芳 and retrieved from the Japanese Ukiyo-e image database. The translated terms, names, explanations, etc. were displayed in English pages. Multiterm queries were treated as words: the artist's full name *Utagawa Kuniyoshi*, was treated as 歌川 (Utagawa) and 国芳 (Kuniyoshi) but not as 歌川国芳. As illustrated in Fig. 11, users will be able to enter a query in English (2) after clicking the Search button (1). The query *Kuniyoshi* is translated as 国芳 when the Begin Search button is clicked (3), and the translated query is retrieved from the Japanese Ukiyo-e image database. Lastly, the user will be able to access the webpage (4) that displays detailed information of a certain Ukiyo-e print, where the metadata in Japanese are translated and displayed in English.

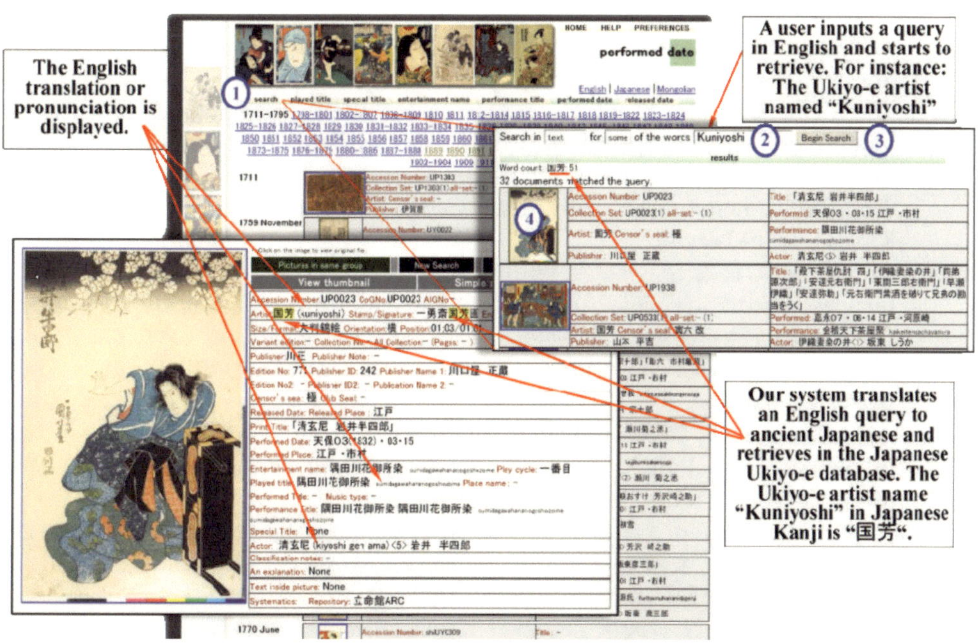

Fig. 11. Using an English query to search Japanese Ukiyo-e databases.

5. Summary

In this chapter we presented some of our work related to integrated information access technology for digital libraries. We developed technologies providing information access across different languages, periods, and cultures. These technologies will be particularly important for large digital library collections that include contents written in different languages and spanning a wide range of periods and diverse cultures. The systems presented in this chapter were developed primarily for humanities researchers but might also be useful to ordinary users because much of the knowledge and wisdom in old documents is not available in modern-language documents.

6. Acknowledgements

This work was supported in part by the Grant-in-Aid for the Global COE Program "Digital Humanities Center for Japanese Arts and Cultures (DH-JAC)" from the Ministry of Education, Culture, Sports, Science and Technology (MEXT) of Japan, MEXT Grant-in-Aid for Strategic Formation of Research Infrastructure for Private University "Sharing of Research Resources by Digitization and Utilization of Art and Cultural Materials"(Grant Number: S0991041), and MEXT Grant-in-Aid for Young Scientists (B) "Research on Information Access across Languages, Periods, and Cultures" (Leader: Akira Maeda, Grant Number: 21700271).

7. References

Batjargal, B.; Khaltarkhuu, G.; Kimura, F & Maeda, A. (2010a). An Ancient-to-modern Information Retrieval for Digital Collections of Traditional Mongolian Script. *Proceedings of the 12th International Conference on Asia-Pacific Digital Libraries (ICADL2010)*, pp. 25–28, ISBN 978-3-642-13653-5, Gold Coast, Australia, June 2010, Springer-Verlag, Berlin Heidelberg

Batjargal, B.; Khaltarkhuu, G.; Kimura, F & Maeda, A. (2010b). An Approach to Ancient-to-modern and Cross-script Information Access for Traditional Mongolian Historical Collections. *Conference Abstracts of Digital Humanities 2010*, pp. 279–282, ISBN 978-0-9565793-0-0, London, UK, July 2010, Centre for Computing in the Humanities, King's College London

Batjargal, B.; Kimura, F. & Maeda, A. (2010c). Approach to Cross-Language Retrieval for Japanese Traditional Fine Art: Ukiyo-e Database. *Proceedings of the 14th European Conference on Research and Advanced Technology for Digital Libraries (ECDL2010)*, pp. 518-521, ISBN 978-3-642-15463-8, Glasgow, UK, September 2010, Springer-Verlag, Berlin Heidelberg

Chan, L. M. & Zeng, M. L. (2006). Metadata interoperability and standardization - A study of methodology, Part I: Achieving interoperability at the schema level. *D-Lib Magazine*, vol. 12, no. 6, (June 2006), ISSN 1082-9873

Choimaa, S. & Shagdarsuren, T. (2002). *Qad-un ŭndŭsŭn quriyangγui altan tobči, (Textological Study)*, Volume I, Centre for Mongol Studies, National University of Mongolia, ISBN 99929-0-119-5, Ulaanbaatar (in Mongolian)

Ernst-Gerlach, A. & Fuhr, N. (2007). Retrieval in text collections with historic spelling using linguistic and spelling variants. *Proceedings of the 7th ACM/IEEE Joint Conference on*

Digital Libraries, pp. 333–341, ISBN 978-1-59593-644-8, Vancouver, British Columbia, Canada, June 2007, ACM , New York, USA

Gotscharek, A.; Neumann, A.; Reffle, U.; Ringlstetter, C. & Schulz, K. (2009). Enabling information retrieval on historical document collections: the role of matching procedures and special lexica. *Proceedings of the 3rd Workshop on Analytics for Noisy Unstructured Text Data*, pp. 69–76, ISBN 978-1-60558-496-6, Barcelona, Spain, July 2009, ACM, New York, USA

Hauser, A.; Heller, M.; Leiss, E.; Schulz, K. & Wanzeck, C. (2007) Information Access to Historical Documents from the Early New High German Period. *Proceedings of the 20th International Joint Conference on Artificial Intelligence*, Hyderabad, India, January 2007

Kawashima, M.; Akama, R.; Yano, K.; Hachimura, K. & Inaba, M. (2009). *New Directions in Digital Humanities for Japanese Arts and Cultures*. Nakanishiya Shuppan, ISBN 978-4-7795-0324-5, Kyoto

Khaltarkhuu, G. & Maeda, A. (2006). Retrieval Technique with the Modern Mongolian Query on Traditional Mongolian Text. *Proceedings of the 9th International Conference on Asian Digital Libraries (ICADL2006)*, pp. 478–481, ISBN: 3-540-49375-1, Kyoto, Japan, November 2006, Springer-Verlag, Berlin Heidelberg

Khaltarkhuu, G. & Maeda, A. (2007). Building a Digital Library of Traditional Mongolian Historical Documents. *Proceedings of the 7th ACM/IEEE Joint Conference on Digital Libraries (JCDL2007)*, p. 483, ISBN 978-1-59593-644-8, Vancouver, Canada, June 2007, Springer-Verlag, Berlin Heidelberg

Khaltarkhuu, G. & Maeda, A. (2008). Developing a Traditional Mongolian Script Digital Library. *Proceedings of the 11th International Conference on Asia-Pacific Digital Libraries: Universal and Ubiquitous Access to Information*, LNCS, vol. 5362, pp. 41–50, ISBN 978-3-540-89532-9, Bali, Indonesia, December 2008, Springer-Verlag, Berlin Heidelberg

Kimura, F. & Maeda, A. (2009). An Approach to Information Access and Knowledge Discovery from Historical Documents. *Conference Abstracts of the Digital Humanities 2009(DH09)*, pp. 359–361, ISBN 978-061-52-9929-7, College Park, MD, June 2009, Maryland Institute for Technology in the Humanities

Kimura, F.; Toba, T.; Tezuka, T. & Maeda, A. (2008). Federated Searching System for Humanities Databases Using Automatic Metadata Mapping. *Proceedings of 9th International Conference on Dublin Core and Metadata Applications*, pp. 139–140, ISSN 1939-1366, Seoul, Korea, October 2009, the Dublin Core Metadata Initiative

Kitamura, M. & Matsumoto, Y. (1996). Automatic Extraction of Word Sequence Correspondences in Parallel Corpora, Proceedings of the 4th Workshop on Very Large Corpora, pp. 79–87

Koolen, M.; Adriaans, F.; Kamps, J. & Rijke, M. (2006). A Cross-Language Approach to Historic Document Retrieval. *Proceedings of the 28th European Conference on IR Research: Advances in Information Retrieval*, LNCS, vol. 3936, pp. 407–419, ISBN 978-3-540-33347-0, London, UK, April 2006, Springer-Verlag, Berlin Heidelberg

Pilz, T.; Ernst-Gerlach, A.; Kempken, S.; Rayson, P. & Archer, D. (2008). The Identification of Spelling Variants in English and German Historical Texts: Manual or Automatic. *Literary and Linguistic Computing*, vol. 23, no. 1, November 2008, pp. 65–72, ALLC, ACH, Oxford University Press, ISSN 0268-1145, Oxford, UK

Shagdarsuren, T. (2001). *Study of Mongolian Scripts (Graphic Study of Grammatology)*, Enlarged second edition. ISBN 99929-5-347-0, Urlakh Erdem Khevleliin Gazar, Ulan Bator (in Mongolian)

Tanaka, T. (2002). Measuring the Similarity between Compound Nouns in Different Languages Using Non-Parallel Corpora, Proceedings of the 19th COLING, pp. 981–987, ISBN 978-1-55860-896-2, Morgan Kaufmann Publishers, December 2002, Taipei, Taiwan

The Dublin Core Metadata Initiative (2008). Dublin Core Metadata Element Set, Version 1.1. http://dublincore.org/documents/dces/

Tsevel, Y. (1966). *Mongol helnii tovch tailbar toli.* Ulsiin Khevleliin khereg erkhlekh Khoroo, Ulan Bator (in Mongolian)

Tungalag, D. (2005). *Mongol ulsiin undesnii nomiin san dahi Mongoliin tuuhiin gar bichmeliin nomzuin sudalgaa*, Volume 1. ISBN 99929-6-313-1, Time Printing, Ulan Bator (in Mongolian)

Zeng, M. L. & Jian, Q. (2008). *Metadata*, ISBN 978-1-85604-655-8, Facet Publishing, London

3

Bringing the Digital Library Design into the Realm of Enterprise Architecture

A. Abrizah and A.N. Zainab
Digital Library Research Group,
University of Malaya, Kuala Lumpur
Malaysia

1. Introduction

Previous digital library research and initiatives have conceptualized and proposed several frameworks for the design, development, evaluation and interaction of digital library systems. Levy and Marshall (1996) discussed a work-oriented perspective of digital library research that is based on the work people do, and how digital libraries assist in the completion of work related tasks. Their framework highlights three crucial characteristics of digital libraries: document, technology and work (which involves research and service). Moen and McClure (1997) identified a framework of five interacting dimensions in digital library of Government Information Locator Service (GILS): policy, users, technology, contents, and standards. The evaluation framework also includes three perspectives, representing the "views" of the stakeholders in the GILS: users, agencies, and the government. Marchionini and Fox (1999) identified four dimensions of digital library development: community, technology, service and content. Saracevic and Covi (2000) presented a framework, consisting seven levels, for examining digital libraries: social, institutional, individual, interface, engineering, processing and content. Another holistic framework is presented by Fuhr et al. (2001) consisting four major dimensions, namely data/collection, system/technology, users and usage. Sandusky (2002) developed a list of six attributes in framing digital library usability research: audience, institution, access, content, services, and design and development. Soergel (2002) offered a digital library research framework consisting of three guiding principles and eleven specific themes for research and development. Gonclaves et al. (2004) introduced 5S and formalisms for Streams, Structures, Spaces, Scenarios, and Societies – as a framework for providing theoretical and practical unification of digital libraries. All these frameworks emphasize the importance of a holistic approach rather than examine digital libraries as a single view, which would be limited in their utility.

However, the absence of common frameworks in the digital library development practices undermines the ability to develop and design digital library systems efficiently, to create large-scale collaborative activities, and to communicate the value of the systems to other communities. Gladney et al. (1994) wrote that the broad and deep requirements of digital libraries demand new frameworks and theories in order to understand better the complex interactions among their components. Supporting this claim, the summary report of the Joint NSF-European Union (EU) Working Groups on Future Directions of Digital 1 Libraries Research recommended that "new frameworks and theories be developed in order to understand the complex interactions between the various components in a globally distributed digital library" (Schauble and Smeaton, 1999). Formal frameworks are crucial to specify and understand clearly and unambiguously the characteristics, structure, and behavior of complex information systems such as digital libraries. The Digital Library Federation (DLF) in 2005 sponsored the formation of the Service Framework Group (SFG) to consider a more systematic, community-based approach to align the functions of digital libraries in fulfilling the needs of information environments (Lavoie, Henry and Dempsey, 2006). DLF envisaged that digital library functionalities be generated from the library business processes, considering the architectures as information systems with specific business requirements (Castelli and Fox, 2007). It is in this context, and in recognition of visions already underway to align digital library development with the emerging perspective of the Enterprise Architecture (Borninha, 2007), the authors conducted a study that seeks to understand and model the digital library services adopting a framework that give preference to scopes, goal requirements and processes - those concepts already common in Enterprise Architecture processes

Abdullah and Zainab (2008) regard a digital library as an enterprise that requires architecting. An Enterprise Architecture for the digital library is a framework or blueprint which shows how the digital library organisation carries out an intended task and how the digital library will or can improve the processes. It shows how a digital library represents a special workspace for the user community, not only for search and access but also for the process or workflow management, information creation, sharing and exchange, and distributed workgroup communication. In order to identify what is required of a digital library in a specific context, a sound methodology is needed to establish an understanding of the digital library entire structure. A multi-faceted information services such as digital libraries may be examined along different dimensions and from different perspectives or views of the stakeholders. There is a need to identify potential users, their involvement and roles in the digital library, their attitude towards the technology, their perception of its potential use and how it fits within the digital library goals in general. In order to do this, a digital library enterprise is required, which is derived and based on empirical data and stand up to conceptual reasoning. This chapter shows how an established Enterprise Architecture can be adopted as a formal framework to guide the research, design and development of digital libraries, providing a precise specification of requirements against which the implementation can be compared for correctness.

2. Enterprise Architecture

In general, Enterprise Architecture is a framework that describes how an organisation develops, manages and uses information technology to optimally support its business functions (Kahn and Wilensky, 1995). Sometimes, the term refers to the group of people responsible for modeling and then documenting the information architecture; other times the term denotes the process of doing this work. More commonly, Enterprise Architecture refers to the models, documents and reusable items (such as components, framework and objects) that reflect the actual architecture (McGovern et al., 2003). In the EACommunity (http://www.eacommunity.com/) Enterprise Architecture is a framework or blueprint for how the organisation achieves the current and future business objectives. It examines business processes, information technology, software and hardware, local and wide area networks, people, operations and projects with an organisation's overall strategy. Each of

these strategies has a separate architectural discipline (such as business, information, application, technical and product) and Enterprise Architecture is the "glue" that integrates each of these disciplines into a cohesive framework (Bolton, 2004) as depicted in Figure 1.
From these definitions, it is understood that Enterprise Architecture consists of the various structures and processes of an organisation. Following this understanding, it is known that an Enterprise Architecture model is a representation of those structures and processes. A good Enterprise Architecture model will depict the organisation both as it is today and as it is envisioned in the future, and will map the various views representing the architecture to one another. These views include both business-oriented perspectives as well as technical perspectives. The blueprint or framework of the enterprise would reveal detailed statements and processes that characterized architectural drawings. The detail drawings would be in any form, such as rich pictures, structured charts, data flow diagrams, Unified Modelling Language (UML) activity diagrams, database tables and entity-relationship model.

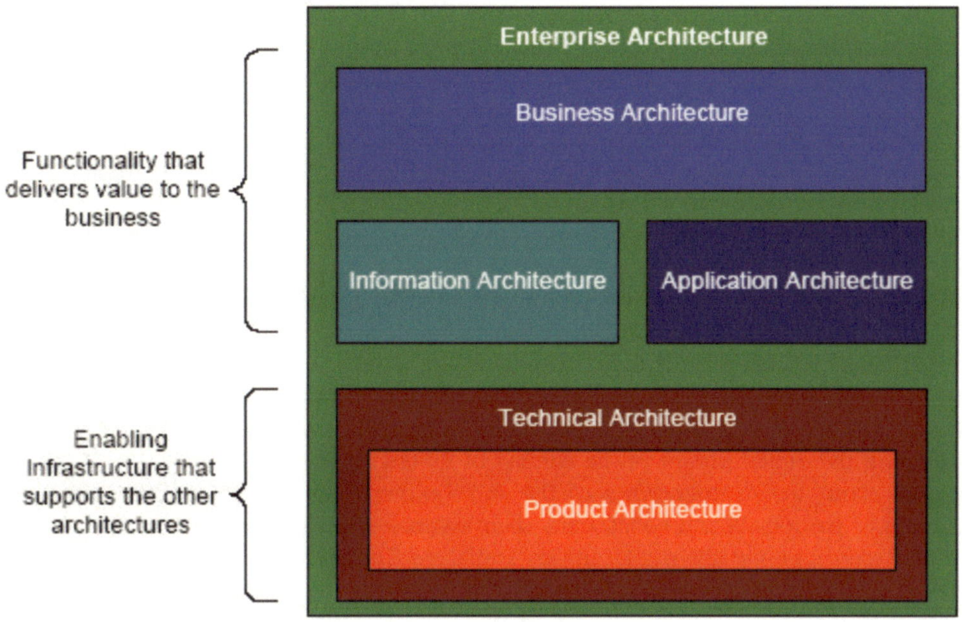

Fig. 1. Enterprise Architecture Relationship (Source: Bolton, 2004)

3. Zachman Framework for Enterprise Architecture

The Zachman Framework is a logical structure for classifying and organising the descriptive representations of the enterprise that are significant to the management of the enterprise, as well as to the development of the enterprise' systems (Zachman, 2002). The framework uses a grid model to provide a logical structure for classifying and organising the descriptive representation of an enterprise, in six different dimensions, and each dimension can be perceived in five different perspectives. In this framework, the architecture is described across two independent aspects, the rows represent the views of five different types of stakeholders (planner, owner, designer, builder and sub-contractor) and the columns represent six different aspects of the architecture (data, function, network, people, time and motivation). The points of intersection between the rows and the columns (between the views and the aspects) form cells. Each of these cells holds important information of the enterprise (also known as artifacts) that needs to be understood and explicitly declared. The Zachman Framework's enterprise design model is presented in Figure 2.

The Zachman Framework for Enterprise Architecture is found suitable to investigate the initial requirements and define the digital library organisation, processes, technology and information flows, as well as ground the design of digital libraries for the following reasons:

a. The framework helps to explicitly show the many perspectives that need to be addressed by the digital library. It requires the planner, owner and designer of the digital library to involve the stakeholders to ensure that it meets their needs and will be used. It holistically controls the approach to investigate the user requirements and guides the data gathering techniques.
b. The framework requires the involvement of stakeholders, not just the enterprise architects and developers. and ideally this practice is what digital library designers and developers should follow. This aligns with the need to involve stakeholders in digital library design and development.
c. The framework is robust enough. It explicitly shows and requires the designer to consider all aspects (What, How, Where, Who, When, Why) of the digital library design.
d. The framework is generic in nature (Pereira and Sousa, 2004) and can be applied perfectly to digital library organization. As such it is a flexible framework and it does not impose a method or restrict any user to a set of pre-defined artifacts.

This chapter shows, through a case study, how the three tiers of Zachman Framework – the contextual (scope) or planner's perspectives (Figure 2 Row 1), the conceptual (business model) or the owner's perspectives (Figure 2 Row 2) and the logical (system model) or the designer's perspectives (Figure 2, Row 3) – are used to design a digital library. The first two rows or layers are referred to as the Business Architecture (Figure 1) for they describe the functions a business performs and the information it uses. The third row refers to the information and the application architecture (Figure 1). The planner is concerned with positioning the digital library in the context of its environment. This is when the planner enquires about the demographics of the stakeholders, ICT individual differences, their readiness to participate and collaborate, their awareness of the concept of digital libraries and their perception of the digital library initiative. The owner is interested in the digital library's deliverable and how it will be used. The designer is concerned with how the digital library is to perform its functions. This involves investigating the resources that are used, the user behaviour of seeking for resources, the experience of searching, the relevance perceived and the problems encountered. The possible sets of constructs or artifacts to represent the cell content for each cell in the top three rows or layers of the Zachman Framework are presented in Table 1.

Row 6 of the framework represents the physical manifestation of the end product itself. Zachman (2003) says that technically Row 6 is not an architecture because it is not a representation (it is the actual thing), however it is useful to incorporate it into the framework graphic as it completes the architectural picture. For an enterprise employment of the framework, Row 6 represents the Functioning Enterprise, which is the end result of the architectural process. In this research, the end result is to ensure that Row 6 represents what the owners have in mind for the digital library enterprise at Row 2. Therefore it is important to incorporate users assessment to evaluate the viability of a useful and enduring digital library system for the user community. This would involve assessment of the usefulness and usability of the system in terms of resources (data), processes (function), location (network), user community (people), time and goals (motivation).

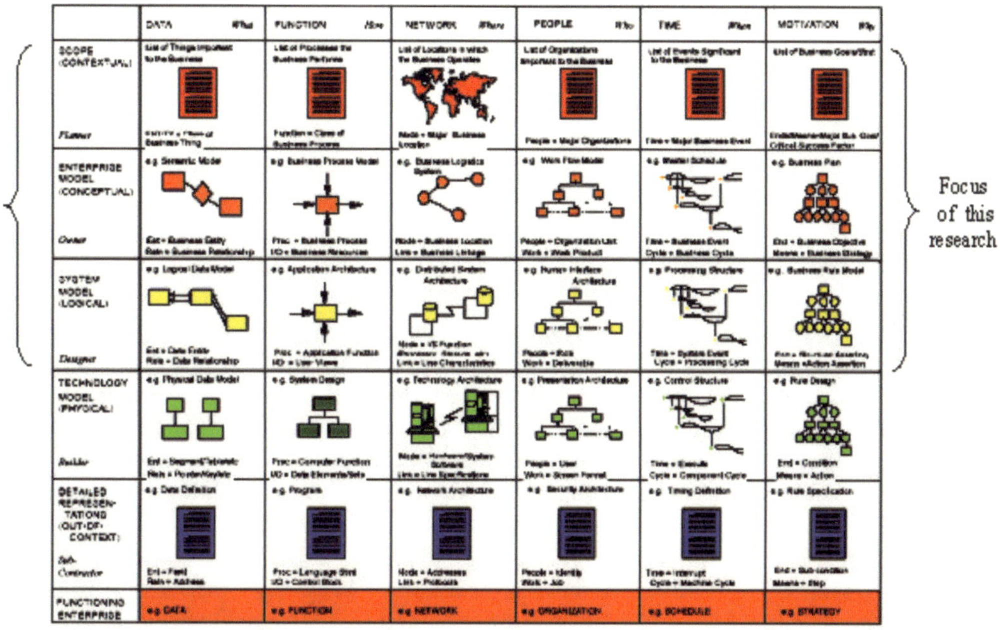

Fig. 2. The Zachman Framework for Enterprise Architecture
(Source: http://www.zifa.com, 2006)

	What	How	Where	Who	When	Why	
SCOPE (Contextual) Planner	List of things important to the business	List of processes the business perform	List of location in which the business operate	List of people involved in the business	List of events significant to the business	List of business goals and objectives	SCOPE (Contextual) Planner
BUSINESS (Conceptual) Owner	Semantic Model	Business Process Model	Business Logistic Model	Work flow model	Master Schedule	Business Plan	BUSINESS (Conceptual) Owner
SYSTEM (Logical) Designer	Logical Data Model	Application Architecture	Distributed System Architecture	Human Interface Architecture	Processing Structure	Business Data Model	SYSTEM (Logical) Designer
TECHNOLOGY (Physical) Builder							
DETAILED PRESENTATION (Out-of-context view)							
FUNCTIONING ENTERPRISE – The prototype	**Data**	**Function**	**Network**	**People**	**Time**	**Motivation**	FUNCTIONING ENTERPRISE – The prototype

Table 1. Zachman Framework at the Contextual, Conceptual and Logical Systems Architecture

4. Formulation of an integrated framework for the collaborative digital library

Collaborative digital libraries are constructed, collected and organized by a community of users and their functionalities support the information needs and uses of that community. Renda and Straccia (2004) viewed a digital library as a collaborative working and meeting space of people sharing common interests. Through a case study method, Zachman Framework is used as a basis to investigate the existing stakeholder's conditions and environment that would ensure the reception of a collaborative digital library for urban secondary schools use in Malaysia. In this digital library environment, students collaboratively build the digital library resources, which indirectly allow members of the community to be aware and be actively involved in local content development. The collaborative digital library would benefit both the students who would be the creator and publisher of digital project works and the teachers who would be given the experience of managing digital resources. The multi-method approach used in the case study, to ensure the consideration of all the aspects (dimensions) of a digital library system and the relationship of these dimensions in the framework used, has been reported elsewhere (Abdullah and Zainab, 2008). Findings were used to populate the Zachman Framework with contextual, conceptual, logical and module diagrams at every intersection between the columns (why, what, who, how, where, when) and the rows (scope, business model, system model). The framework abstracts the characteristics and features of the digital library based on the following six dimensions:

- Motivation factor, requiring the planner and owner to solicit answers to the "why" question, why there is need for the digital library? Why does the current business process need special handling such as those provided by the digital library?
- Data factor abstracts the "what" aspects of the digital library. What data that is currently handled by the stakeholders? What format would the data take in the digital library environment? What are the characteristics of the data used, processed, stored and presented or disseminated in terms of quality, accuracy, usability, description and organization?
- People factor looks at the "who" questions or the roles of people in the digital project environment. Who will be instructing? Who will be handling the data? Who will be reporting the collated or processed data? Are the players in the digital library environment "ready" to participate and contribute to the digital library initiative? Are they able to do so?
- Function or Process factor defines the "how" of the activities in the digital environment. How will users search for data, how will they store the data? How will students write, present and submit their project report? How will the teachers ensure that the students know what is required? How do they grade the reports? How will they keep the reports submitted for the specified time required by the Malaysian Ministry of Education? How can the school library or resource centre accommodate these reports?
- Place or Networks looks at the "where" factor. Where will the digital library be located? Where will it be accessed by the stakeholders?
- Time looks at the "when" aspects of the digital library. When will submission of reports take place? This is useful for designing schedules, the processing and control architecture and timing systems.

The next section illustrates the use of Zachman Framework in design of the digital library, focusing on all six dimensions of the framework from three perspectives. Each of these dimensions is investigated from the perspective of the planner (Row 1), owner (Row 2) and designer (Row 3) of the digital library. These perspectives help ensure that everything relevant to the digital library enterprise is covered. The columns, comprising the six dimensions, are arranged so that the most important column or the focus of attention is presented first. At the end, the outcome would be in the form of listings and diagrams depicting the scope, business and system model of the digital library. Rows 4, 5 and 6 are beyond the scope of this chapter.

5. Case analysis of Zachman framework for the collaborative digital library

5.1 Motivation: why the digital library is needed

Why (Motivation) column of Zachman Framework extracts the motivation of the people that support the realization of the digital library. This reveals the reasons for creating the digital library, as well as the establishment of goals, objectives and business plan of the digital library. The authors felt motivation aspect (stakeholders' motivation) of the framework should be first populated and given the most importance. The case study revealed that the educational community is ready to collaboratively build the digital library as reflected by the following findings (Abdullah and Zainab, 2006):

- Students are "Internet ready", as indicated by (a) high home computer ownership as such they are ready to utilize the digital library; (b) high Internet penetration either at home, school, cyber cafes or friend's houses; (c) a high number of students either have 3-4 years or more than 5 years experience in computer usage; (d) students regularly go online, between either every alternate days or everyday.
- Students are "digital ready" as indicated by their awareness, experience in using and preferring digital sources. The survey indicates that all students know how to word process; they know how to prepare slide presentations or draw using the computer, edit images, create multimedia and scan images, create web pages, database or undertake simple programming. This results show that they are aware and competent in handling digital resources, which is necessary when using digital library.
- Students are also moderately "Web ready" as they know how to use the web. Although most had no formal training, they learn how to use the Web by self-teaching, from books and people. The students also learn how to find sources on their own, from their parents and siblings or from their classmates and friends.
- Students are ready to collaboratively develop digital resources as they indicated sharing the resources they create or found with their friends either by e-mailing the URLs of websites, informing others through chat room or social networks or creating links to websites.
- Some students are "ready web publishers", as many of them either maintain a group web page, have their own personal web page or have been creating page pages for others. The results also show that the students have experience in creating digital resource over the Internet using webpage creator tools or HTML to develop their sites.
- Students do use the Internet for school related assignments or as a major source for their school project. Students sampled highly use the Internet resources to get information for the following subjects, History, Science and Geography. The results indicate that students believe that the Internet helps them with their school work.
- All students feel that there is a need for digital library of local information and feel that this would definitely benefit them. The results indicated very significant correlation between positive perception of the digital library with high Internet use, length of

Internet experience, accessibility of Internet from home high self ratings of Internet skills.

- Teachers in the case study see the value of digital resources and online publishing for their students. They expressed the willingness to play the role as a facilitator in the digital library environment. They were keen on the digital library because students could contribute original works to be shared with other students, especially where some local contents are not available in textbooks. They believed students would be more careful in preparing their project report if they make it available to wider audience in the digital library environment.
- Teachers felt that a digital library would solve problem of storage and retrieval of reports submitted since project reports kept in resource room could only be retrieved by class name and level, and difficult to be retrieved by subject or topics of report or by specific student's name.
- The school's infrastructural facilities are ready to support a digital library as students can gain access to computers at self-accessed learning centres, especially for students and teachers who do not have computers or Internet access at their homes.

The above findings indicated that the readiness factors serve as motivating indicators, goals and objectives that support the plan for developing the digital library. Figure 3 presents the motivating factors that support the plan of the collaborative digital library.

The findings of the case study were plugged into the first three rows of the motivational aspect of Zachman Framework. In Row 1, the Planner's goals and objectives are defined in the form of vision statement that provides the strategic direction for the digital library. The digital library will support secondary students' information needs in conducting research projects through project-based learning (PBL). In PBL, students interpret, analyze, synthesize, generate, and evaluate information about a topic, collaborate with others, and produce a report (Blumfeld et al, 1991). To support students in these types of activities, a full complement of tools is needed to meet the unique needs of learners, and Internet technologies such as digital libraries have the affordances to support students in these activities. Based on this premise, as well as building from various illustrations of digital library initiatives' vision statement, the planner establishes the vision of the collaborative digital library to populate Row 1 of the Motivation column. The planner's vision of the digital library is as follows:

> *"The collaborative digital library should enable secondary students conducting history*[1] *school projects to access the information they need any time and any where, in a friendly, efficient and effective way, by overcoming the barriers o distance and language. The digital library should enable students to collaboratively contribute resources as the digital library is seen as a growing repository on Malaysian local history for education".*

With the vision in mind, the planner establishes the following goals for developing and implementing the collaborative digital library:

a. the development of local historical resources;
b. provision of resources for lifelong learning;
c. provision of round-the clock access; and
d. development of community of users.

---

[1] History has been chosen as the domain of the digital library test-bed based on the survey findings that indicated the students surveyed mainly use Internet resources to get information for their History project. As such the domain of the digital library is collections of History project reports submitted by the secondary school students.

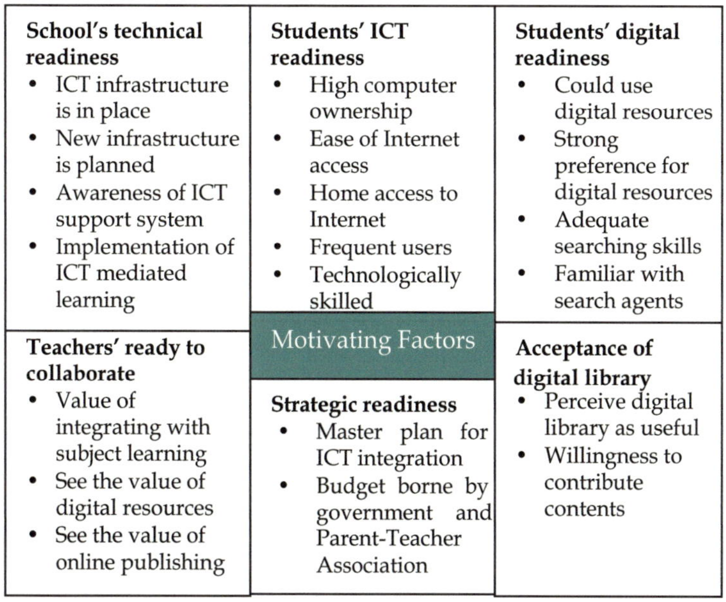

Fig. 3. Motivating Factors that Support the Plan for Realization of the Digital Library

In this capacity, it establishes "a digital library service environment" - that is, a networked, online information space in which students can discover, locate, acquire access to and, increasingly, use information. The objective of the digital library is therefore to provide a learning environment and resources network for history education which is:

a. designed to meet the information needs of learners, in both individual and collaborative settings (enable the creation, organisation and maintaining of local history resources);
b. constructed to enable use of a broad array of materials for local history learning, primarily in digital format submitted by the educational community themselves (they themselves become resource providers); and
c. managed actively to promote reliable access anytime - anywhere to quality collections and services (provided over the Internet), available both within and outside the network.

Row 2 of the Motivation column identifies the owners' business plan that is the approach to use the collaborative digital library. The digital library is modelled to focus on serving students information needs in conducting research projects. As such, in the implementation of this digital library project, the use of the online resources would be an integral part of history projects-based learning activities. The digital library may move the student community towards an emerging digital resources and the submission of reports in the electronic form is therefore feasible. The implementation of the business plan (Figure 4) is consistent with the Ministry of Education's implementation and evaluation of History project, which will make the accomplishment of the goals and objectives feasible. The teachers on the other hand will be given the opportunity to validate the quality of submissions to maintain the quality of the digital library, grade the report online and add links to resources found on the Internet.

Row 3 spells out the the designer's perspectives which expressed the motivation of the digital library in the form of behavioural objectives. The objectives of the collaborative DL from the designer's perspectives are to:

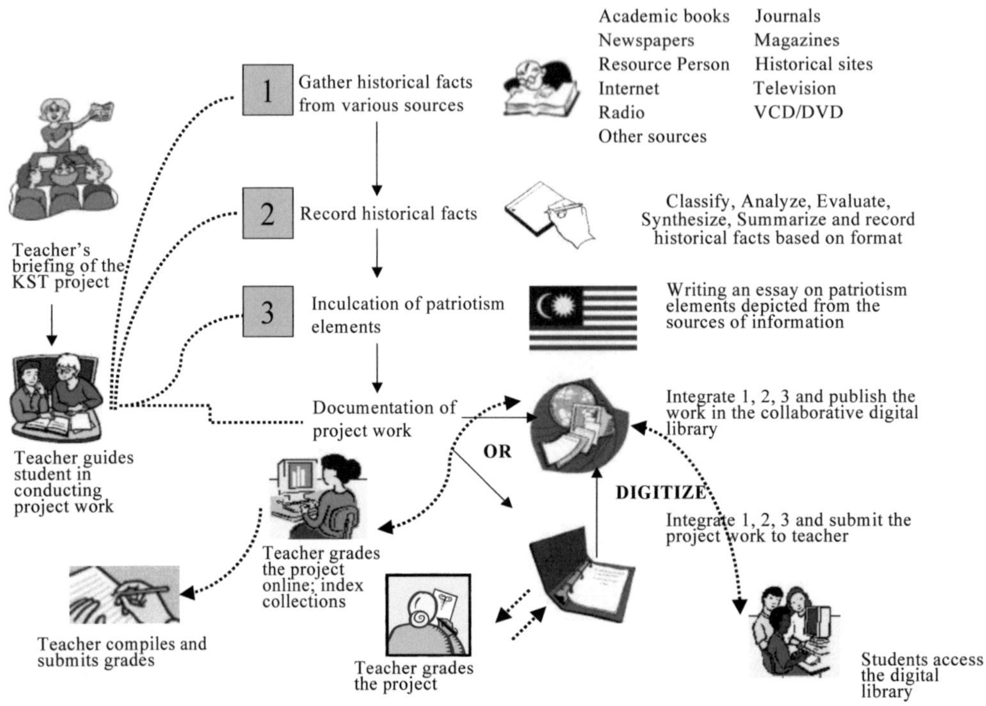

Fig. 4. The Business Plan to Use the Collaborative Digital Library
(Owner's View of Motivation)

a. Enable students to search and browse the digital library resources through various access points regarding the topics they are exploring
b. Allow the students to sequence and organize their project reports in various styles, construct references and append digital objects or pictures to their report.
c. Provide the students with the experience of publishing their project report, allow teachers grade and their friends to view the repot. The motivation for this is to satisfy their innate need to share their work, so that their peers can give comments for improvements before the report is finally submitted.
d. Allow teachers to check the suitability of submissions, maintain quality of contents of the digital library and grade the submissions.
e. Allow teachers and students to provide metadata for resources submitted to the digital library. A metadata schema (Dublin core) will be applied for this purpose.
f. Enable students and user groups to register as members to login and submit and describe resources
g. Allow users to submit feedback or submit useful links to other resources in the Internet.
h. Guide and assist users in using the digital library functions and services.
i. Allow authorized users to add, modify or delete submitted resources to the digital library.

These behavioural objectives of the digital library would assist the designer (Row 3) in developing the required digital library. The motivation and objective statements subsequently assist in the development of the user requirement and detailed definitions of the digital library services required in the Function (How) column of the Framework.

5.2 Data: what resources constitute the digital library

What (Data) column of the Zachman Framework describes the digital library resources students used to fulfill their research needs. The data component, at the macro level identifies the information resources included or covered in the collaborative digital library, and at the micro level, concerned the collections, quality, accuracy, usability, description and organisation of the resources in the digital library. Findings from the case study revealed that the students and teachers emphasized the needs for contents to be "clear, accurate, adequate, organised, valid, reliable, informative and resourceful"

To cater for students' information needs, in Row 1, the planner describes the three main categories of resources (Figure 5), without policy-controlled access. The types of resources are (a) resources that are born digital; (b) digitised resources or digital proxies for physical items; and (c) Links to other resources relevant to the domain focus of the digital libbrary. The digital library collections incorporates not only digital resources in different media types such as text, images, web documents, audio and video, but also in different formats with different levels of content quality and metadata.

Row 2 of the Data column is a contiguous model of the resources expressed in terms of domain focus and topics seen by the owners of the digital library. History has been chosen as the domain of the digital library test-bed based on the survey findings that indicated the students surveyed mainly use Internet resources to get information for their History project.

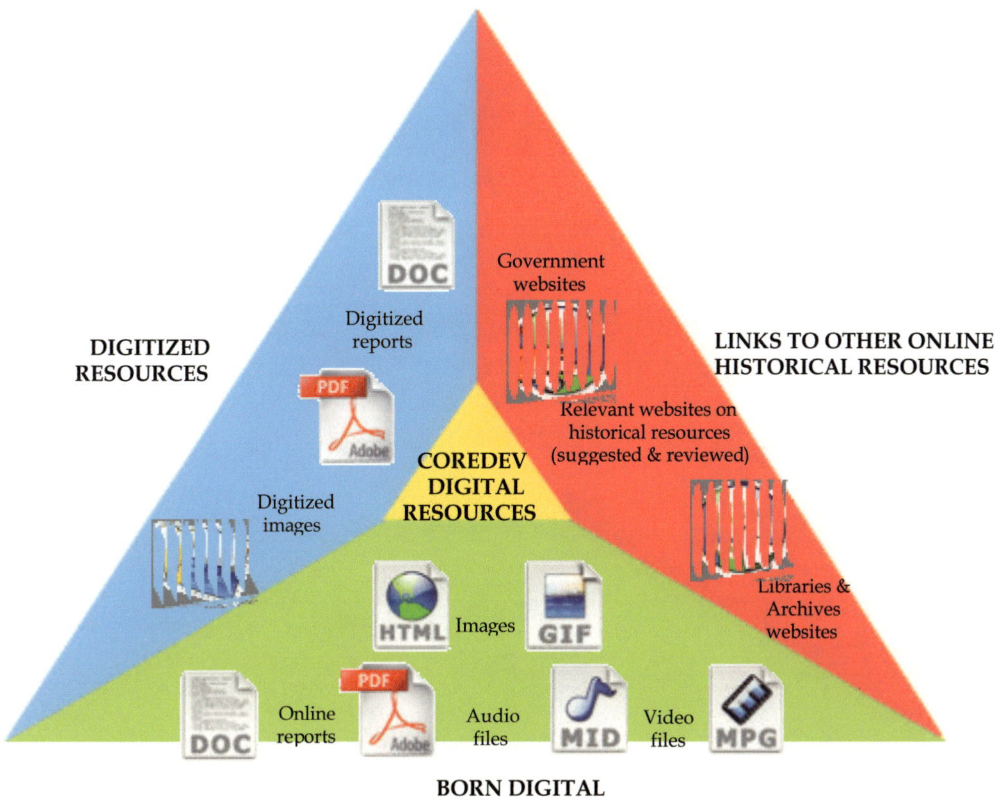

Fig. 5. The Digital Library Resources in Various Media Types and Format (Planner's View of Data)

Case findings revealed that the project reports are typically made available in the form of collections, which refers to groups of resources organised around three themes or topic namely prominent personalities, historical events and historical buildings. Figure 6 presents the semantic description of the domain focus, contents, content criteria and scope of the collaborative digital library, which populates the Data component of the Zachman Framework. The stakeholders' needs for contents to be "clear, accurate, adequate, organised, valid, reliable, informative and resourceful" are therefore used as a set of general guidelines or selection criteria of resources accepted for submission.
From the designer's perspective (Row 3), the data of the digital library is expressed as table definition for the digital library data (comprising digital objects data and metadata, user information, annotation and static information pages) and metadata profile for the digital object resource description (comprising administrative, technical and descriptive metadata). Administrative metadata is created by the author, technical metadata is automatically-generated and descriptive metadata is assigned by the content access provider (human indexer). The descriptive metadata schema used for the object data description is the Dublin Core (DC) Metadata. The digital library has altogether 16 metadata elements and incorporates DC's 14 out of 15 elements, namely title, creator, subject, description, publisher, contributor, date, type, format, identifier, language, relation, coverage and rights. The DC source metadata element is not used. Two other elements incorporated are Collection and Ranking metadata.

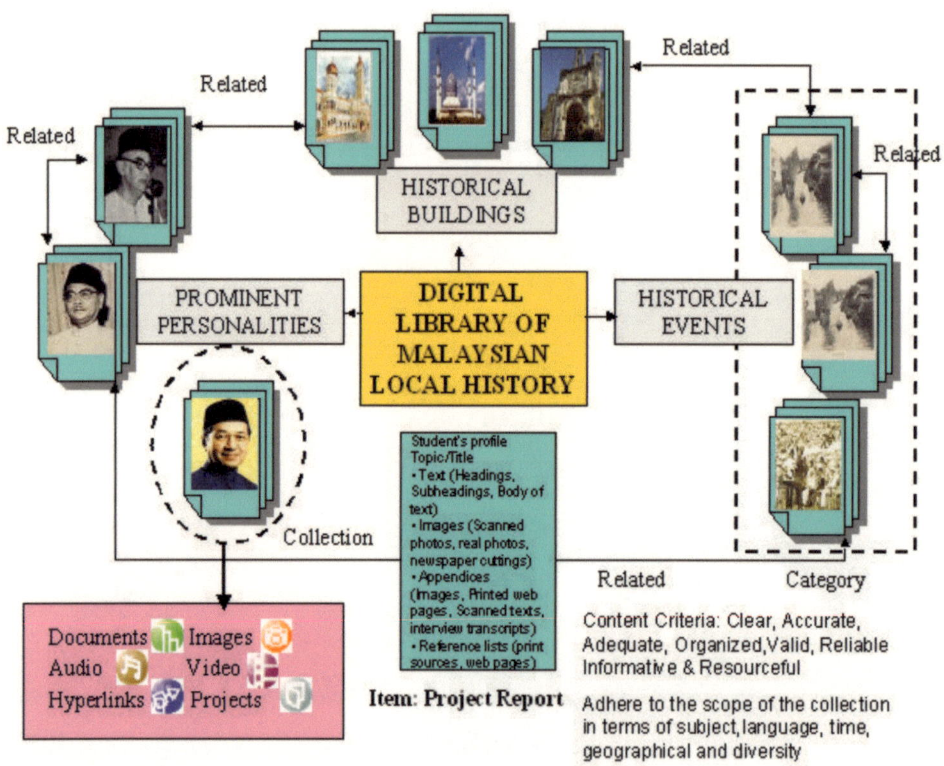

Fig. 6. Domain Focus, Contents, Content Criteria and Scope of the Collaborative Digital Library (Owner's View of Data)

5.3 People: who interacts with / within the digital library

Who (People) column represents the stakeholders or the people within the digital library enterprise to which the digital library assigns responsibility for work. Thus, this component concerns the identification of the digital library users, their information needs, their usage of the Internet and online digital resources and their roles in the enterprise. The design of the enterprise has to do with the allocation of work and the structure of authority and responsibility. This column also deals with human-machine interfaces and relationships between the people and the work they perform.

In Row 1, the planner identifies the audience and the digital library organization. There are three types of audiences within the collaborative digital library enterprise, categorized as partners, guests and affiliate members (Figure 7). The planner identified these groups of people in the form of digital library organisational structure.

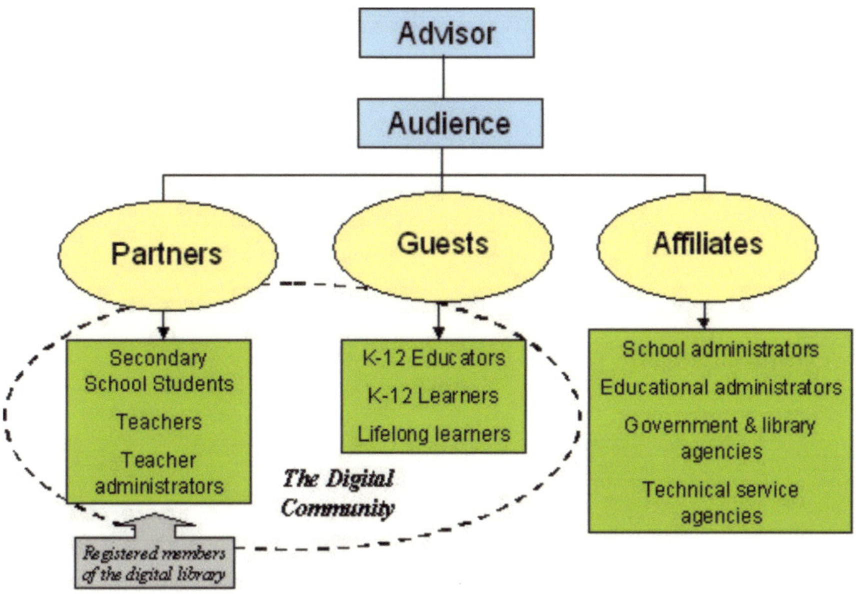

Fig. 7. The Digital Library Organisational Structure (Planner's View of People)

From the owner's perspective, Row 2 of the People Column illustrates the four main classes of people or actors and their respective roles in the collaborative DL. In this Consumer - Content Provider - Content Manager - Administrator model, each class of actors represents a particular generic role. The digital community follows certain rules and their members play different roles, as consumers, content developers or providers, content access providers and content manager (Figure 8).

In Row 3, the designer fleshed out the interaction between actors and technology into a rich picture linked to the functional requirements (Figure 9). Here, the digital library community includes people as well as computers, agents, network connections, files and operating systems, user interfaces, communication links, and protocols, which either use or support the digital library services. The communities of autonomous agents and computers instantiate functions upon requests by the actors of the digital library. To operate, these agents and computers need structures of vocabulary and protocols. They act by sending streams of queries and retrieving streams of results. The digital library system uses the

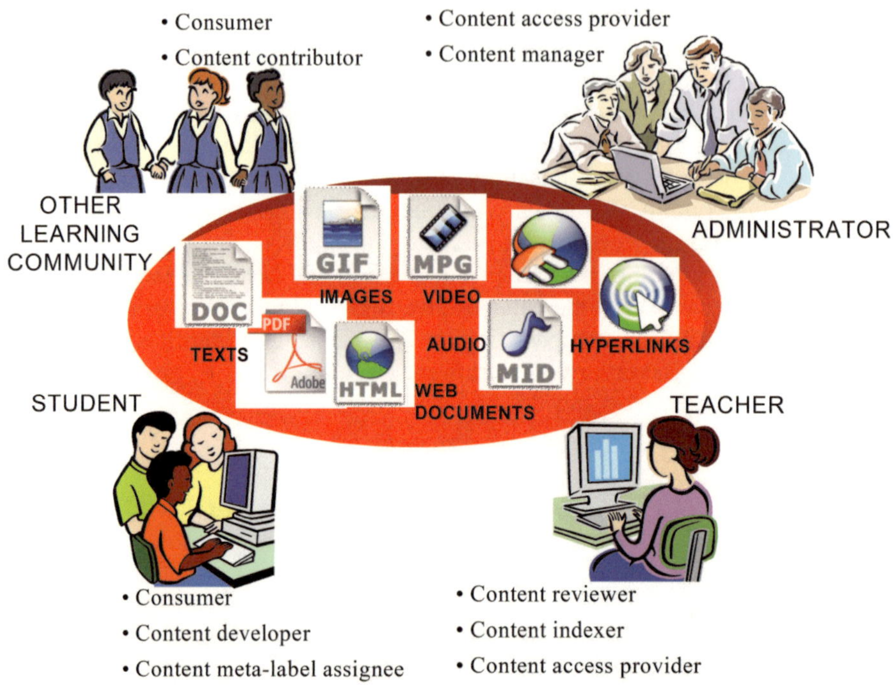

Fig. 8. The Digital Library Actor-Roles Diagram (Owner's View of People)

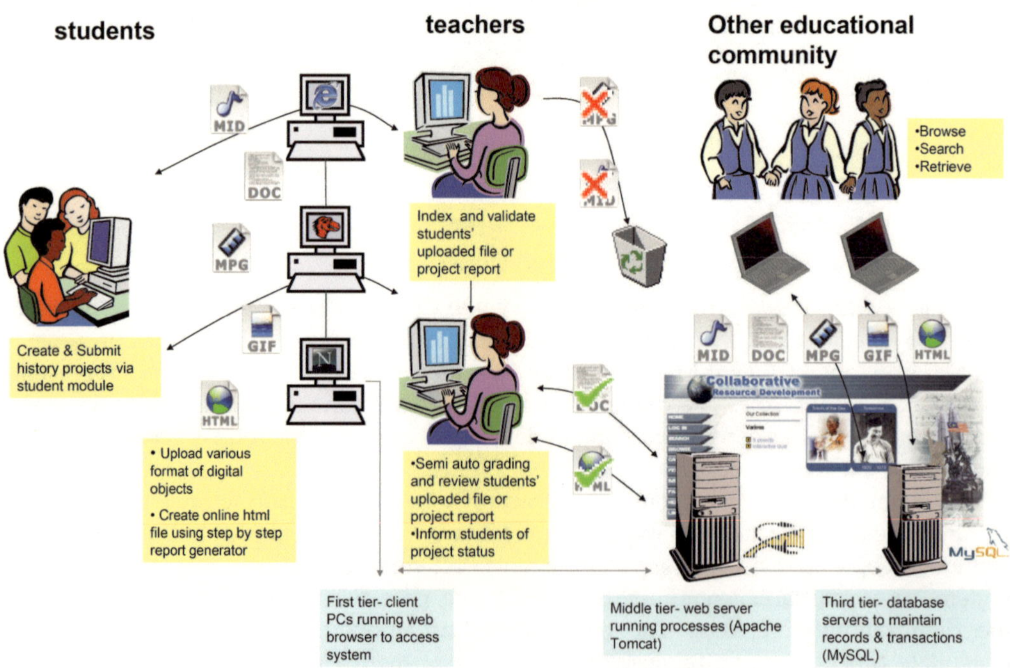

Fig. 9. Actors and Their Roles Depicted in the Digital Library Three-Tier Client-Server Architecture (Designer's View of People)

three-tier client-server architecture. As depicted in Figure 9, the client tier comprises computers with web browsers such as Internet Explorer (4.0 or above), Netscape Navigator, Mozilla Firefox and Opera. User interfaces are provided for clients to process their application and manipulate their data. All application programmes reside in the middle-tier (web server). The web server processes the request from the client and then returns required result in web page format. It processes data request by linking to a database server (such as authenticating and validating users that login into the system). It is also linked to transaction server, especially when clients are uploading files to the web server. The third tier consists of the database server and transaction for maintaining data records.

5.4 Function: what happens in the digital library?

How (functions) defines the functions or activities the digital library enterprise is concerned about relative to each perspective. In Row 1, the planner describes the students' research activities that take place, which encompass the entire information seeking process (from recognizing the need for information to finding, using and presenting it) and the submission and evaluation of the information in the form of project report. This is presented in the form of rich pictures Basically, the students do solitary information seeking, have spontaneous interactions with other people such as parents, siblings and friends and ask for help, and work with information in a group. The description of the activities when conducting history projects are then transformed into the online activities the students and teachers would be able to perform in the collaborative digital library. Figure 10 presents the workflows and processes the collaborative digital library enterprise should conduct. These processes are also in line with the owner's plan to use the digital library for school project (Row 2 of Motivation). The function component refers to the activities students perform in their research, such as choosing topic, searching for information, organising resources, writing, presenting, submitting and teachers grading of project work.

Using data from analysis of the activities culled from the research (Row 1 of Function), formulation of behavioural objectives of the digital library (Row 2 of Motivation) as well as from the analysis of digital library functional requirements (Row 3 of Motivation), the planner develops the user requirement expressed in terms of functions and present it as services in a contiguous structured chart, The structured chart is comprehensible to the owner as the conceptual model of the digital library services (Figure 11). This structured chart populates Row 2 of the Function Column and describes the process of translating the objectives of the digital library enterprise into successively more detailed definitions of its services. Feedback from the stakeholders on the potential features of a service and digital library design implication derived from the analysis of the case study have helped to ascertain the main features required by the collaborative digital library.

In Row 3, the designer portrays the digital services in terms of data transforming processes, described exclusively in terms of definition of programme modules and how they interact with each other. The three system modules, namely administrators (including teachers), students and guests, provide different access types for different level of users. Along with this are specific definitions of security requirements, in terms of who (which role) is permitted access to what function, in the form of structured charts and detailed description of the modules menu.

Fig. 10. Activities Performed in the Collaborative Digital Library (Planner's View of Function)

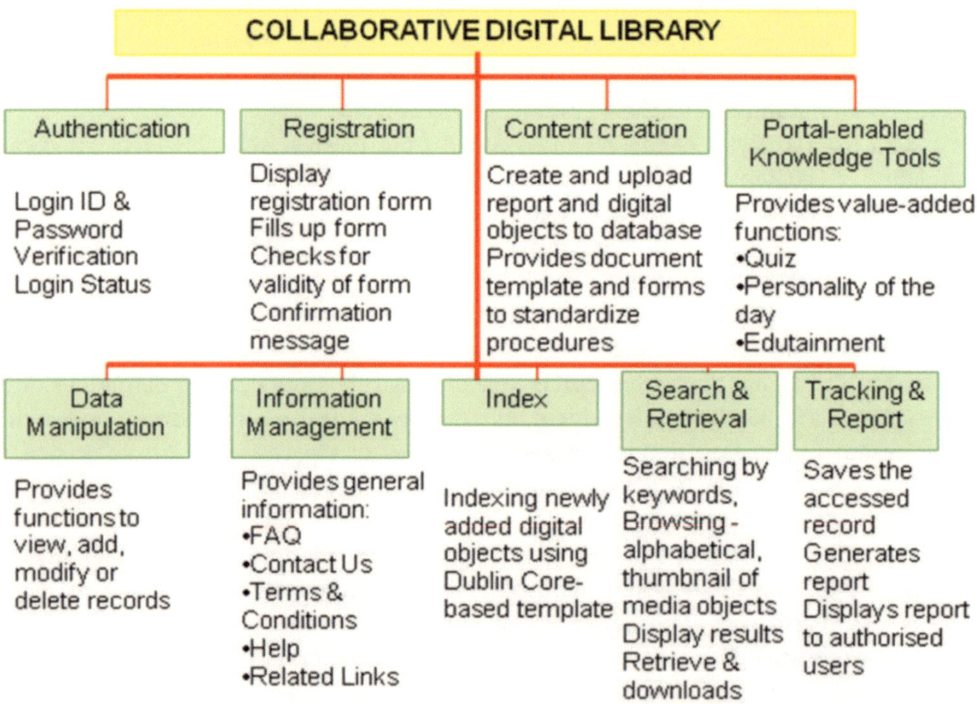

Fig. 11. Conceptual Model of Services in the Digital Library (Owner's View of Function)

5.5 Network: where can one access the digital library

Network (Where) shows the sites or geographical locations and the interconnections between activities within the digital library enterprise. It illustrates the network-related aspect of the digital libraries in terms of the physical locations of members in the digital library which spread over a geographical area. The planner provides the big picture of the digital library as a centralized system with the control for the whole structure at the Faculty of Computer Science and Information Technology University of Malaya (FCSIT UM) as the developer of the digital library system (Figure 12). FCSIT UM group manages the centralized database server. School A is the content collaborator and joint owner of the system and other potential future collaborators such as School B, Education Departments, Ministry of Education, as well as other repositories, would be able to utilise the application server running locally to fetch the required data from the database server.

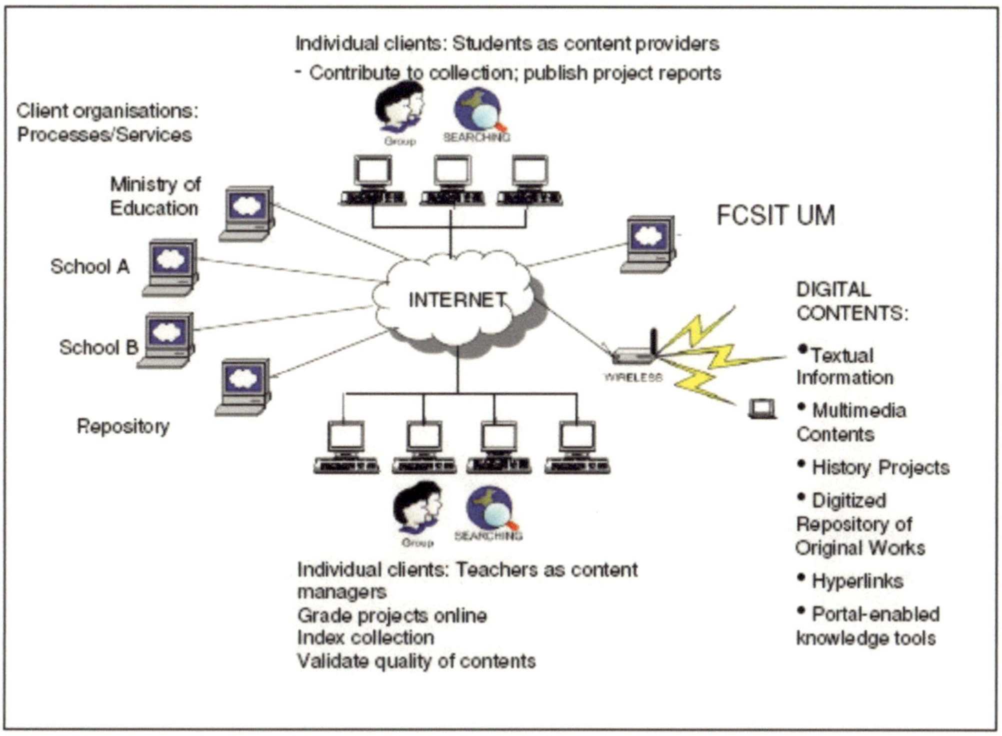

Fig. 12. The Physical Network of the Collaborative Digital Library (Planner's View of Network)

The owner is interested in the conceptual model of "Where" which includes the location of access and place where the primary stakeholders, namely the students and teachers use the digital library (Figure 13). It illustrates the collaborative digital library deployment expressed in term of location of access and computing facilities and network. The school community may access the collaborative digital library system from any 10 locations in the school, as all computers there are connected to the network.

From the designer's perspective, the Network Column presents the logical model of the network component of the collaborative digital library which depicts the types of systems facilities and controlling software at the nodes and lines such as processors/operating systems, database and lines/line operation systems. The notional distributed systems architecture (Figure 14) shows servers supporting the digital library services served from the regional (FCSIT) and local data center environment to the school's three primary locations of access. It is referred to as a notional architecture since the extent of the ability to remotely serve specific applications in both the baseline state and the target state remains to be established.

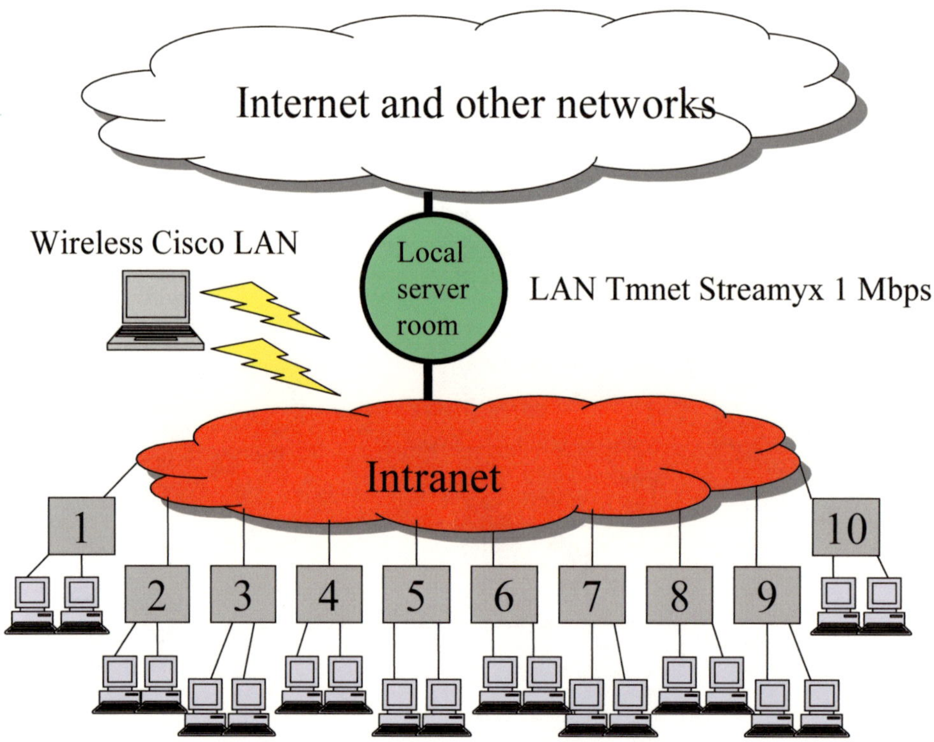

1	Self-Access Learning Centre	10	**6**	Staff room 1	4
2	School Resource Centre	5	**7**	Staff room 2	4
3	Computer Laboratory	40	**8**	Department Heads' Office	4
4	Information Technology Laboratory	40	**9**	Subject Panels' Room	4
5	Language Laboratory	20	**10**	Main Office	10

Fig. 13. The School's Network Diagram Positioning the Location of Access for the Digital Library (Owner's View of Network)

5.6 Time: when can one use the digital library (when do things happen)

The last column, "When" represents time, or the events to which the digital library responds in relation to time. This is useful for designing schedules, the processing architecture, the control architecture and timing systems. It is difficult to describe or address this column in isolation from the others, especially Column 2 (Process). At the strategic level, the planner describes Time as the business cycle and overall business events. As has been delineated in the digital library goals and objectives (Motivation Column), the digital library provides round-the-clock access. As the Internet is a 24/7 medium, the digital library is available 24 hours a day, 7 days a week.

In the detailed model of owner's perspective, the Time Column defines when activities or processes are to happen. Based on the findings of the case study regarding the school's approach in using the digital library, the chronology of events (such as teacher's notification and requirement of the project, students choose topic, gather information, create report, obtain teacher's feedback, edit and submit report) indicating the processes that take place in the digital library environment populates owner's view of the Time Column. The designer defines the business events or the processes in the digital library, which cause specific data transformations and entity state changes to take place (Table 2). The business events populate the designer's view of the Time Column of the Zachman Framework used.

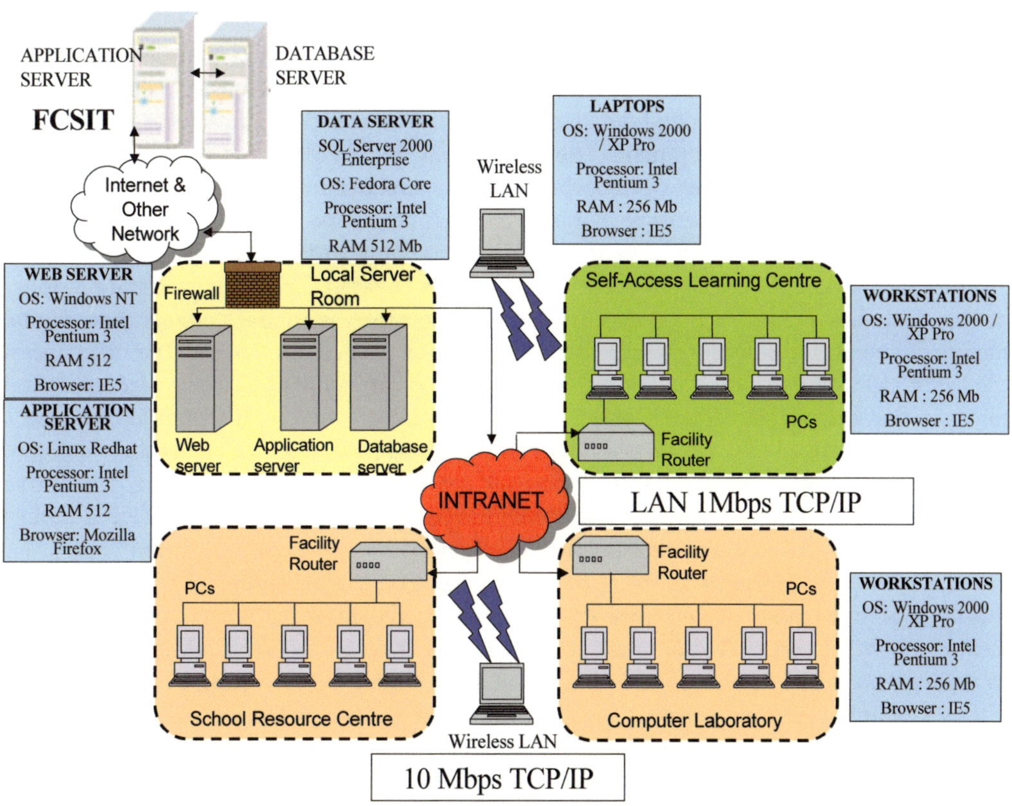

Fig. 14. The Digital Library Notional Distributed Systems Architecture (Designer's View of Nework)

The Process	Data transformations and entity state changes to take place.
Students register	Students receive automatically generated e-mail notifying membership of the digital library
Students create and submit report	Teachers and Administrators receive automatically generated e-mail notification indicating a new report has been submitted and ready to be viewed, graded or indexed.
Students create and submit report	Students receive automatically generated e-mail notification indicating that they have successfully submitted their project report.
Administrator registers teachers	Teachers receive automatically generated e-mail notification which indicates their User ID and Password.
Teacher evaluate and grade report	Students receive automatically generated e-mail notification indicating their projects have been evaluated.

Table 2. Business Events in the Digital Library (Designer's View of Time)

6. Conclusion

This chapter has provided a detailed mapping between the first three layers of Zachman Framework for Enterprise Architecture and the concepts utilized in formulating the requirements and design of a digital library, based on a case study and analysis on building a collaborative digital library to meet the needs of the stakeholders. It has also illustrated the possibility of using the Zachman Framework as an instrument for requirements analysis and evaluation in digital development. The framework highlights the need to involve all possible stakeholders in the development of the architecture, not just the enterprise architects and developers, to ensure that it meets their needs and uses.

The perspectives and artifacts established from the framework have helped ensure that everything relevant to the digital library enterprise is covered. Table 3 shows the mapping of the Zachman Framework perspectives and dimensions with the collaborative digital library deliverables/aspects. The planner's perspective reflects the context that establishes the list of relevant constituents that must be accounted for in the descriptive representation for the other perspectives (owner and designer). The descriptive representation of owner's perspective reflects the usage characteristics of the digital library, what the owner is going to do with it and how they will use it once they get it in their possession. The descriptive representation of designer's perspective forms the basis for the design of the digital library system, as well as the features for manipulating the tangible aspects of the digital library.

Using Zachman Framework as the approach to design a digital library has contributed to the field of Enterprise Architecture by highlighting the fact that fusion of information technology with business is important and these two aspects should be addressed together in organizations. It has also contributed to another dimension of a framework for digital library research and development and "a structured vision for the development of new ideas" (Soergel, 2002). The collaborative digital library adheres to Soergel's guiding principles and ten themes for digital library research and development, as well as incorporates the dimensions of others' framework but instead of listing them as requirements or ticking against a checklist, the authors have embedded the requirements in a system's architectural framework and present them more systematically, taking into

DIMENSIONS	ZACHMAN FRAMEWORK	THE DIGITAL LIBRARY
	LEVEL 1: Objectives /Scope – Planner's View	
Motivation (Why)	Identify and list goals and objectives - requirements analysis based on identified objectives	Motivating factors diagramme Vision statement List of DL goal List of DL objectives
Data (What)	Identify & list features /data important to the repositories using needs survey from stack holders	**DL resources in various media types and format**
People (Who)	Identify & list all stack holders and their roles in handing & processing data - Roles analysis	DL organisational structure
Function (How)	Identify & list processes the data performs - stack holder's information use survey	Activities students perform when conducting history project in the DL
Location (Where)	Identify & list locations where the enterprise operates - information flow survey	The physical network of the DL
Time (When)	Identify & list business events cycles - events use analysis	Access to the DL (24/7)
	LEVEL 2: Business Conceptual Model – Owner's View	
Motivation (Why)	Business Plan Business plan - flow diagram / rich picture	Rich picture showing owners' approach to use the DL List of perceived benefits to use the DL
Data (What)	Entity relationships diagrams - rich picture	DL Subject scope, collection and resource criteria
People (Who)	0rganisation charts, roles, set of skills & security issues - box charts / rich picture	DL actor-roles diagram
Function (How)	Business process model - flow diagram / rich picture	Conceptual model of services in the DL
Location (Where)	Logistics network - nodes and links	Owner's network diagram positioning the location of access for the DL
Time (When)	Business master schedules -rich picture	Chronology of events in the DL environment
	LEVEL 3: System Model – Designer's View	
Motivation (Why)	Business rule model	Behavioural objectives as DL mandatory functional requirements
Data (What)	Data model - entity diagrams	Table definitions for the DL data; metadata profile for the digital objects resource description
People (Who)	System interfaces architecture indicating roles, data, access	Actors and their roles depicted in the DL's three-tier client-server architecture
Function (How)	Data flow diagram showing application of data in the architecture	Structured chart for programme modules; users' menu
Location (Where)	Diagram indicating how data is distributed	The DL notional distributed systems architecture
Time (When)	Process structure with dependency diagrams, entity life history	Business events in the DL

Table 3. Mapping the Digital Library Deliverables to the Zachman Framework Perspectives and Dimensions

account the following details, aligned with the emerging perspective of the Enterprise Architecture:

a. The vision, goals, objectives, business plans and the functional requirements of the digital library;
b. The types of resources, domain focus, collection and data definition of the digital library;
c. The stakeholders and users, their roles and functional roles in the digital library;
d. The activities users perform, service conceptual model and the digital library programme modules
e. The location of access, the network diagram and the notional distributed system architecture;
f. The availability, business cycle and overall business events

In alignment with the vision already expressed by the DLF (2005), the authors felt that digital library developers should "get out of the box" and give more attention to the development of conceptual frameworks giving preference to scopes, goals requirements and processes, in the sense as those concepts are already common in the classic Enterprise Architecture processes and Zachman Framework for Enterprise Architecture can be a very simple comprehensive reference for this. Perhaps is time for the digital library researchers and practitioners to recognize that the focus of the digital library should move from the perspective of the engineer, who are responsible for systems design, to the perspective of the architect who prepares, plans and develops specifications, that bridge the gap between the systems (that the engineers design) and what the community needs. Although this chapter defines the design process and constructs necessary for the development of a collaborative educational digital library for secondary schools with a particular focus in Malaysia, illustration of the detailed mapping between the first three layers of Zachman cells and the dimensions utilized in formulating the requirements and design of the digital library can facilitate design transferability so that it could also be applied in another country setting.

7. References

Abdullah, A & Zainab A.N. (2006). Ascertaining factors motivating use of digital libraries and formulating user requirements using Zachman Framework. *Malaysian Journal of Library Information Science* Vol.11 No 2: 21-40, ISSN 1394-6234

Abdullah, A. & Zainab, A.N. (2008). The digital library as an enterprise: The Zachman approach. *The Electronic Library*,Vol. 26, No. 4, 446-467, ISSN 0264-0473.

Blumenfeld, C., Soloway, E., Marx, R. W., Krajcik, J. S., Guzdial, M., and Palincsar, A. (1991). Motivating project-based learning: Sustaining the doing, supporting the learning. *Educational Psychologist.* Vol. 26, No. 3&4, 369-398, ISSN 0046-1520

Bolton, G. (2004). What is Enterprise Architecture? Available at http://www.eacommunity.com/resources/whitepapers.asp

Borbinha, J. (2007). It is the time for the digital library to meet the enterprise architecture, *Proceedings of the 10th International Conference on Asian Digital Libraries: looking back 10 years and forging new frontiers, ICADL2007.* Lecture Notes in Computer Science, pp. 176-185, ISBN 978-3-540-77093-0, Hanoi, Vietnam December 10-13, 2007, Springer-Verlag, Berlin

Castelli, D. & Fox, E.A. (2007). Series of workshops on Digital Library Foundations. *D-Lib Magazine,* 13, 9/10 (Sept/Oct 2007), ISSN 1082-9873, Available at: http://www.dlib.org/dlib september07castelli/09castelli.html

Fuhr, N.; Hansen, P.; Mabe, M.; Micsik, A. & Solvberg, T. (2001). Digital libraries: A generic classification and evaluation scheme. In *Proceedings of the 5th European Conference on Research and Advanced Technology for Digital Libraries, ECDL2001.* Lecture Notes in Computer Science, pp. 187-199, ISSN 0302-9743, Darmstadt, Germany, September 4-9 2001, Springer-Verlag, Berlin

Digital Library Federation. (2005). DLF service framework for digital libraries: A progress report for the DLF steering committee. Available at: http://www.diglib.org/architectures/serviceframe/dlfserviceframe1.htm

Gonçalves, M. A.; Fox, E. A.; Watson, L. T. & Kipp, N. A. (2004). Streams, structures, spaces, scenarios, societies (5s): A formal model for digital libraries. *ACM Trans. Inf. Syst.* Vol. 22, No. 2 (Apr. 2004), 187-199, 270-3122163, Springer-Verlag, Berlin

Gladney, H.; Fox, E. A.; Ahmed, A.; Ashany, R.; Belkin, N. J. & Zemankova, M. (1994). Digital library: Gross structure and requirements: Report from a March 1994 Workshop. In *Proc. 1st Annual Conf. on the Theory and Practice of Digital Libraries,* IBM Research Report RJ 9840

Kahn, R. & Wilensky R. (1995). *A framework for distributed digital object services.* Available at: http://www.cnri.reston.va.us/cstr/arch/k-w.html

Lavoie, B, Henry G. and Dempsey. L. 2006. A service framework for libraries. *D-Lib Magazine,.* Vol. 12, no 7/8, (July/Aug, 2006) ISSN 1082-9873. Available at: http://www.dlib.org/dlib/july06/lavoie/07lavoie.html

Levy, D. & Marshal, C. (1995). Going digital: A look at assumptions underlying digital libraries. *Communications of the ACM.* Vol. 38 , No. 4, 77-84, ISSN 0001-0782

Marchionini, G. & Fox, E. A. (1999). Progress toward digital libraries: Augmentation through integration. *Information Processing & Management.* Vol. 35, No. 3, 219-225, ISSN 0306-4573

McGovern, J.; Ambler, S.W.; Stevens, M.; Linn, J.; Sharan, V. & Jo, E. (2003). *The practical guide to Enterprise Architecture.* ISBN-10: 0131412752, Englewood Cliffs, N.J. : Prentice-Hall

Moen, W.E. & McClure, C.R. (1997). *An evaluation of the U.S. Government's implementation of the Government Information Locator Service (GILS).* Available at: http://www.unt.edu/slis/research/gilseval/gilsdocs.htm

Pereira, C.M. and Sousa, P. (2004). A method to define an Enterprise Architecture using the Zachman Framework. *ACM Symposium on Applied Computing 2004,* Nicosia, Cyprus, March 14-17.

Renda, E. M. and Straccia, U. (2004). A personalized collaborative digital library environment: a model and an application. *Information Processing and Management.* Vol. 14, No.1, 5-21, ISSN *0306-4573*

Sandusky, R. J. (2002) Digital library attributes: Framing usability research. In Blandford, A. and Buchanan, G. (eds.) *Proceeding Workshop on Usability of Digital Libraries at JCDL'02.* (p. 35-38)

Saracevic, T. & Covi, L. (2000). Challenges for digital library evaluation. In Kraft, D. H. (ed.), ASIS 2000: *Proceedings of the 63rd ASIS Annual Meeting,* Vol. 37 (p. 341-350). Medford, NJ: Information Today

Schauble, P. & Smeaton, A.F. (1998). *Summary report of the series of joint NSF-EU working groups on future directions for digital library research: An international research agenda for digital libraries*. Available at: http://www.ercim.org/ publication/ws-proceedings

Soergel, D. (2002). A framework for digital library research: Broadening the vision. *DLib Magazine*. Vol. 8, No. 12 (Dec 2002), ISSN 1082-9873. Available at: http://www.dlib.org/dlib/december02/soergel/ 12soergel.html.

Zachman, J. A. (2002). *Zachman International Enterprise Architecture*. Available at: http://www.zachmaninternational.com/Default.htm

4

Integrating Disparate Digital Libraries using the WASSIT Mediation Framework

Faouzia Wadjinny, Imane Zaoui, Ahmed Moujane and Dalila Chiadmi
Computer Sciences Department, Mohammadia Engineering School, BP 765
Rabat Agdal,
Morocco

1. Introduction

Nowadays, there is a trend to integrate several digital libraries (DLs) to offer richer information. However, the following three characteristics of DLs make their integration a difficult task (Hasselbring, 2000): (i) Distribution: geographical spread; (ii) Heterogeneity: difference at both the technical level (e.g., hardware platform, operating system, etc.) and conceptual level (e.g., data model, query language, etc.); (iii) Autonomy: DLs are self-sufficient, as opposed to being delegated a role only as components in a larger system. Therefore, challenges faced when integrating DLs include interoperability (among different DLs) and resource discovery (selection of the best sites to be integrated). There are two different types of interoperability for DLs integration (Shen, 2006): syntactic interoperability and semantic interoperability. Syntactic interoperability is the application-level interoperability that allows multiple software components to cooperate even though their data model, query language, interfaces, etc. are different. Semantic interoperability is the knowledge-level interoperability that allows digital libraries to be integrated, with the ability to bridge semantic conflicts arising from differences in implicit meanings, perspectives and assumptions, thus creating a semantically compatible information environment based on agreed-upon concepts.

To deal with the interoperability problem, two solutions can be used: warehousing and mediation systems. In the warehouse approach (Rundensteiner and al., 2000), information is in some way periodically extracted from different sources, processed, merged with information from other sources, and then loaded into a centralized data store. Queries are posed against the local data without further interaction with the original sources. Modifications are filtered (e.g. for relevance or update-time) and propagated in some manner to upgrade the data warehouse. The main advantage of the warehousing approach is the performance of query processing. The main drawbacks are that the data may not be fresh and adding new data source requires reconsidering the warehouse schema. Thus, concerns about data quality and consistency must be addressed.

In mediation systems (Wiederhold, 1992), data remains at the sources and queries to the integrated system need to be translated, at run time, into a sequence of sub-queries to the underlying data sources. Data is not replicated and is guaranteed to be fresh at query time. However, a considerable performance penalty must be paid because sources are contacted for every query. Besides, in heterogeneous environments, especially in the context of DLs,

sources may have diverse and limited query capabilities. Thus, not all of the translations are feasible. Therefore, another challenge faced when integrating DLs is how to generate efficient and feasible query plans to retrieve data from DLs.
Our solution for integrating disparate DLs is a mediation framework, called WASSIT *(frameWork d'intégrAtion de reSSources par la médIaTion)*. In this chapter, we describe the features of WASSIT. In particular, we present how DLs are selected and ranked according to the user quality requirements. Since syntactic interoperability is treated implicitly in mediation systems (by using a common data model and wrappers), we will focus on our solution for semantic interoperability. Generating feasible and efficient query plans, by WASSIT, is also part of this chapter.

Chapter overview

In Section 2, we describe the high level architecture of our mediation framework WASSIT. We present how WASSIT selects pertinent DLs that satisfy the user quality preferences in section 3. In section 4, we present our solution for semantic interoperability. Our approach for optimizing queries over DLs with limited capabilities is presented in section 5. Performances evaluation is discussed in section 6. We conclude and present our future works in section 7.

2. High-level architecture of WASSIT

Our mediation framework WASSIT relies on the well-known mediator architecture (Wiederhold, 1992). WASSIT defines an infrastructure which provides the generic structure and the behaviour of a set of reusable components in an information mediation context (Zellou, 2008). Our framework is mainly made up of two principal components: Mediator and Wrappers. The Mediator, which is the query processing core of the framework WASSIT, has to decompose a user query into a set of sub-queries targeted to the sources. Each sub-query is transmitted to the corresponding source via the associated wrapper. The answers delivered by the wrappers are then combined to form the response to the initial query. The high level architecture of WASSIT is shown in figure 1. In this architecture, we distinguish three levels: the source level including the data sources and the wrappers, the mediation level containing the mediator, and finally the user level containing the user interface. In the mediation level, WASSIT is composed of six modules and a knowledge base.

2.1 Our technological choices for WASSIT

DLs generally differ with respect to the structures they use to represent data (e.g. tables, objects, files, and so on). We use XML as a common data model in WASSIT to reconcile sources' heterogeneous data models because it provides a common format for expressing both data structures and contents. Thus, it can integrate structured, semi-structured and unstructured data. XQuery (Fernández and al., 2007) is the query language we adopt in WASSIT since it is the W3C standard for querying XML documents. In order to achieve efficient query processing, we represent the queries according to an algebraic model. The one we have chosen is XAT (Wadjinny & Chiadmi, 2006). XAT algebra offers SQL operators such as union, join, etc. It offers also specific operators such as navigate, tagger, etc. Ontologies in WASSIT are used at two levels: to represent schema mappings and to capture the semantic of each source since we address semantic heterogeneity. We adopt OWL (Deborah and al., 2004), the Ontology Web Language, to represent these ontologies.

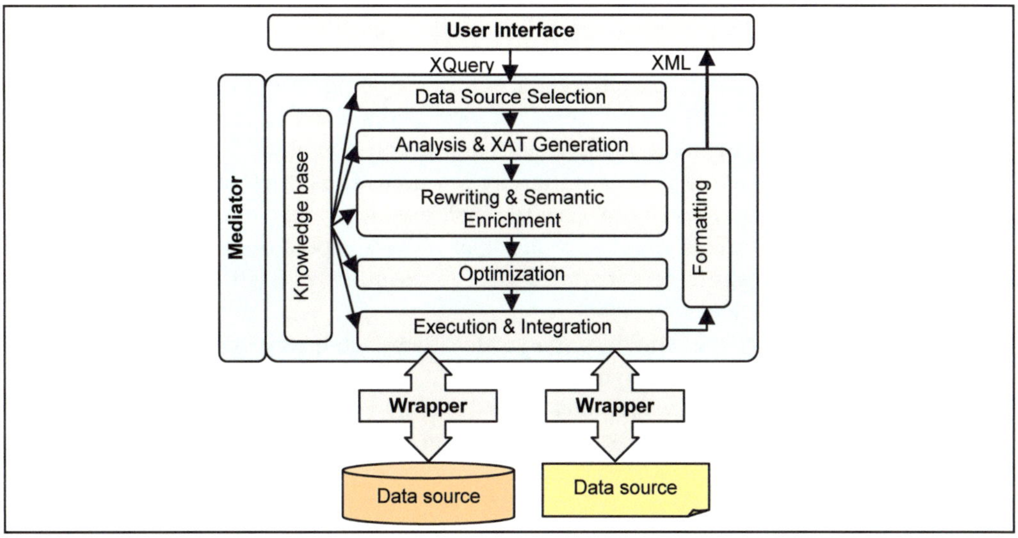

Fig. 1. High level architecture of WASSIT

2.2 Description of WASSIT's components

As cited earlier in this section, WASSIT is made up of a user interface, a mediator which contains six modules and a knowledge base, and wrappers. In the following, we will present each entity of WASSIT.

User Interface*:* It is a QBE (Query By Example) interface which frees the user from the knowledge of the XQuery language. In addition, this interface allows users to formulate their queries using the concepts of the global ontology. After the reception of a query by this interface, the corresponding XQuery query is generated. Moreover, the user interface allows users to express their preferences and needs through a user profile.

Data Source Selection **module**: To select the most relevant sources, this module performs quality matching between a user's profile and sources' profiles. The selected sources are then integrated to get a personalized response that respects user's quality requirements. More details about this module are given in section 3.

Analysis & XAT Generation **module:** This module has to analyze the user's queries. It rejects the syntactically incorrect ones. It eliminates also the queries that refer to unavailable concepts. This is achieved by using the knowledge base. User's queries are then transformed into XML algebra trees in order to be treated. Each node of a XAT tree is an algebraic operator.

Rewriting & Semantic Enrichment **module:** Let's remind that our framework aims to access a set of heterogeneous information sources. Every source has its local schema that describes its structure in a data model. The query submitted to the framework is formulated in terms of mediated schema (global schema). To have the query executed, the framework must rewrite the user's query formulated in terms of mediated schema as a query execution plan (QEP). Each QEP is presented in the form of a tree, where leafs are sub-queries that will be sent to the wrappers, and nodes are reconstruction operators that will be used by the mediator to integrate the results. The *Rewriting* module generates a QEP through three steps; each step is processed by one sub-module (Gounbark and al., 2009). These sub-modules are described in the following.

(1) *Global views substitution* module: This module has two features. First it ensures global views substitution, which consists in replacing each global view reference by the definition of this view. Views definitions are retrieved from the mapping definition. Then global paths (used to define global query) are projected on local paths (used to define local views). (2) *Union and join Operator ascending* module: Join and union operators, having distinct views from distinct data sources, can't be executed by a source. Thus, these operators have to be executed by the mediator. In order to schedule their execution, they are moved at the top of the algebra tree. (3) *Bindings adjustment* module: moving operators across the plan tree (previous step) makes parameters inappropriate. Consequently, this module has to adjust binding operators' parameters.
Moreover, in this step, we enrich semantically each sub-query (when possible) with synonyms, hyperonyms and hyponyms.
***Optimization* module:** The *Optimization* module takes as input the QEP obtained after query rewriting. After extracting sub-queries from this QEP, the *Optimization* module constructs a plan according to query capabilities of the underlying DLs. More details about this module are given in section 5.
***Execution & integration* module:** This module takes as input the sub-queries delivered by the *Optimisation* module and sends them to the appropriate wrappers using the localization information given by the knowledge base. It is composed by three sub-modules (Gounbark and al., 2009), which are described in the following.
(1) *XQuery Query Generator* module: sub-queries are represented by a XAT tree. This module translates each XAT tree sub-query to a XQuery query. (2) *Sub-queries Execution* module: this module ensures the actual execution of XQuery queries. It sends the XQuery queries to the right wrapper which translates the XQuery query to the underlying data source querying language. (3) *XAT Table Generation* module: This module constructs a XAT table from the XML results returned by the wrappers. The resulting XAT tables are combined according to the optimized QEP to form the answer to the user query.
***Formatting* module:** In this module, the result returned by the *Execution & Integration* module is formatted in order to form the answer which will finally be returned to the end user.
The knowledge base: The knowledge base is associated to the mediator, it stocks the general information used for query processing in the framework. It contains global ontology, local ontologies, users' profiles, sources' profiles, physical localization of sources, source descriptions, localization of wrappers, source capabilities, etc. More details about the construction of global ontology are given in section 4.
Wrappers: At a given wrapper, a sub-query expressed in XQuery is translated into the source query language. The wrapper has also to format the results returned by the source in an XML format. In WASSIT, two wrappers are developed: an XQuery/SQL wrapper (Benhlima & Chiadmi, 2003) and an XQuery/SOAP wrapper (El Marrakchi, 2009).

3. Digital libraries selection in WASSIT

Because of their increasing number and their heterogeneity, digital libraries may contain redundant information that differs by their quality characteristics. Since WASSIT answers user's queries by combining responses from different DLs, the final response quality relies on the quality of the sources involved. The perception of quality differs also from a user to another. For example, user A may ask for actual data, when user B looks for historical one.

To summarize, the concept of quality makes the difference between several DLs treating the same subject. It can be used to personalize the mediator's responses according to the user's preferences by selecting the most relevant DLs. The objective is to give a response that meets the user's quality requirements. In this section, we present our solution for DLs selection according to user's quality requirements in WASSIT. Our approach consists in building a multi-dimensional user's profile which stores the knowledge about a given user, especially his identity and quality preferences (Zaoui and al, 2009). We also construct a source profile which contains source definition, content, location, and quality characteristics (Zaoui and al, 2010). Both user's profiles and source's profiles are stored in the knowledge base. In the remaining of this section, we begin by presenting related works in section 3.1. In section 3.2, we define the quality paradigm in the domain of DLs. In section 3.3, we present our quality model to evaluate both user's quality requirements and source's quality characteristics. We use this model to select the most relevant DLs involved during the integration process in section 3.4. We illustrate our approach trough an example.

3.1 Related works

Several systems have been developed to integrate disparate and heterogeneous DLs. The majority of them addresses the problem of source selection following two approaches (Paltoglou, 2009). The first approach considers the source as a big document constructed via document concatenation, so the source selection becomes a simple problem of document retrieval. The most used source selection algorithm named CORI (Callan, 2000), is based on this assumption, GIOSS (Gravano & Garcia-Molina, 1995) and K-L divergence based algorithms (Xu & Croft, 1999) belong also to this category. The second approach considers the source as a repository of documents so the selected sources are those who are the most likely to return the maximum of relevant documents. ReDDE (Si & Callan, 2003) algorithm and the DTF (decision theoretic framework) (Nottelmann & Fuhr, 2003) give a source ranking by estimating the number of relevant documents for each query. The estimation is based on calculating a cost function which include quality and time factors. Both approaches require a source representation in their selection and ranking process. The source characteristics used are either given by the source, for example the protocol STARTS requires digital libraries to provide an accurate description of their content and quality, or discovered automatically through sampling queries (Callan, 2000). Our source selection and ranking algorithm is inspired from the second approach. We estimate the quality of each source using sampling queries and we build a quality model to perform a personalized source selection. The main contribution is that the source selection and ranking is not based on user queries but on user's profiles. The selection is performed by matching user's preferences and sources' characteristics. So, for each user, the selected set of candidate sources meets the user's quality requirements and it is also independent from the queries. These sources are used later on in the rewriting process to give a personalized response.

3.2 The quality paradigm

Many researches have been conducted to define the quality paradigm in DLs, but no single definition or standard exists. Usually, the concept of quality is the aggregation of multiple criteria organized into dimensions or categories. These dimensions may concern the quality of software, the quality of web sites, the quality of services, the quality of documents and data, and the quality of sources (Burgess and al, 2004). In the literature, there are a multitude of quality criteria depending on the domain and the application. Taxonomy of quality indicators is presented in (Burgess and al., 2002). The authors define quality using three factors: (i) Utility, which measures the satisfaction of user's requirements; (ii) Cost, which reflects the payment given by the user and/or the system to satisfy the user's requirements; (iii) Time, which means how long the user waits to get an appropriate answer and how long the system takes to provide it. Naumann and Leser (Naumann & Leser, 1999) present other parameters concerning especially the quality of data like viability, freshness, consistency and understandability. The quality of sources is measured in most cases using factors like popularity, completeness, freshness and extent (Wang & Strong, 1997). All these quality factors could be divided in two categories. (1) Subjective quality factors, which depend on user's preferences, and vary according to the context of interaction. They are usually expressed explicitly with a score given by the user, or via a natural language using words like "good", "bad", "excellent", etc. (2) Objective quality factors, which are considered as measurable metrics, collected implicitly through statistical and data mining algorithms. To sum up, the variety of existing quality indicators makes it difficult to build an appropriate quality model. First, we need to select the most useful quality indicators that WASSIT will use to select relevant sources. Then, we have to organize them into dimensions in order to facilitate their exploitation. In the next, we give our quality model based on two dimensions. We choose the corresponding metrics and explain how to get their values.

3.3 WASSIT quality model.

To introduce our quality model, let us consider a user asking about children stories. The result may be different depending on the selected sources. If we select only a specialized source in Harry Potter editions, the result is clearly incomplete because we omit all other kid stories and novels. But if we select the most popular kids' digital library, this user may be satisfied about the completeness of the result. The result differs also depending on the user preferences. For example, user A is more interested on old stories whereas user B prefers the last published ones. From these examples, we can say that defining a quality model in a digital library integration system depends on two dimensions, which are the user's quality preferences and the source's quality characteristics.

3.3.1 User's quality preferences

We define a preference as the desired level of quality that may satisfy the user's needs. User's quality preferences are related to the quality of retrieved documents, the quality of integrated sources and finally the quality of service depending on the retrieving process and the source capabilities. In the next, we study only the user's quality preferences related to the quality of sources since our objective is to select the most appropriate ones.

We define a model where the user expresses his quality preferences in three steps. First, he chooses his desired quality criteria from a global list available in the WASSIT's user interface. Second, he gives a ranking of these criteria from the most important one to the less using weights. Weighting quality criteria helps the system to emphasize the priority of the quality criterion to satisfy. Third, he states his desired values for each criterion. Usually, user's preferences values are expressed using a numerical score in an appropriate scale, a percentage, words like "good", "bad", etc. or even a predicate (e.g., I prefer sources having recent articles than those published before 2004). In this case, the user expresses his preference about the freshness of the source. He considers that sources having only documents published before 2004 are not fresh enough. To simplify our model, we suppose that the user states required preferences via WASSIT's user interface either by putting a score directly or by a slider on an appropriate scale. The position of the slide gives the corresponding score.

3.3.2 Source's quality characteristics

We define the source's quality characteristics as the main quality criteria that make a significant difference between data sources. In our model, the source's quality characteristics are stored in source profile. In the next, we focus on four information quality metrics which are reputation, freshness, completeness and time of response.

Reputation

Reputation, also called popularity, means the degree to which a source is in high standing (Naumann & Leser, 1999). Reputation of a source is related to several factors: (i) the quality and quantity of information and documents in the source; (ii) the authority and credibility of the source's owner (e.g., an official DL have a higher reputation than a wiki web site, a specialized DL in a given field such as computing science have a higher reputation than a DL treating all subjects); (iii) the quality of service including time of response, cost and security parameters. Indeed, a source having a good response time and a lower cost is more appreciated by the users.
Source's reputation depends on the user's judgment. It's a highly subjective criterion. For this reason, we consider that the reputation of a source S expressed by the user U is measured by a score from 1(bad reputation) to 5 (very high reputation). In the following, we denote this score by Reputation_Score(U,S).
We need now to measure the reputation of a source S. For this purpose, we define a metric called Global_Reputation_Score which is the average of all Reputation_Scores expressed by a set of users U={U_1, U_2...U_n}. The Global Reputation Score is computed using formula 1.

$$\text{Global\_Reputation\_Score}(S) = E[\textstyle\sum_{i=1}^{n} \text{Reputation\_Score}(Ui, S)/n\,] + 1 \qquad (1)$$

Freshness

There are various definitions of source freshness in the literature, as well as different metrics to measure it. (Bouzghoub & Peralta, 2004) gives a state of the art of these definitions and presents taxonomy of metrics to measure it depending on the domain of application. For example, in data warehouse systems, one of the metrics used to measure source freshness is currency (Segev & Weiping, 1990). Currency reflects the degree of change between data extracted and returned to the user and data stored in the source. In our model, we consider that freshness refers to the age of information in the source and the update of its' content. To measure this factor, we use the Timeliness factor (Wang & Strong, 1996), which expresses how old is data in the source since its creation or update. This factor is bounded with the update frequency of the source. We define a metric called Timeliness_Score which measures the time elapsed since data was updated. For example, a "Timeliness_Score=2 years" means that the source contains documents published after 2008. We also suppose that sources give the Timeliness_Score as a meta-data in their descriptions.

Completeness

Completeness is the extent to which data is not missing and are of sufficient breadth, depth, and scope for the task at hand (Naumann and al, 1999). In other words, it expresses the degree to which all documents relevant to a domain have been recorded in the source. Completeness of a source is also called in the literature: coverage, scope, granularity, comprehensiveness and density. For example, a scientific digital library is more complete than a non specialized one. We measure completeness using sampling queries which estimate the coverage of a source regarding some specific topic. We define a metric called Completeness_Score which represent the percentage of relevant documents returned by the source S out of the size of this source. Completeness_Score is given by formula 2, Where Size(S) is the number of documents stored in S and Size(D) is the number of documents that answer the sample queries.

$$\text{Completeness\_Score}(S) = \left(\frac{\text{Size}(D)}{\text{Size}(S)}\right) * 100 \quad (2)$$

Time of response

Time of response is the time that a source takes to answer a given query. It is calculated in seconds. Time of response could be very high if the source is saturated or doesn't have the capability to answer the query. In this case, we use our *Optimization* module to solve this problem. For the next, we suppose that the problem of source capabilities is resolved, so the time of response depends only on the communication process with the source. We use sample queries to determine this factor. Let SQ= $\{SQ_1, SQ_2,\ldots,SQ_k\}$ be the set of sample queries. For each sample query SQ_i, we measure the time of response denoted Query_Time_of_Response. The Time of Response of the source S is then computed as the maximum of all Query_Time_of_Responses using formula 3.

$$\text{Time\_of\_Response}(S) = \max_{i=1}^{k}(\text{Query\_Time\_of\_Response}(SQ_i)) \quad (3)$$

More quality factors could be found in the literature (Burgess and al, 2002). For example, understandability, credibility, precision, correctness, etc. All these factors could be added in our model easily. The user then chooses those who meet his quality requirements. In this step of work, we think that the quality factors defined are sufficient for WASSIT to make a quality aware source selection and ranking. To attempt this goal, we need to make a compromise between all defined criteria. We face two major problems. First, the source quality scores are not homogenous: we have a percentage, a time, a number. So, we need to scale the scores to make them comparable. Second, users set their quality preferences by selecting quality criteria, then stating importance weightings for each selected criterion. Finally, they state preference values for each desired criterion. So we need to select the relevant sources according to the preference values. Then, we have to rank the selected sources using the preference weightings. In the next section, we present our source selection and ranking algorithm.

3.4 Source selection and ranking algorithm

The quality of sources is measured with several criteria. Thus, source selection is a multi-attribute decision making problem (MDMP). In the literature, several methods have been developed to resolve this problem such as SAW, TOPSIS and AHP (Naumann, 1998). We choose to apply SAW (Simple Additive Weighting) (Hwang and Yoon, 1981), because it's one of the most simple but nevertheless a good decision making procedure. SAW results are also usually close to more sophisticated methods (Naumann, 1998). The basic idea of SAW is to calculate a quality score for each source using a decision matrix and a vector of preference weights. Although SAW solves the problem of the heterogeneity of quality criteria by scaling their values, this method ranks sources considering only the user's quality preferences weights. This ranking is based on the priority and importance of quality criterion but does not consider the preference's values. Consequently, we could not select the best sources unless the user defines a limit of the acceptable source's scores or a number of desired sources. To overcome these limitations, we develop a selection and ranking algorithm that respect both the user's quality preferences weights and values. The values defined by the user correspond to the criteria thresholds. Our algorithm is performed in two stages: source selection and source ranking using SAW method. It is described in the following.

Input: $S=\{S_1,S_2,..,S_n\}$: Set of candidate sources
$Q=\{Q_1,Q_2,..,Q_m\}$: set of source's quality metrics.
$M=[v_{ij}]_{(n*m)}$: the decision matrix, where v_{ij} is the value of Q_j measured on source S_i
$W=[w_i]_m$: the vector of user's quality preference weights
$T(Q_i)$: threshold defined by user for each Q_i
Output: $S'=\{S'_1,S'_2,..,S'_k\}$: Set of selected and ranked sources
Begin
// **Stage 1:** Source Selection
1. for all Q_i select the one having the highest weight and call it Q_{max}
2. from S, select S_i having Q_{max} value $\geq T(Q_{max})$

// **Stage 2:** Source Ranking using SAW Algorithm
1. Scale v_{ij} to make them comparable using some transformation function. With this scaling all source's quality values are in [0, 1]. We obtain a scaled decision matrix $M'=[v'_{ij}]_{(n*m)}$ where:

$$v'_{ij}=\frac{v_{ij}-\min_i(v_{ij})}{\max_i(v_i)-\min_i(v_i)}$$

2. Apply W to M'
3. Calculate sources' scores; the score of source S_i is given by: $\text{Score}(S_i) = \sum_{j=1}^{m}(v'_{ij}.w_j)$
4. Rank sources according to the sources' scores obtained in step3.

End

To illustrate our algorithm, let's consider the following example. We aim at integrating six DLs dealing with scientific field. We suppose that each DL is a single source. The integrated sources have different values of quality parameters summarized in the decision matrix (cf. Table 1).

	Global_Reputation_ Score	Timeliness_Score (years)	Completeness_Score (%)	Time_of_Response (s)
S_1	1	10	20	1
S_2	3	2	60	0.5
S_3	2	60	40	0.3
S_4	5	20	50	1
S_5	4	5	10	2
S_6	5	30	80	1

Table 1. The quality decision matrix

Consider a user who requires a Global_Reputation_Score>3. This criterion is mandatory, he also prefers sources with a Completeness_Score>30%. This criterion is desirable and he doesn't care about the other quality factors. We suppose that the user sets his preference priorities based on the following scale: {0.4: mandatory, 0.3: desirable, 0.2: not desirable, 0.1: indifferent}. The corresponding user quality preferences of this user are given in table 2.

	Global_Reputation _Score	Timeliness_Score (years)	Completeness_Score (%)	Time_of_Response (s)
Weight	0.4	0.1	0.3	0.1
Value	>3	Ø	>40%	Ø

Table 2. User's quality preferences (weights and values) (Ø means no preferred value for the criterion)

Remind that our main objective is to identify the sources that best fit with the user's quality preferences. For this purpose, we apply our source selection and ranking algorithm.
Stage 1. We select only sources having a Global_Reputation_Score>3. The remaining sources are: S_2, S_4, S_5 and S_6. Then we select only sources having a Completeness_Score>40%. The corresponding sources are: S_2, S_4 and S_6.
Stage 2. We apply SAW to the selected sources S_2, S_4 and S_6. We scale the decision matrix to make the quality values comparable. Then, we apply the vector of user's weights W to the scaled matrix. The scaled decision matrix, the vector of user's weights and the sources' scores are presented in table 3.
Sources' scores give the following ranking: S_6 is more appreciated than S_4 and finally S_2. As shown in this example, our source selection and ranking algorithm returns to the user a set of relevant sources that satisfies his quality preferences both in terms of quality weights and quality values.

	Global_ Reputation_Score	Timeliness_ Score (years)	Completeness_ Score (%)	Time_of_ Response (s)	Source Scores
S_2	0	0	0.333	0	0.0999
S_4	1	0.642	0	1	0.5642
S_6	1	1	1	1	0.9
Weight	0.4	0.1	0.3	0.1	

Table 2. Calculating sources' scores using SAW

4. Semantic interoperability in WASSIT

Semantic interoperability in DLs means the capability of different information systems to communicate information consistent with the intended meaning (Patel and al., 2005). The NSF Post Digital Libraries Futures Workshop (Larsen & Wactlar, 2003) identified it as being of primary importance in digital library research. One of the well accepted mechanisms for achieving semantic interoperability is the utilization of ontologies (Gruninger, 2002). Structure knowledge embedded in ontologies supports information retrieval and interoperability. Ontologies also help investigation of correspondences between elements of heterogeneous data sources (Shen, 2006). In WASSIT, we use ontologies to achieve semantic interoperability. Since DLs are heterogeneous, they may have local schemas or ontologies expressed in various formalism degrees, going from the informal definitions up to rigorously formal descriptions. However, the availability of a coherent formal ontology within the mediation system facilitates semantic query rewriting by enriching terms with semantically related ones. This is a key issue for data integration. In the remaining of this section, we present in section 4.1, related works for constructing formal ontology in mediation systems. In section 4.2, we present our approach for building ontologies in WASSIT. We illustrate our approach through an example.

4.1 Related works

The most used approaches for constructing formal ontology in mediation systems are mapping and integration. We present those approaches in the following.

Ontology mapping. Mapping is a crucial process in schemas and ontologies integration as well as in semantic conflicts resolution between ontologies and between heterogeneous data sources. It is defined (Pavel & Euzenat, 2005) as being the set of operations permitting to define relationships between the elements of two schemas (or ontologies) having a semantic correspondence. We distinguish two types of mapping (Bruijn & Polleres, 2004): one-way and two-ways mapping. The first one consists in defining an expression of a destination ontology terms according to a source ontology terms, whereas the two-ways mapping operates in both directions. In our works, we are interested in the two-ways mapping, between schemas and local ontologies.

Ontology integration. The integration process consists in creating a new ontology from two or more ontologies in order to replace or to unify and then to share their vocabulary. This can be achieved using operations such as union and intersection. The intersection approach consists in producing a reduced ontology based on the terms having common semantics. The advantage of this approach is that it makes possible to obtain, easily, a reduced shared vocabulary. However, its disadvantage lies in information loss that can result from this approach. This last is used in Observer (Mena and al., 2000) where the intersection between the ontologies is measured by a percentage indicating information quantity loss during the query translation process between the different system nodes. The union approach is used when we want to get only one global ontology containing all the terms contained in these ontologies. This approach has the advantage to allow easy query rewriting since the necessary vocabulary is kept in the resulting global ontology without any information loss. It has the disadvantage to need a lot of efforts to elaborate the union task. Furthermore, adding or deleting ontologies is quite difficult. Several mediation systems use this approach. We can mention Picsel (Rousset and al., 2002) and SIMS (Arens and al., 1996).

We have adopted this last approach to build our knowledge base ontologies. But we extended it by using generalization and specialization operators. However, to palliate to its disadvantage, we propose a solution for semi-automatic integration of the local ontologies.

4.2 Building ontologies in WASSIT

To resolve semantic conflicts, we adopt hybrid architecture for the knowledge base development. Our approach combines local data sources ontologies and a global ontology that provides a shared vocabulary. This architecture offers adaptability and extensibility for new sources addition since every source has its own local ontology.

To build our ontologies, we follow the process represented in figure 2. The global ontology construction process takes place in two phases: the mapping of local schemas and ontologies, and the merging of local ontologies. The mapping of the local schemas and

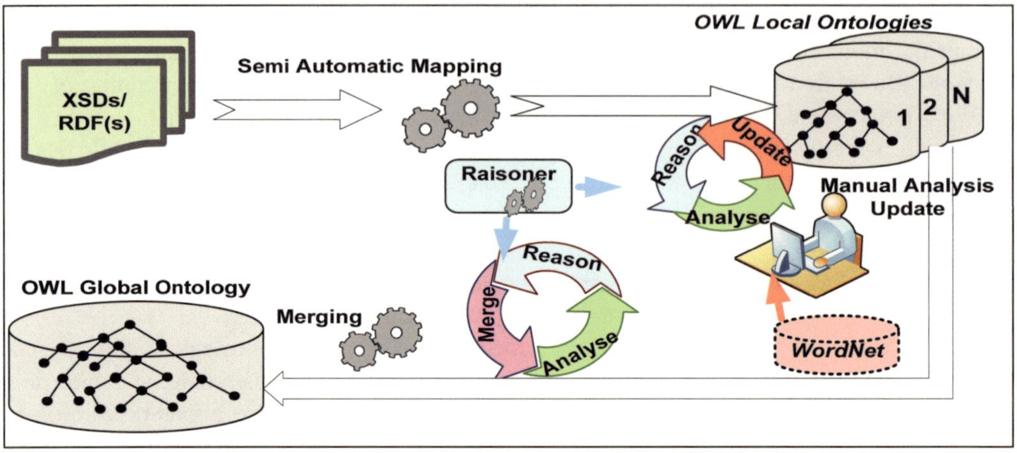

Fig. 2. The Construction process of local and global ontologies for WASSIT

ontologies of each local source in an OWL local ontology is achieved in order to permit a transparent and uniform merging of the local ontologies. At the end of this process, a mapping table is generated. It contains mapping information between local schemas and ontologies.

The merging of all OWL local ontologies resulting from the first step is achieved to build the global ontology. During the merging process, the mapping table is updated by the correspondence information between local ontologies and the global one. To illustrate our approach, we take the example of the local schemas given in figures 3 and 4. Through this example, we present the three phases of our approach, which are: *Mapping local schemas to local ontologies*, *Merging local ontologies into the global ontology* and *Consistency checking*.

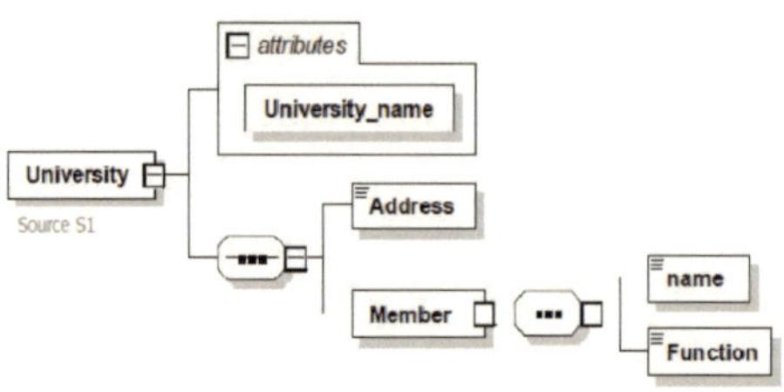

Fig. 3. Local XML Schema S_1

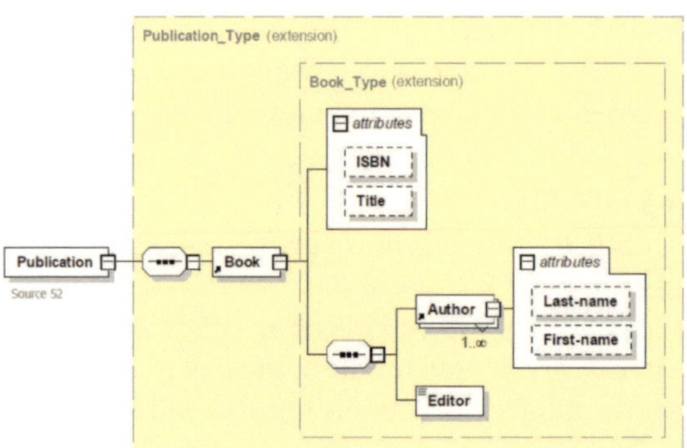

Fig. 4. Local XML Schema S_2

4.2.1 Mapping local schemas to local ontologies

Each source to be integrated is described by its local schema or its local ontology that we enrich by metadata, to add rich semantics about this data source (format, communication protocol, access rights, etc.), about its capacities and about its content.

The construction of local ontologies is accomplished by mapping local schemas and ontologies that can be represented under various formats (XML schemas, DAML-OIL, etc.). In this chapter, we limit our study to the case of the local schemas described in XML schemas.

As we adopted the OWL language for our knowledge base ontologies representation, a mapping between the XML schemas and OWL syntax is necessary (cf. Table 4). Several works for mapping between XML Schemas and OWL exist. We were inspired from the one introduced by Bohring and Auer (Bohring & Auer, 2005).

Moreover, the syntax mapping must be coupled with another one for concepts names contained in the local schemas to avoid ambiguousness that can be produced by this transformation. Indeed, an XML schema document has an ordered hierarchical structure that allows two elements to have the same identifier (name) so long as they are not in the same node. However, the order between these elements won't be taken in consideration after the mapping, because OWL doesn't define any order between properties. The OWL syntax components, rdfs:range and rdfs:domain, alone don't enable removing the generated ambiguity while transforming these elements and non-global attributes of the XML schemas toward OWL.

XSD	OWL
xsd:elements, containing other elements or attributes.	owl:Class, coupled with owl:ObjectProperties
xsd:elements, with neither sub-elements nor attributes	owl:DatatypeProperties
xsd:attribute	owl:DatatypeProperties
xsd:complexType	owl:Class
xsd:SimpleType	owl:DatatypeProperties
xsd:minOccurs	owl:minCardinality
xsd:maxOccurs	owl:maxCardinality
xsd:choice	combination of owl:intersectionOf, owl:unionOf and owl:complementOf
xsd:sequence, xsd:all	owl:intersectionOf

Table 4. Mapping between XML schema and OWL elements.

The definition of non ambiguous identifiers to keep a two ways mapping between the local schemas and the local ontologies is essential to permit an applicable user's query resolution. Therefore, we adopted the following process:

- The id of a local element is composed of the name of the complex type in which the element is declared +"." + its_local_name (e.g., "Book_Type.Editor").
- The id of a local attribute is composed of the name of the complex type in which the attribute is declared +".$" + its_local_name (e.g., "Book_Type.$ISBN").
- The id of a global attribute is composed of its namespace + "$"+ its_local_name.

- The id of an anonymous type is defined by the name of the element in which the definition of the type is declared +"."+ Anonymoustype (e.g., "Book_Type.author.anonymoustype").

4.2.2 Merging local ontologies into the global ontology

The goal of this phase is to generate a global ontology related to the mediated sources domain. As our objective is to achieve a virtual integration of distributed, autonomous and heterogeneous data sources, the user query must be expressed against the global ontology. Thus, this ontology must contain the whole domain concepts contained in the integrated data sources. To this end, we follow a hybrid integration of the ontologies by union completed by generalization and specialization operations. However, before performing this integration, a set of issues rises: What are the concepts and the classes to generate? What are the specializations and/or generalizations to conceive? Do these generalizations also affect properties? To answer these questions, we took into account the following constraints:

- Equivalence degree must be maintained, since a pair of concepts considered equivalent can vary a lot semantically. For example, the merging process considers "member" in the University.XSD as semantically equivalent to "Author" in Publication.xsd, although Member can be more general than author. In general, a Member cannot be an Author.
- Semantic relationship that requires one-to-many mapping (and inversely many-to-one) must be expressed correctly. For example, member.name in University.XSD is semantically equivalent to the union of the two concepts Author.first-name and Author.last-name in the Publication.XSD (Bohring & Auer, 2005).

Therefore, our approach is not reduced to a simple union of local ontologies, because we carry out specializations and/or generalizations of the concepts and properties. We use the lexical ontology WorldNet (Fellbaum, 1999) for this purpose.

4.2.3 Consistency checking

The reasoning mechanisms on ontologies allow to derive and to deduce new knowledge not described explicitly by the ontology. It can be achieved for OWL ontologies using a reasoner. The inferred information can be used to improve query resolution. In our system, we used these reasoning capacities to verify the consistency of the ontologies resulting from the mapping and merging procedures. We use the RacerPro reasoner <http://www.racer-systems.com/> to accomplish these tasks.

5. Optimizing queries over DLs with limited capabilities

In the context of digital libraries, sources may have diverse and limited query capabilities. For example, users of an online bookstore get information on books via forms. These forms allow several types of keyword based queries including search by title, subject, author, ISBN, price, etc. If we consider the web source Amazon.com <http://www.Amazon.com/>, this bookstore does not support any query that specifies conditions on the price attribute because this attribute is absent in the search form. Let us consider another web bookstore, Books.com <http://www.Books.com/>. This bookstore supports queries that specify the price attribute. However, it cannot support queries where the attribute publisher is mentioned. Consider now a third web bookstore Books-a-million.com <http://www.booksamillion.com/>. As opposed to the above mentioned online bookstores, it does not offer search neither by price nor by publisher.

As shown in the example above, DLs have diverse and limited query capabilities. These restrictions have many reasons, including the concerns of efficiency of query processing, simplicity of the query interface and security. In such situation, DLs must inform the mediator which queries they can support, so that the mediator can construct query execution plans (QEPs) that contains only feasible sub-queries. This is known as the Capability-Based Rewriting (CBR) problem. In order to be able to perform capability-based rewriting, the mediator needs formal descriptions of the query capabilities of DLs. A capability-based rewriter takes as input these descriptions and the query, and it infers query plans for retrieving the required data that are compatible with the source query capabilities. Solving the CBR typically produces more than one candidate plans for the query. Choosing the optimal plan is done using a cost model.
The problem we address in this section is how to generate efficient query plans that respect the limited and diverse capabilities of DLs in WASSIT. For this purpose, we model the source capabilities through *Capabilities Tables* and propose an algorithm to generate query plans respecting DLs capabilities. We propose also a cost model which we will use while constructing query plans. This section is structured as follows. In section 5.1, we give an overview of related works. We present in section 5.2 our solution which is made up of formalism for describing data source capabilities, a cost model and an algorithm for generating query plans.

5.1 Related works

Few mediation systems have addressed the capability-based rewriting problem. Some of these systems (e.g., GARLIC (Haas and al., 1997)) use exhaustive search methods to construct the optimal query plan according to the adopted cost model. However, the exponential complexity of these search methods limits the number of integrated data sources. Other systems, like e-XMLMedia (DANG-NGOC, 2003), verify the feasibility of the sub-queries after constructing the QEP. For each sub-query addressed to a source, the mediator checks its feasibility by consulting the source's capabilities. If a sub-query cannot be processed at a given source, the mediator attempts to download the entire source. Such an attempt is not only expensive but also may not be allowed by the source. Another category of mediation systems (e.g., DISCO (Tomasic and al., 1996)) initially ignores the limited sources' capabilities to generate possible query plans. It then checks the query plans against the sources' capabilities and rejects those containing unsupported queries. This strategy could be very expensive compared to capabilities-based rewriting as the latter ensures that the queries issued to the sources are answerable by these sources.
While developing our solution, we took into account the disadvantages that we have just quoted. Since the number of integrated DLs may be important, we use heuristic search algorithms. These algorithms construct QEPs that minimize as much as possible the cost of treatment, in a time less than that spent by the exhaustive search algorithms. In addition, the QEP generation process is based on sources capabilities descriptions. Thus, QEPs contains only feasible sub-queries. In the following, we present our solution for the capability-based rewriting problem.

5.2 Our solution

We illustrate our solution with a running example presented in section 5.2.1. Trough this example, we present our formalism for describing sources' capabilities in section 5.2.2, our cost model in section 5.2.3 and our algorithm for constructing efficient query plans in section 5.2.4.

5.2.1 A running example

Suppose that we have three sources S_1, S_2 and S_3 and that each of them provides a local view. Let V_1, V_2 and V_3 be their local views respectively, with: V_1=(ISBN, Price, Subject), V_2=(ISBN, Author) and V_3=(ISBN, Publisher).

Sources S_1, S_2 and S_3 have limited capabilities for query processing. These capabilities are expressed as follows:

- Queries sent to S_1 must either provide the Price or the Subject field. In both cases, the set of attributes returned by the source is {ISBN, Price, Subject};
- Queries sent to S_2 must provide the ISBN field. The set of attributes returned by the source is {ISBN, Author};
- Queries sent to S_3 must provide the ISBN field. The set of attributes returned by the source is {ISBN, Publisher}.

Let BooksGV(ISBN, Price, Subject, Author, Publisher) be a global view offered by WASSIT when integrating the three data sources. BooksGV is defined as follows: $((V_1\ Join_{ISBN}\ V_2)\ Join_{ISBN}\ V_3)$. Suppose we formulate a query (Q), at WASSIT's user interface, to find all books dealing with "Linux", whose author is "Radi" and whose publisher is "Elsevier". The condition attached to the query Q is: Subject = "Linux" Λ Author = "Radi" Λ Publisher = "Elsevier".

5.2.2 Describing source capabilities

To describe source capabilities, we use a table that we call *Capabilities Table*. A *Capabilities Table* of a source S enumerates the conditions expressions that can be evaluated by S, and the set of attributes returned by S after evaluating these expressions. For example, table 5 describes capabilities of source S_1. Each row in the table describes a condition expression C that S_1 can evaluate, and the set of attributes returned by the source S_1 when processing this condition expression. For example, row 1 states that S_1 can evaluate condition expressions like (Subject= "XML") and returns the set {ISBN, Price, Subject}. *Capabilities Tables* of the integrated DLs are stored in the knowledge base of WASSIT.

	Evaluated_Attributes			Returned_Attributes		
Operator	ISBN	Price	Subject	ISBN	Price	Subject
Λ	0	0	1	1	1	1
Λ	0	1	0	1	1	1

Table 5. *Capabilities Table* of source S_1

We define a function called R_Attr(C) (for Returned_ Attributes) which returns the set of attributes returned by a source when evaluating a condition expression C. If a condition expression is not supported, then R_Attr(C) returns the empty set. For example, R_Attr (Price=P) = {ISBN, Price, Subject} and R_Attr (Subject=S Λ Price =P) =Ø.

5.2.3 Our cost model

In order to obtain the cost of a plan, one must have statistics about the underlying data, such as sizes of relations and sizes of domains. It is also necessary to have a cost formula to calculate the processing cost for each implementation of each operator. Because data sources are autonomous, it may not be possible to have statistics about the sources or unreliable ones, preventing a direct application of cost models approaches developed for homogeneous systems. Several approaches have been proposed for cost based query optimization in mediation systems (DANG-NGOC, 2003). In this paper, we propose a simple cost model that we use while constructing query plans.

In mediation systems, the cost of a plan may be approximated by the sum of communication cost, source query processing costs and mediator processing cost, as expressed in formula 4.

$$cost(plan) = Communication\_cost + mediator\_cost + sources\_costs \quad (4)$$

Furthermore, in the context of web data integration, communication cost dominates source query processing costs and mediator processing cost (DANG-NGOC, 2003). If the plan consists of N sub-queries (SQ_i) executed sequentially, then the cost of a plan is expressed by formula 5. In this formula, R_i is the response corresponding to sub-query SQ_i. Minimizing the cost given in formula 5 involves reducing the number of sub-queries. This observation will be used while constructing QEPs.

$$cost(plan) = \sum_{i=1}^{N}(communication\_cost\ (SQ_i) + communication\_cost\ (R_i)) \quad (5)$$

5.2.4 Constructing query plans

When a query is formulated at the WASSIT's interface, the corresponding XQuery query is generated. This query is processed by the *Analyse & XAT Generation* module and the *Rewriting & Semantic Enrichment* module. The output of this second module is a QEP. As the global view is a join of the local sources views, the QEP generated, let be P_1, consists in sending the sub-queries SQ_1 (subject="Linux"), SQ_2 (author="Radi") and SQ_3 (Publisher="Elsevier") respectively to data sources S_1, S_2 and S_3. After retrieving results, a double join on the attribute ISBN is done at the mediator level Note that this plan is not feasible because sources S_2 and S_3 cannot answer SQ_2 and SQ_3 because of their limited query capabilities.

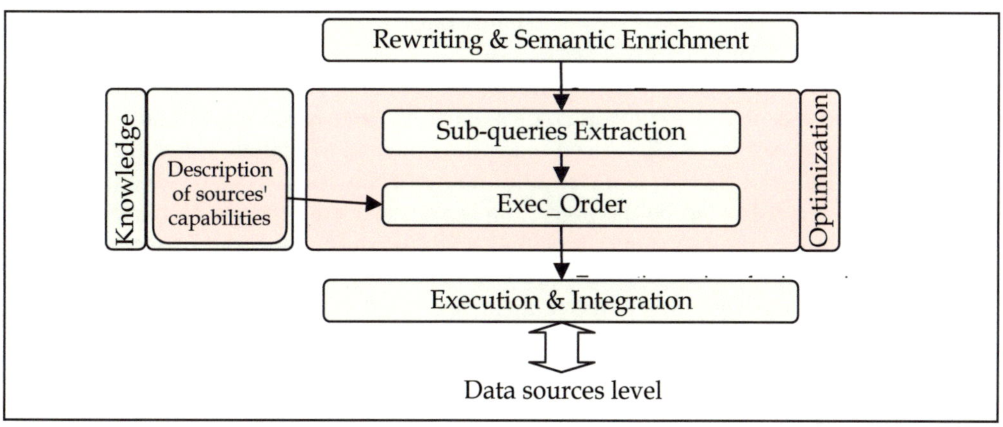

Fig. 5. *Optimization* module Architecture

Since the generated QEP contains sub-queries that are not feasible, the role of the *Optimization* module is to construct a QEP with feasible sub-queries. To this end, the first operation performed by the *Optimization* module, when receiving a QEP, is the extraction of its sub-queries. This operation is performed by the *Sub-queries Extraction* module (cf. figure 5). The extracted sub-queries are then processed by the *Exec_Order* module. The role of this module, based on the algorithm described below, is to find an execution order of sub-queries which takes into account the limited query capabilities of the integrated data sources and that minimizes the cost of the generated QEP. To illustrate this concept of execution order of sub-queries, consider a second QEP, let be P_2. This plan consists on sending the sub-query SQ_1 (Subject = "Linux") to source S_1. For each $ISBN_i$ returned, a sub-query SQ_2 (ISBN= $ISBN_i$) is sent to source S_2. For each $ISBN_j$ returned satisfying the condition Author="Radi", a sub-query SQ_3 (ISBN= $ISBN_j$) is sent to S_3. In plan P_2, sub-queries are executed in chain. Each sub-query uses the results of the sub-query already executed.

According to our cost model, minimizing the cost of a plan involves reducing the number of its sub-queries. Suppose that source S_1 contains 30 books on "Linux" and that source S_2 contains 3 books on "Linux" whose author is "Radi". For simplicity, we count the communication cost by calculating the number of sub-queries sent to a source. For each sub-query sent to a source, we take a cost equal to 1. If we consider plan P_2, the first sub-query executed is SQ_1 (Subject="Linux"). Since each sub-query has a cost equal to 1, the communication cost of SQ_1 is equal to 1. For each $ISBN_i$ returned, the sub-query SQ_2(ISBN=$ISBN_i$) is sent to source S_2. Since S_1 contains 30 books on "Linux", 30 sub-queries are sent to S_2 with a cost equal to 30. For each $ISBN_j$ returned satisfying the condition Author="Radi", a sub-query SQ_3 (ISBN= $ISBN_j$) is sent to S_3. Since S_2 contains 3 books on "Linux" whose author is "Radi", 3 sub-queries are sent to source S_3 with a cost equal to 3. Thus, the communication cost of plan P_2 is: 1+30+3 = 34. In the cost of plan P_2, SQ_1 has the minimal cost (1) because it is executed in block. Therefore, in our algorithm we seek all sub-queries that can be executed in block. A join between these sub-queries constitute the first entity in the chain. In the next section, we present our algorithm.

Algorithm for constructing QEPs

To illustrate our algorithm, we use the running example given in section 5.2.1. Let SQ_1, SQ_2 and SQ_3 be the sub-queries extracted from the plan generated by the *Rewriting* module. Let C be the condition attached to the user query. C is: Subject = "Linux" Λ author = "Radi" Λ Publisher = "Elsevier". Let Attr(C) be the set of attributes of the condition C. This set is noted A, where A = {Subject, Author, Publisher}.

The algorithm developed is a greedy algorithm. Its idea is to find, at each iteration, a sub-query that can be executed using the attributes of set A. After executing this sub-query, the function R_Attr() (cf. section 5.2.2) is used to get the returned attributes. These attributes are added to set A. This treatment is repeated until no more sub-queries can be executed. Thus, the execution plan constructed by this algorithm is a chain of sub-queries. However, the first sub-query constituting the chain may be either a simple query or a join between multiple sub-queries. In fact, seeking the first sub-query in the chain may lead to several sub-queries. Since sub-queries at the beginning of the chain are executed in block, their execution reduces the communication cost. Therefore, these sub-queries must be executed simultaneously; a join on their results is performed at the mediator. This will constitute the first element of the chain. To sum up, the algorithm consists of three stages:

Stage 1. In this stage, the algorithm checks if all sub-queries can be executed using the attributes of set A. This test is based on *Capabilities Tables* of the integrated data sources. If so, the sub-queries are sent to data sources without any additional processing. If one of the sub-queries cannot be answered using set A, the algorithm proceeds to the second stage.

Stage 2. This stage uses the result of the first stage: all sub-queries that can be answered using the attributes of set A, form the first element of the plan. Thus, these sub-queries will be executed in parallel. A join of their results is performed at the mediator level. The attributes returned after the execution of these sub-queries are added to set A.
In the running example, only the sub-query SQ_1 can be executed. It is the first sub-query in the chain. The attributes returned by SQ_1, which are ISBN and Publisher are added to set A. A becomes = {Subject, Author, Publisher, Price, ISBN}.
Stage 3. In this stage, we seek among the remaining sub-queries, a sub-query that can be executed using set A. If this sub-query exists, the set A is enriched with the attributes returned after its execution. In the example, SQ_2 is selected and A becomes A = {Subject, Author, Publisher, Price, ISBN}. The same process is repeated until no more sub-queries must be executed. If at a given step, no sub-query can be executed using the attributes of set A, then there is no plan to execute the target query. Below, we give a formal description of the algorithm.

```
Input:   Set of sub-queries SQ={SQ1, SQ2,.., SQn}
         Set A
Output:  Plan (if exists)
Begin
  // Stage 1
    Plan ← Ø, B ← Ø
    For each (SQi )i=1 to n
         if SQi can be answered using A
                   B ← SQi
         if (B==SQ)
                   Plan ← {SQ1, SQ2,.., SQn}
         Else
                   Plan ← Ø
  // Stage 2
    If Plan == Ø
         Plan ← Plan . [B]    // B contains sub-queries that will be joined
         A ← A U {attributes(B)}
         SQ ← SQ - {B}
  // Stage 3
    While SQ ≠ Ø
         For each SQi
                   if SQi can be answered using A
                             N←SQi
                             Break
                   Else
                             Return (Ø)     //The plan does not exist
         Plan ← Plan . [N]
         SQ ← SQ - {N}
         A ← A U {attributes(N)}
    Return (Plan)
END
```

6. Performance evaluation

In this section, we analyze the performances of our framework WASSIT, when integrating DLs, through simulation. The performance index that we evaluate is the response time. For this purpose, we present the key parameters that have an impact on the response time in section 6.1. Then, we present and discuss the most important results in section 6.2.

6.1 Performance parameters

We study the influence of the key parameters on the response time, which is defined as the time elapsed between submitting a query to WASSIT and getting a response. In mediation systems, response time may be important (Travers, 2006) (Langegger and *al.*, 2008). This is due to communication cost, source query processing costs and mediator processing cost. Furthermore, additional processing time is introduced by our *Optimization* module. But this is still tolerable since we give to the user the guaranty to get a response in a finite time. Without our *Optimization* module, the mediator may not answer some queries because of the limited query capabilities of the underlying DLs. Response time depends also on the bandwidth of the communication network, between mediator and data sources. The system load, which lies principally on queries frequency and size of sources' responses, has also an impact on the response time. We summarize these parameters in table 6.

Parameter	Meaning
N	Number of integrated sources
R_Size	Response size (Bytes)
F = 1/T	Queries frequency: number of queries addressed to WASSIT per time unit. T is the period of query arriving (seconds)
BW	Network Bandwidth

Table 6. The key parameters for studying the system performances

6.2 Results analysis

We remind that our objective is to evaluate the performances of WASSIT. Due to the lack of space, we present only the most important simulation results. In the first simulation scenario, we study the impact of the *Optimization* module on the response time. (cf. figure 6). In the second scenario, we evaluate the response time for different values of bandwidths (cf. figure 7). The third scenario consists on analyzing the influence of the responses' sizes variation and the period of query arriving on WASSIT's performances (cf. figure 8 and figure 9). We present results analysis below.

Figure 6 shows an exponential increase of response time depending on the number of integrated sources. This is due to the processing time introduced by the *Optimization* module. We also deduce that the system has good performances if we integrate less than six sources. As the number of sources increases, these performances degrade and for more than 20 sources, the system begins to crush.

Figure 7 shows that response time decreases when the bandwidth increases. Indeed, increasing the bandwidth reduces communication cost, which is the most penalizing cost in mediation systems. Consequently, communication networks with good bandwidth would help to integrate more data sources.

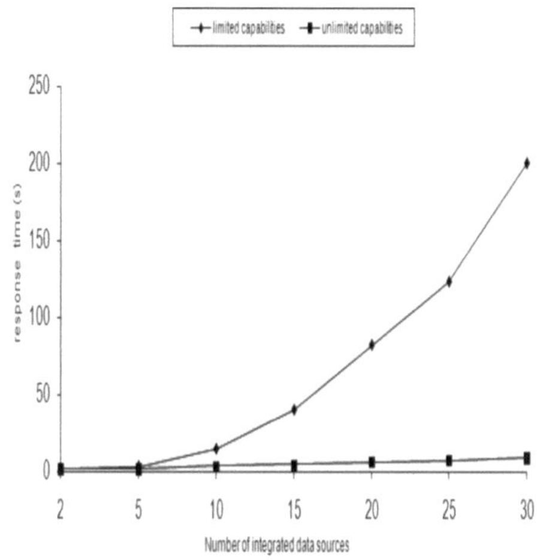

Fig. 6. Response time depending on N

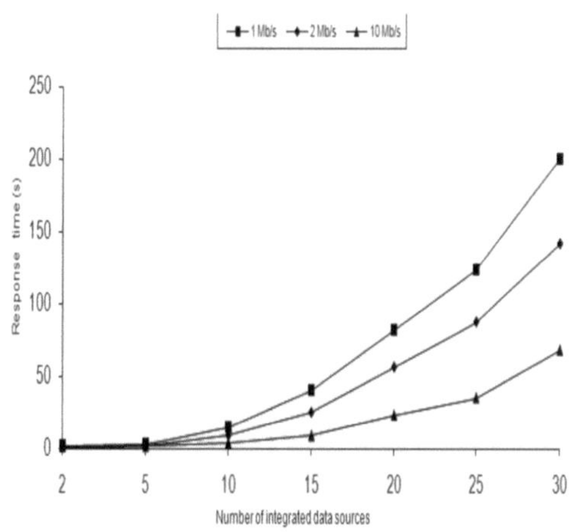

Fig. 7. Response time for 3 values of BW

Figure 8 shows that reducing responses sizes implies reduction of response time. Indeed, the reduction of responses sizes minimizes communication cost. Thus, when the responses returned by the integrated data sources have small sizes, the system performances are improved.

Figure 9 shows that, for periods greater than 12 seconds, the response time remains constant. This indicates that for these periods, the system goes idle waiting for new queries. The figure shows also that for periods less than 4 seconds, the response time increases exponentially. This induces performance deteriorating and the mediator becomes a bottleneck for the system.

To summarize, to improve WASSIT's performances, we can either reduce the number of integrated sources or reduce the system load. This can be performed if responses sizes are smaller, and if queries frequency is reduced. In addition, communication networks with good bandwidth would help to have better performances.

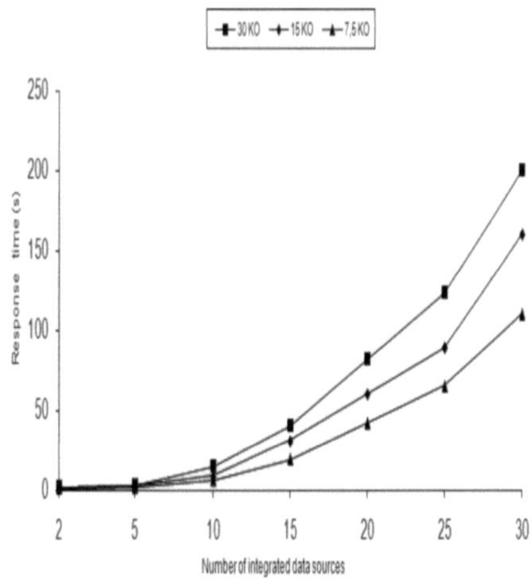

Fig. 8. Response time for 3 values of R_Size

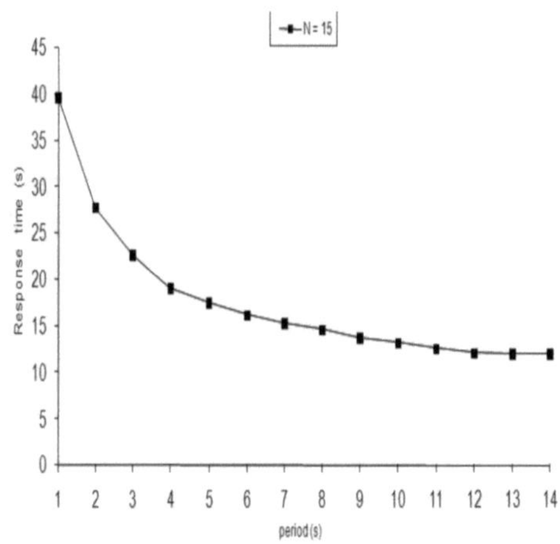

Fig. 9. Response time depending on T

8. Conclusion and future works

In this chapter, we use the mediation framework WASSIT to integrate disparate DLs. The main challenges faced in this integration are selecting DLs according to the user quality requirements, dealing with semantic interoperability and constructing query plans with respect to the limited query capabilities of the underlying DLs. To select DLs, we define a quality model based on two dimensions, which are the user's preferences and the source's quality parameters. We develop an algorithm that selects and ranks the sources respecting the user's preferences. The ranking is performed using the well known SAW method. To deal with semantic interoperability, we use ontologies. To build our ontologies, we apply the union approach to local ontologies. We improve the union approach by carrying out specializations and/or generalizations of the concepts and properties. For constructing query plans respecting the limited query capabilities of DLs, we develop a formalism for describing sources capabilities, a cost model and an algorithm for constructing query plans. We perform simulations to evaluate our system performances. The results show an acceptable response time for a given number of integrated sources. However, in some situations, the system becomes a bottleneck when the number of integrated DLs is important. This may occurs in the context of very large digital libraries. Despite the fact that WASSIT's reduces the number of integrated sources via sources selection, the number of selected sources may still high inducing performance degradation. To deal with this limitation, we plan to extend our work in two directions:

- **Using a hierarchy of mediators.** In this architecture, an instance of WASSIT integrates other instances of the same mediator. Each integrated mediator will integrate DLs. We believe that this solution will improve performances because it allows processing parallelization.
- **Using a peer-to-peer architecture.** In this architecture, a peer's network is formed. Each node in the network contains an instance of WASSIT integrating DLs. The absence of a central node avoids bottlenecks. We anticipate that this solution will give us good performance.

9. References

Arens, Y.; Knoblock Craig A. & Hsu, C. (1996). Query Processing in the SIMS Information Mediator, *Proceedings of Advanced Planning Technology, AAAI Press*, California, USA.

Benhlima, L. & Chiadmi, D. (2003). XQuery-SQL wrapper for integrating relational data sources", *Proceedings of COPSTIC'03*, pp 54–57, Rabat, Morocco, Dec. 11–13.

Bohring, H. & Aue, S. (2005). "Mapping XML to OWL Ontologies", *Proceedings of 13. Leipziger Informatik-Tage (LIT 2005), Lecture Notes in Informatics (LNI),* Vol. 72, pp. 147-156, ISBN 3-88579-401-2.

Bouzeghoub, M. & Peralta, V. (2004). A Framework for Analysis of Data Freshness, *International Workshop on Information Quality in Information Systems (IQIQ'2004), co-located with SIGMOD Conference*, Paris, France.

Bruijn, J. & Polleres, A. (2004). Towards an Ontology Mapping Specification Language for the Semantic Web, *Digital enterprise research institute deri,* Technical Report 2004-06-30.

Burgess, M.; Alex Gray, W. & Fiddian, N. (2002). Establishing Taxonomy of Quality for Use in Information Filtering, *Actes de la 19th British National Conference on Databases (BNCOD)*, pp. 103-113, Sheffield, UK.

Burgess, M-S-E; Gray, W.A. & Fiddian, N-J. (2004). Quality Measures and the information consumer. *Proceedings of the Ninth International Conference on Information Quality (ICIQ-04).*

DANG NGOC, T-T. (2003). *Integration of semi-structured data with XML,* Ph.D. dissertation, Versailles Saint-Quentin-en-Yvelines Uniersity, France.

El Marrakchi, M. (2009). *Mise en place d'un adaptateur XQuery/SOAP pour l'interrogation des Web services à partir d'un système de médiation.* M.S Thesis, Computer Sciences Department, Mohammadia Engineering School, Rabat, Morocco.

Fellbaum, C. (1999). *WordNet: An electronic lexical database.* Cambridge, Massashusset, MIT Press.

Fernández, M.; Malhotra, A.; Marsh, J., Nagy, M. & Norman, W. (2007). XQuery 1.0 and XPath 2.0 Data Model (XDM) W3C Recommendation 23, January 2007, Available from http://www.w3.org/TR/xpath-datamodel/

Garcia-Molina, H.; Papakonstantinou, Y.; Quass, D.; Rajaraman, A.; Sagiv, Y.; Ullman, J-D.; Vassalos,V. & Widom, J. (1997). The TSIMMIS approach to mediation: Data models and languages. *Journal of Intelligent Information Systems,* Vol. 8, No. 2, pp. 117-132.

Gounbarek, L.; Benhlima, L. & Chiadmi, D. (2009). Data Integration System: towards a prototype, *The seventh ACS/IEEE International Conference on Computer Systems and Applications (AICCSA-09),* Rabat, Morocco.

Gravano, L.; Chang, C.; Garcia-Molina, H. & Paepcke, A .(1997). STARTS: Stanford proposal for internet meta-searching, *Proceedings of the ACM-SIGMOD International Conference on Management of Data.*

Gruninger, M. & Lee, J. (2002). SPECIAL ISSUE: Ontology applications and design. *Communications of the ACM,* Vol. 45, Issue.2, pp. 39–41.

Haas, L.; Kossmann, D.; Wimmers E.; & Yang J. (1997). Optimizing queries across diverse data sources, *Proceedings of 23rd International Conf. on Very Large Data Bases, VLDB'97,* Athens, Greece, pp. 276–285.

Harrati, R. & Calabretto, S. (2006). Un modèle de qualité de l'information. *Actes des journées Extraction et Gestion de Connaissances (EGC),* p.299-304, Lille, France.

Hasselbring, W. (2000). Information System Integration: Introduction. *Communications of the ACM,* Vol. 43. Issue. 6, pp. 32-38.

Hwang, C.L. & Yoon, K. (1981). Multiple Attribute Decision Making: Methods and Applications. Springer-Verlag, Berlin, Heidelberg, New York.

Langegger, A.; Woß, W. and Blochl, M. (2008). A Semantic Web Middleware for Virtual Data Integration on the Web, *In proceedings of the 5th European Semantic Web Conference,* ESWC 2008, Tenerife, Canary Islands, Spain, June 1-5.

Larsen, R-L. & Wactlar, H.D. (June 2003). Knowledge Lost in Information. *Report of the NSF Workshop on Research Directions for Digital Libraries,* (June 15-17), Chatham, MA, National Science Foundation Award No. IIS-0331314. http://www.sis.pitt.edu/~dlwkshop/

Lenzerini, M. (2002). Data Integration: A Theoretical Perspective. *Proceedings of the 21st ACM SIGACT-SIGMOD-SIGART Symposium on Principles of Database Systems (PODS 2002),* pp. 233–246, Madison, Wisconsin, US.

Mcguinness, D-L. & Harmelen, F-V. (2004). OWL Web Ontology Language Overview. W3C Recommendation 10 February 2004, Available from http://www.w3.org/TR/2004/REC-owlfeatures-20040210/

Mena, E.; Illarramendi, A.; Kashyap, V. & Sheth, A-P. (2000). OBSERVER: An Approach for Query Processing in Global Information Systems Based on Interoperation Across Pre-Existing Ontologies. *Journal of Distributed and Parallel Databases,* Vol. 8, No. 2, pp. 223-271.

Moujane, A. (2006). *La sémantique fondée sur les ontologies pour la plate-forme WASSIT. M.S. thesis,* Computer Sciences Department, Mohammadia Engineering School, Rabat, Morocco.

Naumann, F.; Leser, U. & Freytag, J.C. (1999). Quality -driven integration of heterogenous information systems. *Proceedings of the 25th International Conference on Very large Data Bases (VLDB'99),* pp. 447-458.

Nottelmann, H. & Fuhr, N. (2003). Evaluation different methods of estimating retrieval quality for resource selection. *Proceedings of the 26th Annual International ACM SIGIR Conference on Research and Development in Information Retrieval.*

Paltoglou, G. (2009). *Algorithms and strategies for source selection and results merging (Collection fusion algorithms) in distributed information retrieval systems.* PhD thesis, Department of Applied Informatics, University of Macedonia.

Patel, M.; Koch, T.; Doerr, M.; & Tsinaraki, C. (2005). Semantic Interoperability in Digital Library Systems, *report of DELOS2 Network of Excellence in Digital Libraries,* Deliverable D 5.3.1.

Pipino, L.; Lee, Y. & Wang, R. (2002). Data quality assessment. *Communications of the ACM,* Vol. 45, No. 4, pp. 211-218.

Rousset, M-C.; Bidault, A.; Froidevaux, C.; Gagliardi, H.; Goasdoué, F.; Chantal, R. & Safar, B. (2002). Construction de médiateurs pour intégrer des sources d'information multiples et hétérogènes : le projet PICSEL. *Revue I3 : Information - Interaction – Intelligence,* Vol. 2, No. 1, pp. 5-59.

Rundensteiner, E.; Koeller, A. & Zhang, X. (2000). Maintaining Data Warehouses over Changing Information Sources, *Communications of the ACM,* Vol. 43, No. 6, pp. 57-62.

Segev, A. & Weiping, F. (1990). Currency-Based Updates to Distributed Materialized Views, *Proceedings of the 6th International Conference on Data Engineering (ICDE'90),* Los Angeles, USA.

Shen, R. (2006). *Applying the 5S Framework To Integrating Digital Libraries,* PhD dissertation, Virginia Polytechnic Institute and State University, Virginia, US.

Shvaiko P. & Euzenat, J. (2005). A survey of schema-based matching approaches. *In Journal on Data Semantics IV,* pp. 146-171.

Si, L. & Callan, J. (2003). Relevant document distribution estimation method for resource selection, *Proceedings of the 26th Annual International ACM SIGIR Conference on Research and Development in Information Retrieval.*

Strong, D.; Lee, Y. & Wang, R. (1997). Data quality in context, *Communications of the ACM,* Vol.40, No 5, pp. 103-110.

Tomasic A.; Raschid L., & Valduriez P. (1996). Scaling heterogeneous databases and the design of DISCO, *Proceedings of the 16th International Conf. on Distributing Computing Systems (ICDCS),* pp. 449–457, Hong Kong.

Travers, N. (2006). *Optimisation Extensible dans un Médiateur de Données Semi-Structurées.* Ph.D. dissertation, Université de Versailles Saint-Quentin-en-Yvelines, France

Wadjinny, F. & Chiadmi, D. (2006). XML Algebra for SIRENE, *Proceedings of MCSEAI'06,* pp 63-568, December 7-9, Agadir, Morocco.

Wang, R. & Strong, D. (1996). Beyond accuracy: what data quality means to data consumers. *Journal on Management of Information Systems*, Vol. 12, No. 4, pp. 5-34.

Wiederhold, G. (1992). Mediators in the Architecture of Future Information Systems. *In IEEE Computer Journal*. Vol. 5, No. 3, pp 38-49.

Xu, J. & Croft, W.B. (1999). Cluster-based language models for distributed retrieval. *Proceedings of the 22nd Annual International ACM SIGIR Conference on Research and Development in Information Retrieval.*

Zaoui, I.; Wadjinny, F.; Chiadmi, D. & Benhlima, L. (2009). Construction d'un profil utilisateur pour un médiateur de bibliothèques électroniques, *Proceeding of WOTIC*, Agadir, Morocco.

Zaoui, I.; Wadjinny, F.; Chiadmi, D. & Benhlima, L. (2010). Towards a personalized data source selection in the context of mediation systems, *Proceeding of the third International Conference on Web and Information Technologies*, Marrakech, Morocco.

Zellou, A. (2008). *Contribution to the LAV rewriting in the context of WASSIT, a resources integration framework.* Ph.D. dissertation, Computer Sciences Department, Mohammadia Engineering School, Rabat, Morocco.

Part 2

Operation and Development

5

Sorting Search Results of Literature Digital Libraries: Recent Developments and Future Research Directions

Sulieman Bani-Ahmad
AlBalqa Applied University
Jordan

1. Introduction

An OLDL (Online Literature Digital Library) is a library in which collections, i.e., publications from one or more domains of study, are stored in *digital formats* (as opposed to print, microform, or other media) and accessible by users through the Internet. Examples of well-known OLDLs are IEEE Xplore (IEEE Xplore, 2008), ACM Portal (ACM Digital Library, 2008), CiteSeer (CiteSeer, 2008), Google Scholar (Google Scholar, 2008), and PubMed (PubMed, 2008). Digital libraries are rapidly growing in popularity. For instance, ScienceDirect (ScienceDirect, 2008), the world's leading scientific, technical and medical information resource celebrated its billionth article download in November'06 since launched in 1999. Besides usage, digital libraries are also rapidly growing in terms of *size* and *diversity of topics*. For instance, (i) in Computer Science, ACM Digital Library (ACM Digital Library, 2008) has close to *one million* full-text publications collected over 50 years, to search and download; (ii) in Electrical Engineering and Computer Science, IEEE Xplore (IEEE Xplore, 2008), another OLDL, provides users with on-line access to more than 1,700 selected conferences proceedings.

These high growth rates introduced several challenges facing the information access capability of OLDLs. Next we list few challenges that probably guides future research related to LDLs.

Challenge 1: Large Sizes and Topic Diversity of Search Output Results. Search outputs of OLDLs tend to suffer from the "topic diffusion" problem, where commonly, keyword-based searches produce a large number of publications over a large number of topics, where not all topics are of interest to the user. One way to solve this problem is to assign scores to search results (i.e., publications). Assigning scores to publications helps OLDLs to present the most important relevant publications to the user first, Citation-based publication score measures (e.g., citation count) are commonly used for ranking publications. At the present time, OLDLs lack effective and accurate publication ranking.

Challenge 2: Lack of Effective Scoring Functions for Publications. At the present time, OLDLs lack effective and accurate publication rankings (Ratprasartporn et al., 2007). Providing accurate publication scores can help users in reducing the time spent in searching OLDLs, and thus enhances the scalability of OLDL usage as users can quickly identify important relevant publications to their topic of interest.

Challenge 3: Lack of Effective Scoring Functions for Search Outputs. In the field of literature digital libraries, citation analysis is employed to order digital library search outputs (e.g., Google Scholar). Examples of citation-based measures are citation-count (Bani-Ahmad & Ozsoyoglu, 2007) and PageRank (Brin & Page, 1998). However, as noticed by (Cho et al., 2005), citation-based measures compute popularity of publications based on the "current" state of a citation graph that continuously changes and evolves. Thus PageRank is effective in capturing the popularity of publications based on the current citation-graph in-hand. In section 4, we show that PageRank may assign inaccurate popularity scores *for both old and recent publications*. And thus PageRank cannot be used to rank OLDL search outputs. We therefore need effective techniques to order search results based on their importance and relevance to users' interests.

This chapter is organized as follows. After the introduction in section 1, we present and evaluate a set of citation-based score functions for publications. We show that they have problems in both accuracy and separability. To solve these problems, section 3 introduces the *Research-Pyramid Model,* a new model for the evolution of research and citation behavior. For that, we present two algorithms from literature for identifying research pyramid structures in publication citation graphs. We show that this model can help in computing accurate and non-skewed publication scores. In section 4 we propose the notion of *publication's popularity*. We also present how the temporal popularity of publications, as computed by the PageRank algorithm for instance, varies over time. For that we validate the *publication popularity growth and decay model.* And finally in section 5 we present a number of future research directions related to the topic of this chapter.

The observations preselected in this chapter are based on real experiment conducted on a literature digital collection of around 15,000 publications that we refer to as the AnthP. AnthP. These publications are from the ACM SIGMOD Anthology (ACM SIGMOD Anthology, 2003). For each paper in the AnthP, DBLP bibliography (DBLP, 2003) is used to extract the titles, authors, publication venue (conference or journal), and publication year info. Information extracted about each paper is the paper's publication venue, the publication year, authors, and citations. The AnthP dataset includes: (a) 106 conferences, journals, and books, (b) 14,891 papers, and (c) 13,208 authors.

2. Evaluating publication scoring functions in digital libraries

This section deals with the issues of defining score functions for publications in digital libraries, and evaluating how good they are. Presently, digital libraries do not assign scores to publications, even though they are potentially useful for (a) providing comparative assessment, or "importance", of papers, and (b) ranking papers returned in search outputs. Using social networks or bibliometrics, one can define a number of publication score functions.

Existing citation-based publication score functions are all based on the notion of prestige in social networks (Wasserman & Faust, 1994) and bibliometry (Chakrabarti, 2003). The well-known PageRank (Brin & Page, 1998) algorithm determines the importance of a publication by the number *and* importances of publications with links to it (i.e. citing papers). The Hyperlink Induced Topic Search (HITS) algorithm (Kleinberg, 1998) is similar to the PageRank algorithm in that HITS involves computing two scores for each publication; hub and authority scores. Authorities represent high-prestige publications, whereas hubs are publications that have links to authorities. Other citation-based score functions can be derived as follows. (a) Use normalized citation count (i.e., how many times a paper is cited by other papers) as the basis for a score function. (b) Revise the score of a paper using the score of its publication venue (conference or journal). (c) Add weights to citations, e.g., citations by an "important" author's work are more significant. (d) Revise the score of a paper using temporal distributions of citations; e.g., citations in the last 10 years are more significant than earlier citations. (e) Revise a paper score using the score of its citation venue; that is, capture the notion of a hub or an authority, e.g., survey journal represents a hub, whereas a research paper represents an authority. (f) Revise a paper score by the score of its author. One can also combine the score functions above. In the next two subsections we present, in more details, and evaluate these citation-based score functions of publications.

2.1 Citation-based publication score functions

In this section we present and evaluate citation-based score functions for publications.

A. PageRank

Importances of papers that cite a particular paper determines its importance. PageRank (Brin & Page, 1998) and HITS (Kleinberg, 1998) were designed based on this assumption. PageRank scores is computed recursively using the formula

$$P_{i+1} = (1-d)M^T P_i + E$$

Where P_i and P_{i+1} are the current and next iteration PageRank vectors respectively. M is a matrix derived from the citation matrix *C* by normalizing all row-sums in C to 1. *C*, in turn, is the adjacency matrix of the graph G formed as follows; the papers represent the graph nodes, and the citation relationships between these papers represent the edges. *C* is of size *N*x*N*, where *N* is the total number of papers in the system. Finally, *d* and (1-*d*) are the future citation probability. Given that an author *A* who is writing a new paper and already cited paper *u* which in turn cites paper *v*, and let *w* be a paper in *AnthP* selected randomly. The parameter *d* represents the probability that *A* will cite *w*, and (1-*d*) is the probability that *A* will cite *v*.
To guarantee the algorithm convergence, it is assumed to have a hidden link between each pair of the graph nodes. This link is represented by the user-defined parameter *E*. A variation of *E* is simply $E_1=d$. Another variation of *E* that is used in (Brin & Page, 1998) is

$$E_2 = d / N \left[1_N \right] P_i .$$

Where 1_N is a vector of N ones.

B. Hubs and Authorities

Authority score of paper P is computed by summing up the hub scores of the papers citing P. Hub score of P is computed by summing up the authority scores of the papers that P cites. Computation is recursive until results converge after a number of iterations. One difference between HITS and PageRank is that the first one works on papers in the result set of a query, while the latter considers all the papers independent of the query [Cakmak, 2003].

C. Citation Count

A paper, normally, does not cite another paper unless the cited paper is relevant. And, large number of citations to a paper gives an indication that the paper is important. Based on this fact, one can use citation count as a measure for paper importance. For a given paper P, let *CitationCount*(P) be the number of times paper P is cited by other papers. Using the number of citations, paper P is as important as those papers that have the same number of citations and more important than those papers that have fewer citations. We will refer to this paper ranking measure as $P_{Citation\_Count}$.

2.2 Evaluating publication score functions

Figure 1 shows the three score functions, namely, PageRank (P_{PgRank}), Authorities scores of HITS (P_{Auth}) and, the Citation-count (P_{CitCnt}). As it is clear from the figure the three functions are highly skewed, and do not separate scores well over the interval [0, 1]. This figure is based on the AnthP digital collection from the field of data management[1]. More details about AnthP can be found in (Bani-Ahmad & Ozsoyoglu, 2007). In (Pan, 2006), the author observed the skewness and inseparability of these functions independently in computer science and life sciences publications (70,000 documents in each) as well. And, it is shown (Render, 2004; Li & Chen, 2003) that distributions of citation-based score functions are also highly skewed and decay very fast. Studies show that the cause is topic diffusion since scores are computed with respect to the full publication set.

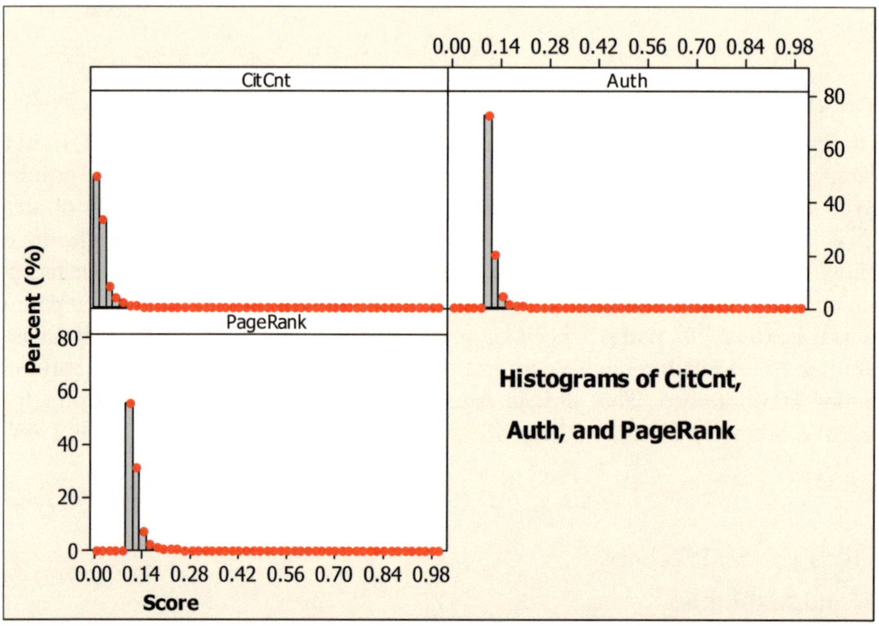

Fig. 1. Skewness of Score distribution of the three main citation-based publication score functions.

In (Bani-Ahmad* et al., 2005), the authors compared and evaluated several publication score functions, including *PageRank* (Brin & Page, 1998) and *Authorities scores* (Kleinberg, 1998), both adopted from the www search domain, and *citation-count scores* from the bibliometrics domain (Chakrabarti, 2003). The authors observed the *separability* problem with all of these

[1] This experimental dataset includes: (a) 106 conferences, journals, and books, (b) 14,891 papers, and (c) 13,208 authors. These papers are obtained from ACM SIGMOD Anthology.

functions which is that none of these scoring functions assigns scores that distribute well over a given scale, e.g., [0, 1]. Instead, distributions of existing publication score functions are highly skewed, and decay very fast (Render, 2004), resulting in a much less useful comparative publication assessment capability for users. This lack of separability is caused by the "rich gets richer" phenomena (Render, 2004; Li & Chen, 2003), i.e., a very small number of publications with relatively high numbers of in-citations have even higher chances of receiving new citations. Yet, these scoring functions are still not very accurate, probably caused by topic diffusion in search outputs (Haveliwala, 2002).

In the following section, and by using the research-pyramid model proposed in (Aya et al., 2005), the authors in (Bani-Ahmad & Ozsoyoglu, 2007) normalize scores of publications within their (the publications) own research pyramids, which allows for a fair comparative assessment of publications as publications are compared to their peers in their own research pyramids.

3. Improved publication scores via research pyramids

Providing accurate publication scores for search results and ranking publications returned as search results accurately can help users in reducing the time spent in searching OLDLs. And, better publication rankings are also useful for comparative assessments of publication venues and scientists as well.

At the present time, OLDLs lack effective and accurate publication rankings (Ratprasartporn et al., 2007). For instance, ACM Digital Library returns rankings of publication search results that are unexplained and not useful to users (ACM Digital Library, 2008). Moreover, search outputs of OLDLs tend to suffer from the "topic diffusion" problem, where commonly, keyword-based searches produce a large number of publications over a large number of topics, thereby producing scores that are nonspecific to topics.

The research evolution model proposed in (Aya et al., 2005) suggests that citation relationships between research publications produce multiple, small *pyramid-like* structures, where each pyramid represents publications related to a highly specific research topic. A *research pyramid* is defined (Aya et al., 2005) as a set of publications that represent a highly specific research topic, and usually has a *pyramid-like* structure in terms of its citation graph (Aya et al., 2005). Publications within an individual research pyramid are (i) *motivated by* earlier publications in the topic area (e.g., our paper (Bani-Ahmad & Ozsoyoglu, 2007) is motivated in part by citations (Ratprasartporn et al., 2007), and (Aya et al., 2005)), or (ii) *use techniques* proposed in publications from other research pyramids (e.g., our paper (Bani-Ahmad & Ozsoyoglu, 2007) in part uses some of the techniques presented in citations (Brin & Page, 1998) and (Kleinberg, 1998)). Other "reasons" for citations may also be observed (Aya et al., 2005).

In this section, our goals are to (a) provide a solution to the OLDL search output ranking problem due to the topic diffusion problem, by grouping search outputs at the most-specific (detailed) topic level and without identifying the topics themselves, (b) eliminate the low separability problem of score functions, and (c) improve the accuracy of three score functions, namely, PageRank, Authorities and Citation Count score functions. The research pyramid (RP-) model is used to improve the separability and accuracy of publication scores, and is based on normalizing publication scores within a limited scope, namely, *within individual research pyramids*. These improvements come from the fact that publications are now compared to their peers within their peer groups, namely, their own research pyramid publications that are on the same topic.

In (Bani-Ahmad & Ozsoyoglu, 2007), two approaches to identify research pyramids are presented and evaualted. The first, called *LB-IdentifyRP*, uses Link-Based Research Pyramid identification, which captures research pyramids by identifying pyramid-like structures *from the citation graph of the publication set*. The second approach, called *PB-IdentifyRP*, uses Proximity-Based Research Pyramid identification, utilizes a graph-based proximity measure, namely SimRank (Jeh & Widom, 2002), to compute similarities between publications, and then restructures the k-most-similar publications into a research pyramid.

3.1 Properties of research pyramid model

In (Bani-Ahmad & Ozsoyoglu, 2007), the authors have observed three properties of research publications in three separate data sets, namely, ACM Anthology which is a collection of 15,000 publications (we refer to this set by the AnthP set in future), and computer sciences and life sciences publication sets, each with 70,000 publications (we refer to these sets by the CSSet and LSSet in future) (Pan, 2006). These properties are utilized in the identification of research pyramids.

Property 1 (*Maximum Citation Age*). In OLDLs, most publications receive most of their in-citations within a fixed number of years after their publication dates. We refer to this value as the *Maximum Citation Age*, and denote it by C_{AgeMax}.

It has been observed in (Bani-Ahmad et al., 2005; Pan, 2006) that, in the *AnthP*, CSSet and the LSSet datasets, most publications receive 90% of their in-citations in 10 years, i.e., $C_{AgeMax}=10$. Figure 2 presents the citation age distributions in AnthP. Below in Property 4, we give a tighter bound for citation age within which topical similarity within an RP is maintained between citing and cited publications.

In rare cases, publications may cite works older than C_{AgeMax}. It is found (Ahmed et al., 2002) that a great proportion of these citations are for historical reasons, which we interpret as: old cited works (a) have coarse similarity to citing papers, and (b) do not belong in the RP of the citing publication.

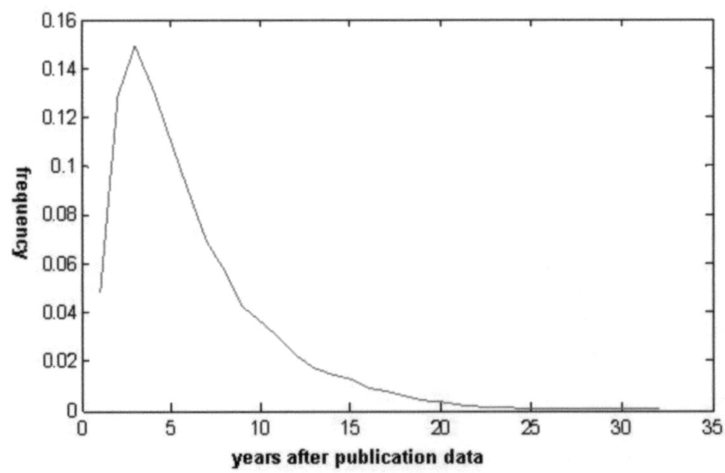

Fig. 2. Citation age distribution curve of AnthP

Property 2 (*Topic Specificity Over Time*). Scientific research publications quickly become very topic-specific over time, usually referable via a highly specific topic.

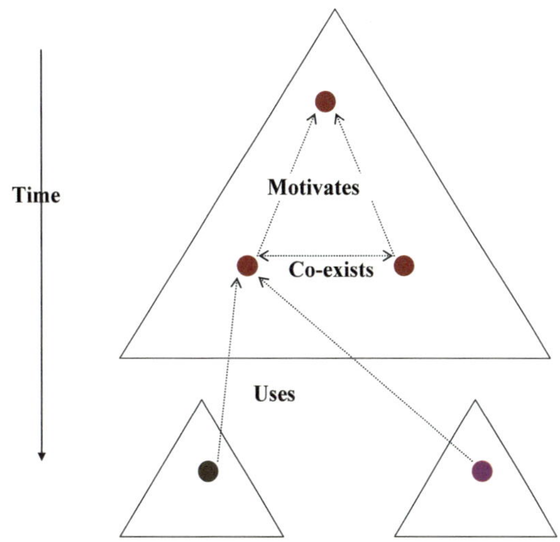

Fig. 3. The RP-Based Model

As illustrated in Figure 3, an old research pyramid that covers a certain research topic leads to instantiations of new research topics, and thus to creations of new RPs, that *use* techniques proposed in the publications of parent RP(s). Again, such old citations carry topical similarity between the citing and cited publication at a coarse granularity level. Possible citation exchanges between different RPs also occur and are of type "uses", i.e., the citing paper *uses* techniques proposed by the cited paper.

Example. Codd's paper *"E. F. Codd, "A Relational Model of Data for Large Shared Data Banks", Commun. ACM 13(6): 377-387(1970)"* is about the topic *relational model,* and cited around 580 times. A new and more specific topic of 2000's (i.e., citation to Codd's work is 30+ years old), say, *rank-aware join algorithms,* is coarsely related to the more general topic *relational model* in that, a publication P in the RP of *rank-aware join algorithms* and citing Codd's paper "uses" the techniques proposed in the RP of the *relational model.*

Property 3 (*Topic Similarity Decay Over Citation Path).* After *very small* citation path distances, topical similarity between papers decays significantly.

From Figure 4, in AnthP, after a citation path of length 3, the topical similarity, as measured by SimRank, significantly decays. We refer to this value by $L_{Max\text{-}TopicDecay}$. *This observation led the authors in (Bani-Ahmad & Ozsoyoglu, 2007) to build RPs of height at most 3 in the experimental results section.*

Property 4 (*Topic Similarity Decay over citation age).* After a certain citation age, topical similarity between the citing and the cited papers significantly decays.

From Figure 5, in the AnthP set, after a citation age of about 5 years, the topic similarity between the citing and cited papers decays significantly. We refer to this value by $C_{AgeMax\text{-}TopicDecay}$. *This observation led the authors in (Bani-Ahmad & Ozsoyoglu, 2007) to build RPs in the experimental results section such that the maximum citation age within an RP is 5 years.*

The two characteristics that identify a *research pyramid RP* are.

RP-Property 1 (*High Topic Specificity*). An RP, usually organizable into a pyramid, is a set of publications that represent a *highly specific research topic.*

We maintain high topic specificity of RPs by applying properties 3 and 4, and keeping the height of research pyramids low (property 3). Note that we make no attempts to identify the

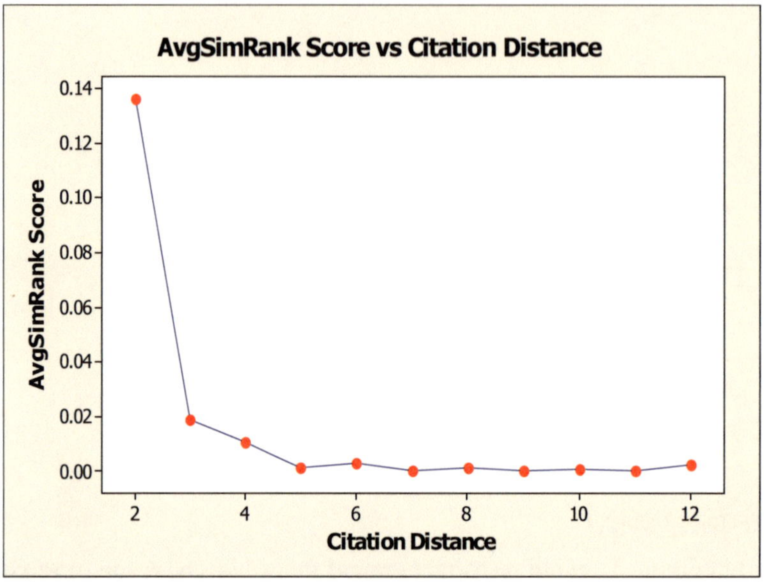

Fig. 4. SimRank score change with citation distance

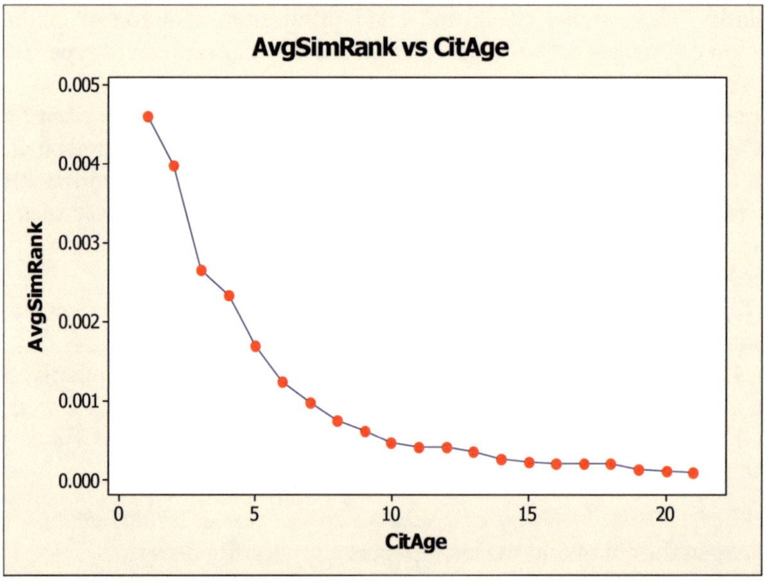

Fig. 5. SimRank score change with citation age

topic associated with an RP, as our approach does not need the topics explicitly. But, in interactive environments, providing topics to users is useful (Ratprasartporn & Ozsoyoglu, 2007).

RP-Property 2 (*Research Pyramid Construction*). RPs are arranged into *pyramid* structures either directly by using citation graphs (i.e., the link-based approach) (Aya et al., 2005) or indirectly using the publication times and close proximity of papers (i.e., the proximity-based approach).

3.2 Research pyramid identification procedures

Based on the properties of publications and characteristics of RPs, next we propose two *offline* research pyramid identification procedures, namely, the link-based (LB) and the proximity-based (PB) RP identification procedures.

Both procedures start by choosing a candidate root node for an RP, called the *cornerstone paper*. The paper that is located at the root of a research pyramid receives more citations than others as other publications within the research pyramid are "motivated" by it, and directly or indirectly cite it. Thus, our approach is to *identify papers with high in-citations as cornerstone papers* (i.e., the roots) of RPs to be constructed.

The *link-based* procedure locates research pyramids by identifying pyramid-like structures in the citation graph of the publication set. In summary, within an individual RP, publications are topically related (Aya et al., 2005), and motivated by each other (see figure 3) (Aya et al., 2005), and we use the four properties to identify citations within RPs—as summarized next.

In *AnthP,* the average number of citations to a paper ("in-citations"), denoted by C_I, is 2.066. Note that, in our experiments, we consider *only* the *AnthP* citations that are completely within AnthP; any citation from a paper within AnthP to a paper that is not in AnthP is removed. Using Property 3 and RP-Property 1, we limit RP heights to 3. Thus, the expected number of papers within a research pyramid RP_P with paper P as the root and with height 3 is $|RP_P| = 1 + C_I + C_I^2 + C_I^3 \approx 15$. Of course, the actual identified RP sizes (the number of papers in RP_P) vary. Some RPs may deal with active research topics, and, in such cases, the number of in-citations of publications are noticeably higher than C_I, leading to noticeably higher RP sizes as well.

Figure 6-(a) presents the link-based *LB-IdentifyRP()* procedure. The proximity-based *PB-IdentifyRP()* is similar, except that the function call to *LB-FormRP()* is replaced by the function call *PB-FormRP()*. The procedure *LB-IdentifyRP()* (a) selects a cornerstone paper P from the existing publication set (originally, say, AnthP) as an RP root, by simply picking the current most-cited publication (only citations that are $C_{AgeMax\text{-}TopicDecay}$ old according to property 4 above), (b) calls *LB-FormRP()* to locate the RP set RP_P of P, and (c) eliminates RP_P from the current publication set *CurrAnthP*, and repeats (a)-(c) again, until no more publications are left in *CurrAnthP*.

Note that our approach in this chapter is to create distinct and nonoverlapping research pyramids. An alternative approach, not reported here due to space limitations, is to allow *overlapping research pyramids* as follows: Do not to eliminate *any* papers from the original publication set (i.e., remove step (c) above); instead, simply *color each* selected publication, and continue until all publications are colored, meaning that, when the algorithm ends, each paper belongs to at least one RP set, and possibly more.

The two main functions of the link-based *LB-IdentifyRP()* procedure are *ChooseRoot()* and *LB-FormRP(). ChooseRoot()* (See Figure 6.b) chooses publications that are cornerstone papers, or roots of research pyramids. The function *LB-FormRP()* (Figure 6.c) forms the RP_P of a root publication P by adding direct citers of P (i.e., *level-1 citers*) into RP_P, and indirect citers of P at a level up to the L_{Max}; in experiments, we choose L_{Max} as 3, by following the property 3. The function *Citers*(P, l, $C_{AgeMax\text{-}Topic\text{-}Decay}$) returns the set of publications that cite P at a level l (which is at most L_{Max}) where the citation age of the citing paper with respect to P is less than the maximum citation age $C_{AgeMax\text{-}Topic\text{-}Decay}$, (Properties 1 and 4). In more detail,

1. Paper-id pid_P of root P along with its level *0* is inserted into RP_P and the queue Q, which holds paper-ids for future expansions and their distances to the root paper P.

2. Two-tuple <P_i, ℓ > in Q is dequeued, and expanded by locating direct or indirect citers of P_i so long as their levels with respect to P is at most $L_{Max\text{-}TopicDecay}$ (i.e., 3) and their citation age with respect to P (the root) is less than the maximum citation age $C_{AgeMax\text{-}TopicDecay}$ (i.e., 5). All expanded publications and their level info with respect to P are inserted into the queue Q.
3. The above two steps are repeated until Q is empty; then RP_P is returned.

```
proc LB-IdentifyRP(AnthP, RP-Sets)
{
 RP-Sets := Ø;
 CurrAnthP := AnthP;
  while (CurrentAnthP = Ø)
  {Root:=ChooseRoot(CurrAnthP);
   RP_Root:=LB-FormRP(Root,L_Max-TopicDecay);
   RP-Sets:=RP-Sets U RP_Root;
   CurrAnthP:=CurrAnthP - RP_Root;
  }
}
```

(a) Procedure LB-IdentifyRP

```
funct ChooseRoot(CurrAnthP)
 return TopCited_TopicDecay(CurrAnthP);
```

(b) Function ChooseRoot

```
funct LB-FormRP(P, L_Max)
{Set RP_P:={P};    Queue Q;
 Q.Enqueue({P},0);
 while(Q is not empty)
 {<P_i, ℓ>:=Q.Dequeue;
  if(ℓ<L_Max) then
  {CiterSet=Citers(P_i, ℓ, C_AgeMax-TopicDecay);

  Q.Enqueue(CiterSet,(ℓ+1));
   RP_P = RP_P +CiterSet;
   } } }
 Return RP_P}
```

(c) Function LB-FormRP()

```
Funct PB-FormRP(P, L_Max)
{Set RP_P={P}; Queue Q;
 Q.Enqueue(P,0);
 while(Q is not empty)
 {<P_i, ℓ>:=Q.Dequeue;
 if(ℓ<L_Max) then
 {CiterSet(P_i):=Citers(P_i, ℓ, C_AgeMax-TopicDecay)

  TopSimSet:=TopSim(P_i, |CiterSet(P_i)|, C_AgeMax-TopicDecay);
  Q.Enqueue(TopSimSet, ℓ+1);
  RP_P= RP_P+TopSimSet;
  } }
  Return RP_P}
```

(d) Function PB-FormRP()

Fig. 6. Functions of LB- and PB-IdentifyRP algorithms

The function *PB-FormRP()* (figure 6.d) of the proximity-based approach utilizes a graph-based proximity measure, namely *SimRank* (Jeh & Widom, 2002), to compute similarities between publications. It captures RP_P of the root publication by locating publications that are most similar to *P* and yet (a) are linked to *P* with a citation path length of at most $L_{Max\text{-}TopicDecay}$, and (b) have a citation time distance less than $C_{AgeMax\text{-}TopicDecay}$. *SimRank* iteratively computes similarity scores between nodes in a graph G following the rule that "two nodes are similar if they are linked with similar nodes". In other words, the *SimRank* similarity between two nodes *a* and *b*, *S(a, b)*, is iteratively computed using the formula (until the similarity scores converge):

$$S(a,b) = \left[C / |I(a)|\,|I(b)|\right] * \sum_{i=1}^{|I(a)|} \sum_{j=1}^{|I(b)|} S(I_i(a), I_j(b))$$

where $I(a)$ and $I(b)$ are sources of in-links of a and b, respectively. C is the decay factor between 0 and 1. We choose C=0.8 (Jeh & Widom, 2002). If $|I(a)| or |I(b)| = 0$ then *S(a, b)*=0 by definition, in the case where a=b, *S(a, b)*=1. The space complexity of the naive SimRank algorithm is $O(N^2)$ where N is the graph size (the citation graph in publication domain). We prune as in (Jeh & Widom, 2002) by considering node pairs that are near each other in the range of radius *r*. We choose *r*=6, which is twice the value of the expected research pyramid height as also explained in Section 3.5.

PB- FormRP() receives as input the root *P*, the maximum level L_{Max} from root, and utilizes the maximum citation age $C_{AgeMax\text{-}TopicDecay}$ (as 5) and returns the RP set RP_P of publication *P* following the same main steps of *LB- FormRP()* with one main difference: the way the two-tuple $<P_i, \ell>$ dequeued from *Q* is expanded, as follows:

- Top $|Citers(P_i, \ell, C_{AgeMax\text{-}TopicDecay})|$ similar papers, based on *SimRank*, to P_i are identified. The number of citers of P_i is used to capture the density of the RP being identified, and thus to expand RP at P_i accordingly.
- The identified similar papers are added to RP_P and also enqueued to *Q* for further expansion, this time with the level increased by 1. Similar to *LB- FormRP()* a maximum level of $L_{Max\text{-}TopicDecay}$ (which is 3) is employed.

Advantage of PB-FormRP() over *LB-FormRP()* is that it successfully captures co-existing members of RP as well as those that are not reachable through any citation path from RP's root (as illustrated in Figure 3.7 above). We give an example.

Example. Figure 7 shows two RPs; RP_1 and RP_2. RP_1 contains two co-existing roots *A* and *B*. Such a case occurs when two researchers work on the same problem simultaneously. At some point of our RP identification process, *A* will probably be recognized as a root of a new RP, say RP_3, as it has more in-citations than *B*. And, since B is not reachable through any path from *A*, *LB-FormRP()* will fail to identify *B* as a member of RP_3. *PB-FormRP()* will succeed to place both A and B into RP_3 in this case as *B* is very similar to *A*. A similar problem will be observed with paper *C* that is not reachable through any path from the root. Furthermore, *LB-FormRP()* may incorrectly identify *F*, that probably "uses" a technique proposed in *A*, as a member of RP_3 when *F* is really a member of RP_2 which co-exists with RP_3. *PB-FormRP()* successfully repels *F* from RP_3 as *F* is not similar to *A* or any of RP_3's members, based on *SimRank*.

We observe here that *PB-FormRP()* may capture *pyramid-like* structures, but not exactly pyramid structures. SimRank computes similarity between two papers P_1 and P_2 by averaging the similarity of the citers of both. However, note that similar papers to a member of an RP will be the other members of the same RP since members of an RP are usually cited by each other (as they are motivated by each other).

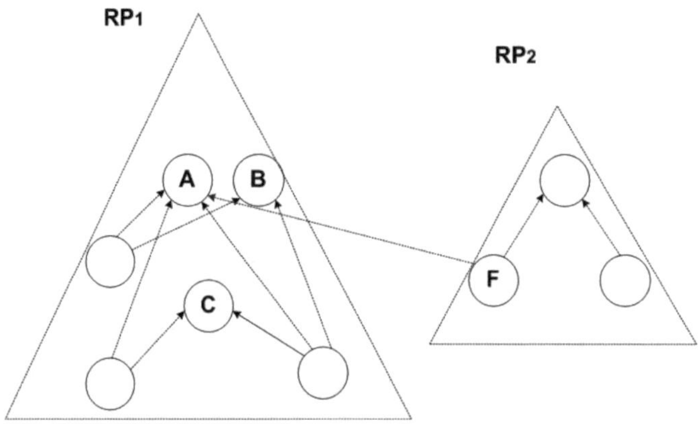

Fig. 7. Examples where *PB-FormRP()* is more successful than *LB-FormRP()*.

3.3 Improved publication scores via the RP-Model

In (Bani-Ahmad & Ozsoyoglu, 2007), the authors have applied the two RP-identification algorithms on the AnthP set. After that, they normalized publication scores within the research pyramids identified. The authors observed that, for RP-based scores, the observed skew values (table 1) range between (-0.05) and (1.88) in the RP-based scores (zero skew indicates that the distribution is symmetric). In comparison, the original scores showed highly skewed values that range between 8.12 and 13.04, which mean that they are sharply left-skewed. They also observed that, for RP-based scores, Kurtosis values (that measure how sharply peaked a distribution is) range between (-0.26) to (2.65) (near zero Kurtosis values indicate normally peaked data). In comparison, in the case of globally normalized scores, Kurtosis values range between (113.28) and (291.10). The enhancement of score distribution comes from the fact that publications are being compared to their peer groups, i.e., publications that belong to the same scope, and thus have the same chances of receiving new citations.

	Mean	IQR	Skewness	Kurtosis
CitCnt	0.02527	0.01845	8.12	113.28
Auth	0.11352	0.01134	13.04	291.10
PageRank	0.12091	0.01733	8.84	134.65
LBCitCnt	0.55698	0.88462	-0.05	-1.81
LBAuth	0.81266	0.37723	-1.02	-0.26
LBPageRank	0.77649	0.46181	-0.80	-0.84
PBCitCnt	0.20802	0.21910	1.88	2.65
PBAuth	0.62386	0.32036	-0.07	-0.58
PBPageRank	0.55653	0.31615	0.30	-0.60

Table 1. The Means, InterQuartile Ranges (IQR), Skewness, and Kurtosis values of the Publication Score Functions applied on the AnthP set.

The above observations on *PageRank* (P_{PgRank} , $P_{PgRank-LB}$, $P_{PgRank-PB}$) also apply to *Authorities* scores (P_{Auth} , $P_{Auth-LB}$, $P_{Auth-PB}$). Here we report only PageRank-related results as we have observed that P_{Auth} and P_{PgRank} scores are highly correlated with a correlation coefficient of 0.98, and the correlation between P_{PgRank} and P_{CitCnt} is 0.74. (Bani-Ahmad* et al., 2005).
The authors in (Bani-Ahmad & Ozsoyoglu, 2007) have also performed multiple searches and manually evaluated the accuracy ranking publication via the RP-Model. They observed that research-pyramid-based scores resulted in 16% - 25% more accurate search outputs than the PageRank-based quality scores. Accuracy was measured for the top-k publications in the result sets, where k is 10.

3.4 Section summary and conclusions

In this section, The Research-Pyramid model proposed in (Aya et al., 2005) is used to solve the separability and accuracy problems of publication score functions. We showed that (i) normalizing publication scores within their research pyramids provides more accurate and less skewed scores, moreover (ii) ranking search results by these scores promises to give higher accuracy compared to ranking by globally normalized publication scores due to reduction of topic diffusion effect.
However, as noticed by (Cho et al., 2005), citation-based measures compute popularity of publications based on the "current" state of a citation graph that continuously changes and evolves. Thus PageRank is effective in capturing the popularity of publications based on the current citation-graph in-hand. In the following section, we show that PageRank may assign inaccurate popularity scores *for both old and recent publications*. And thus PageRank cannot be used to rank OLDL search outputs. We therefore need effective techniques to order search results based on their importance and relevance to users' interests.

4. On popularity quality: growth and decay phases of publication popularities

4.1 Introduction

In the field of literature digital libraries, citation analysis is employed to evaluate the impact of publications and scientific collections (e.g., journals and conferences). It is also employed to order digital library search outputs (e.g., Google Scholar). Examples of citation-based measures are citation-count (Bani-Ahmad & Ozsoyoglu, 2007) and PageRank (Brin & Page, 1998). However, as noticed by (Cho et al., 2005), citation-based measures compute popularity of publications based on the "current" state of a citation graph that continuously changes and evolves. Next we present two scenarios where usage of such popularity scores becomes problematic.
Example 1 (*Scores for recent publications;* Google Scholar (Google Scholar, 2008)). Figure 8 shows a sample search output from Google Scholar, a digital library search tool by Google (Google Scholar, 2008), for keywords "top-k query processing for semistructured data". On the left-side of figure 8, relevant documents are ordered based on text-based relevancy to query terms **and** the citation-based popularity of the document. On the right-side, documents are ordered based on their publication date. The most relevant document to our query, the one entitled by "TopX: efficient and versatile top-k query processing for semistructured data", is published in 2008, and appears at the top of the right-side search output list (where popularity didn't affect the order of the output list). In comparison, this document is pushed down and appeared on page 5 of the left-side search output list of

Google Scholar. Given that users usually check only a few pages of a returned list of documents (Bani-Ahmad & Ozsoyoglu, 2007), this publication may not even have a chance to develop popularity unless, in time, awareness of readers increases, i.e., it becomes known to users.

All Articles

[PDF] Top-k query evaluation with probabilistic guarantees - all 6 versions »
M Theobald, G Weikum, R Schenkel - … Conference on Very Large **Data** Bases (VLDB), Toronto, Canada, 2004 - cse.iitb.ac.in
... error relative to "exactly **top-k**" queries, translatable into guarantees about **query**-result precision ... on algorithms that **process** index lists by ...
Cited by 85 - Related Articles - View as HTML - Web Search

IO-**Top-k**: index-access optimized **top-k query processing** - all 5 versions »
H Bast, D Majumdar, R Schenkel, M Theobald, G … - … of the 32nd international conference on Very large **data** …, 2006 - portal.acm.org
... index-access steps in TA-style **top-k query processing** in the ... In these cases, the **query** optimizer needs to find a ... attributes that are relevant for **top-k** queries ...
Cited by 20 - Related Articles - Web Search - BL Direct

SPIDER: a multiuser information retrieval system for **semistructured** and dynamic **data** - all 3 versions »
P Schäuble - Proceedings of the 16th annual international ACM SIGIR …, 1993 - portal.acm.org.. The retrieval of information from **semistructured data** collections is supported by an appropriate re ... Let q be the user's **query** and let k be the ... The **top k** exact ...
Cited by 40 - Related Articles - Web Search

Recent Articles

TopX: efficient and versatile **top-k query processing** for **semistructured data**
M Theobald, H Bast, D Majumdar, R Schenkel, G … - … VLDB Journal The International Journal on Very Large **Data** …, 2008 – Springer **...** As for our **data** model, we focus on a tree model for **semi- structured data**, thus following the W3C XML ... TopX : **top-k query processing** for **semistructured data** ...
Web Search - BL Direct

IO-**Top-k**: index-access optimized **top-k query processing** - all 5 versions »
H Bast, D Majumdar, R Schenkel, M Theobald, G … - … of the 32nd international conference on Very large **data** …, 2006 - portal.acm.org
... index-access steps in TA-style **top-k query processing** in the ... In these cases, the **query** optimizer needs to find a ... attributes that are relevant for **top-k** queries ...
Cited by 20 - Related Articles - Web Search - BL Direct

[PDF] Top-k query evaluation with probabilistic guarantees - all 6 versions »
M Theobald, G Weikum, R Schenkel - … Conference on Very Large **Data** Bases (VLDB), Toronto, Canada, 2004 - cse.iitb.ac.in
... error relative to "exactly **top-k**" queries, translatable into guarantees about **query**-result precision ... on algorithms that **process** index lists by ...
Cited by 85 - Related Articles - View as HTML - Web Search

Fig. 8. Searching Google Scholar for "top-k query processing for semistructured data"

Example 2 (*Scores for old publications;* CiteSeer (CiteSeer, 2008)): The two plots in Figure 9 show in-citation counts of two relatively highly cited publications from CiteSeer (CiteSeer, 2008) (the observations made in this example do apply to most of the top-cited papers; check the full list posted by CiteSeer (CiteSeer-Lists, 2008)). Notice that the popularities of the two publications have dropped significantly after 2004. We observe that the probability

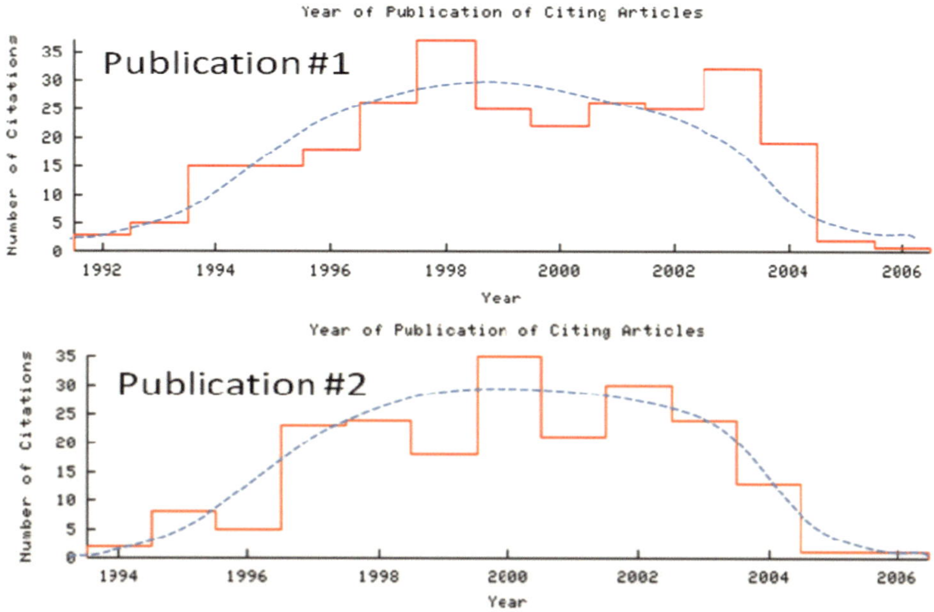

Fig. 9. Citation count per year for two publications that appeared in 1992 and 1994 (from CiteSeer) and cited around 300 times each.

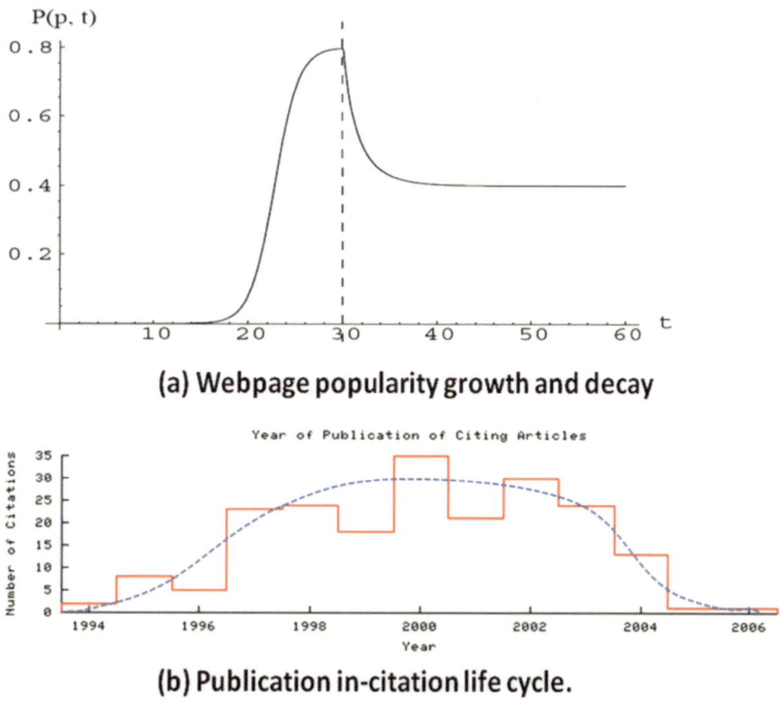

Fig. 10. Popularity drop of webpages, as opposed to observed in-citation life cycle of publications.

that a publication receives new citations drops as it gets older. And, we also observe that PageRank scores of old publications reach a certain value, and do not change after that, even when they are not cited anymore. The reason is that citations do not age or disappear, and as we shall shortly explain, citation graphs around old publications minimally change. We thus conclude that PageRank scores of old publications represent their peak popularity (that they achieved in the ***past***), but not their *current* popularity. This means that, even though old publications may in time be of lower interest to present users, their PageRank scores do not change.

Based on the above two examples, we argue that, although PageRank is effective in capturing the peak popularity of publications, PageRank may assign inaccurate popularity scores *for both old and recent publications*.

In (Cho et al., 2005), a web-user model is introduced and a new *popularity growth model* of webpages is presented. Using the growth model, Cho et. al. derived a quality estimator to compute webpage quality as opposed to its peak-time popularity.

In this section, we experimentally validate the popularity growth phase model of publications proposed by (Cho et al., 2005). Moreover, we observe the following differences between publication citation and web-link graphs that the popularity growth model does not take in consideration: (i) publication citations do not ever disappear like web links, (ii) unlike web links, once two papers are published, no new citations between them are added, (iii) also unlike web links, new citations to old papers are very unlikely to occur, and (iv) indirect citations to a publication are of lesser effect on its PageRank score (Desikan et al., 2005). We observe that these differences result in popularity decay for old publications overtime, which we refer to as the *publication popularity decay phase*. In this section, these differences guide us in extending the popularity growth model to accurately capture popularity decay of publications in technology-driven fields of study where authors tend *not* to cite publications that get older, and publication quality becomes less relevant. We demonstrate that our proposal successfully assigns accurate publication scores that are in turn useful for two tasks:

i. **Ranking search results of user queries in literature digital libraries**. Accurate publication scores may help users retrieve new and yet *promising* publications; and new publications may contain undiscovered ideas at the frontiers of the topic of interest for users. Our extended quality estimator identifies high quality papers, presents them to the user, and thus gives new papers a better chance to accumulate awareness more quickly.
ii. **Modeling popularity life cycle of publications**. Coupled with the probabilistic model of researchers' citation behavior, which we discuss in section 5.4, *popularity life cycle* of publications in different publication venues can be modeled. Cho et. al. analytically verified that the quality estimator they propose can successfully be used for pages with changing quality (growth and decay) (see figure 5.3). However, they did not investigate the popularity decay of pages (Cho et al., 2005), probably because of the difficulties in capturing such web data and the complexity of web-link graph dynamics. Studies show that, for literature digital libraries, the popularity decay phase can be successfully modeled and integrated with the popularity growth phase.

Our two-phase publication popularity model, i.e., the popularity growth and decay model, is in heavily different than the webpage popularity model. To illustrate the differences, figure 10 shows two popularity growth and decay curves, one for a webpage (figure 5.3.a from (Cho et al., 2005)) and another for a publication (figure 10.b from CiteSeer (CiteSeer, 2008)). Notice that the popularity of a webpage keeps increasing as the webpage becomes known and those who "like" it place links to it in other pages (Cho et al., 2005). After the webpage reaches the peak, its popularity decays until it reaches a steady-state popularity value (Cho et al., 2005). In comparison, the decay of publication popularity has a much different curve. Studies show that researchers rarely cite old works, especially in fast-moving fields like computer and life sciences. Consequently, we show that, by properly modeling users' citation behavior along with accurate publication quality estimators, we obtain realistic publication popularity growth and decay curves similar to the dashed curves of figure 10.b. Empirically, we observe that the majority of publication "citation count per year" curves conform to this growth and decay model.

4.2 Page quality and webpage popularity evolution model

Cho et. al. (Cho et al., 2005), via a simple user-web model, developed a formula for the popularity growth of webpages, and then used the formula to estimate page quality.

Publication quality, based on the web-user model, is defined as the popularity of the publication given that all possibly interested authors are aware of it and those who like it have cited it.

After getting published, a paper goes through two main phases:

i. a **popularity growth phase** where its popularity increases as more authors become aware of it and cite it. After some time, the publication's popularity reaches to a certain value. During the growth phase of the publication, (i) researchers develop awareness of the publication, i.e., more authors get to know it, and (ii) research problems inspired by the paper get studied by authors. This means that the longer the growth phase of a paper, the better the quality of the paper; and (iii) the authors who *like* the paper cite it in their works.
ii. a **saturation phase**: after the transient growth phase, the publication's PageRank score settles at a certain value, and minimally changes.

Definition:

1. The ***growth region*** of a publication is the time interval during which the publication popularity grows.
2. The ***saturation region*** of a publication is the time interval that starts at the saturation point; and, afterwards, the publication usually does not receive new citations.
3. The ***popularity function*** $\boldsymbol{P}(p,t)$ of publication p, is a function that computes the popularity of p at time t.
4. ***Publication quality*** $Q(p)$ is the intrinsic and (saturation-time popularity) quality of a publication (Cho et al., 2005).

We empirically calculate an estimation $\tilde{Q}(p)$ for the publication quality $Q(p)$ of publication p as the PageRank score at the saturation region. Or, $\tilde{Q}(p) = PR(p, t_{sat})$ where $PR(p, t_{sat})$ is PageRank score of p at the saturation time point t_{sat}.

The popularity *growth* function $\boldsymbol{P}(p,t)$, proposed in (Cho et al., 2005), is derived as:

$$\boldsymbol{P}(p,t) = Q(p)/(1 + C_1.e^{-\beta t}) \quad (1)$$

Note that the function $\boldsymbol{P}(p,t)$ is monotonically increasing with time t. The constant $Q(p)$ is the intrinsic quality of the publication p (that is estimated as p's PageRank score in the saturation region), constant C_1 is the rate of PageRank score growth in Cho's PageRank score growth model. For new publications, $\boldsymbol{P}(p,0) \cong 0$. In time, the exponent component, $e^{-\beta t}$, approaches zero as t increases, and, consequently, $\boldsymbol{P}(p,t)$ converges to $Q(p)$, the intrinsic quality score of the publication, over time.

Remark: The popularity of a publication p at time t is estimated as the p's PageRank score based on the citation graph at time t. Also, the quality of publication p is estimated as the PageRank score at saturation phase (Cho et al., 2005).

The above remark forms a bridge between the PageRank score change curve and Cho et. al.'s popularity growth model (and our model of publication popularity growth and decay model). (Cho et al., 2005) base their model on the fact that the quality of a page is time-invariant and does not change overtime. Thus; $Q(p)$ is assumed to be a constant estimated at any time as the sum of (a) the current popularity or PageRank score of p, and (b) the relative popularity (PageRank) rate of change, i.e.,

$$\tilde{Q}(p) = PR(p,t) + \frac{1}{c}.\frac{d\boldsymbol{P}(p,t)}{dt}.\frac{1}{PR(p,t)} \tag{2}$$

where $0 < c \leq 1$ is a constant which we choose to be 0.1 as in (Cho et al., 2005).

A high quality publication is one with a scientific value, and one can intuitively estimate the quality of a publication based on its impact on other authors. Quantitatively, the quality can be measured as the conditional probability that an author will like the publication (L_p) given that s/he has became aware of it (A_p). Mathematically, $Q(p) = P(L_p|A_p)$, as defined in (Cho et al., 2005).

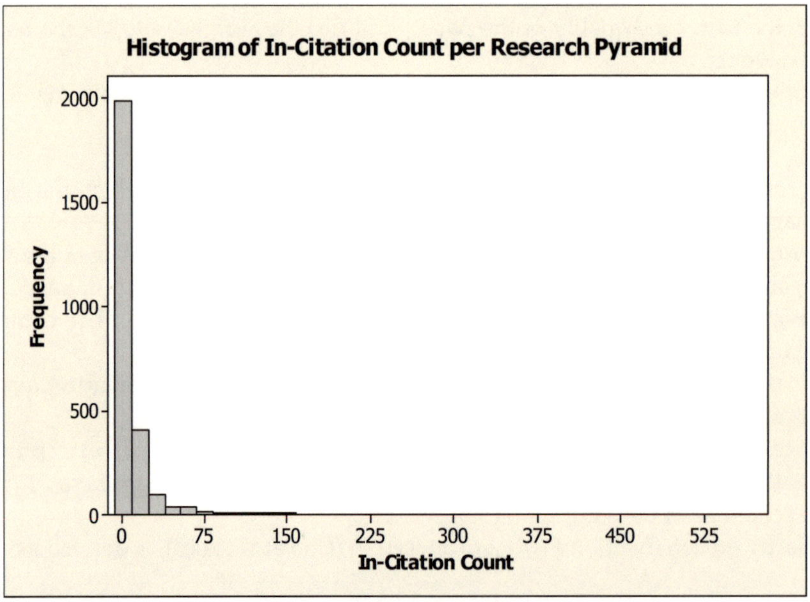

Fig. 11. In-citation per research pyramid (inter-research pyramid citations, i.e. citations from publications outside an RP to ones inside it).

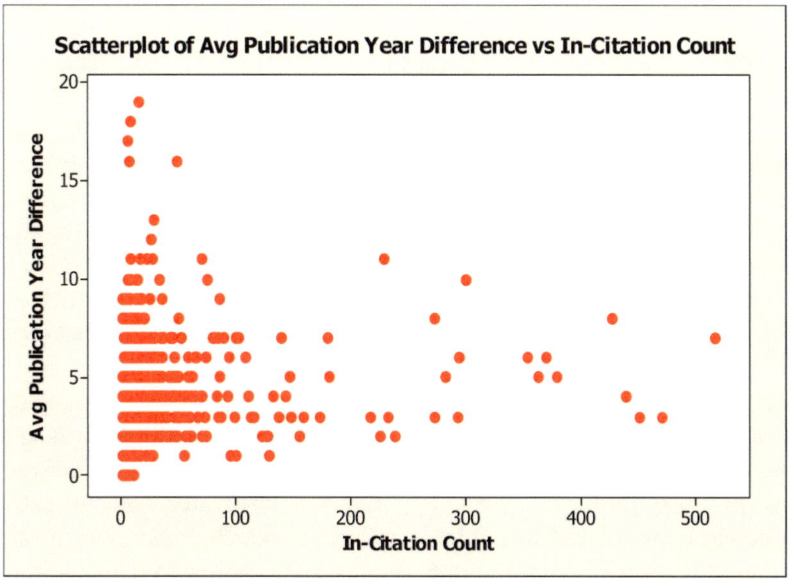

Fig. 12. Inter-pyramid Citation count (x-axis) vs the (average difference in publication dates of publications in a research pyramid).

We argue that we need to distinguish between two measures of quality for a publication.

i. The first measure represents the scientific value of that publication (i.e., how well-written it is, the authors follow a suitable technique to solve the research problem, …, etc). This value is time-invariant and is represented by $Q(p)$ (Cho et al., 2005).
ii. The second measure represents the value of the paper to the user at the time s/he is searching the digital library. This value, in contrast to $Q(p)$, is time-dependent, especially in fast-moving fields of study. We refer to this quality measure as the *Publication Quality with Aging Factor.*

Next in the following subsection, we show that publications go through the popularity growth phase during which publications gain awareness and thus popularity. And in section 5.6, we empirically show the popularity growth curves conform to the "sigmoidal" evolution pattern derived by (Cho et al., 2005). Finally, in section 5.4, we study one aspect of researcher citation behavior, and use it in section 5.5 to propose our notion of *Publication Quality with Aging Factor.*

4.3 Properties of publication citation graphs and research pyramids

In this section we validate Cho et. al.'s popularity growth phase by (i) using PageRank as a popularity indicator, and (ii) utilizing the research-pyramid model of research evolution (Bani-Ahmad & Ozsoyoglu, 2007; Aya et al., 2005), to show that popularity scores of publications converge to a steady-state value that can be estimated by equation (2) above.

We first note one difference between a publication citation graph from a web citation graph: Publication citation graph evolution behavior is to some extent more controlled than web graphs and can be anticipated. A webpage that has been on the web for a relatively long time may still receive new links (citations); old publications, however, are rarely cited (Ahmed et al., 2002; Bani-Ahmad & Ozsoyoglu, 2007; Case & Higgins, 2000). Consequently, publication citation graphs are highly unlikely to face structural changes around relatively old publications. This special characteristic of publication citation graphs allows for developing accurate mathematical models for changes to publication's PageRank scores, and thus better estimation of publication quality. In contrast, a web graph may face abrupt structural changes at any time in any part of the graph. Studies show that, every week, around 8% web pages are replaced and that about 25% new links are created (Ntoulas et al., 2004).

Next we describe the research-pyramid (RP-) model (Bani-Ahmad & Ozsoyoglu, 2007; Aya et al., 2005) of publications that also suggests time-dependent growth patterns in publication citation graphs. The RP-Model is based on the observation that citations between research publications produce multiple, small pyramid-like structures, where each pyramid represents publications related to a highly specific research topic (Aya et al., 2005). A research pyramid is defined as a set of publications that represent a highly specific research topic, and usually has a pyramid-like structure in terms of its citation graph (Aya et al., 2005; Bani-Ahmad & Ozsoyoglu, 2007).

The RP-Model suggests that publication citation graphs evolve in a time-controlled manner through the stimulation of most-specific research topics from one another as follows. A publication that deals with a new specific research problem appears, and proposes the first solution for it. More publications appear after that publication, addressing the same problem and proposing enhanced or refined solutions to that problem. In time, the research problem (i) is either solved, (ii) settles down with "good-enough" solutions, or (iii) subdivided into more specific research problems (i.e., new research pyramids) (Bani-Ahmad & Ozsoyoglu, 2007).

Publications within an individual research pyramid are (i) motivated by earlier publications in the topic area, or (ii) use techniques proposed in publications from other research pyramids. We have observed that citations between different research pyramids conform to a highly left-skewed distribution, (figure 13), which indicates that as research pyramids of a particular research topic is formed and new research pyramids are instantiated, the RPs already formed receive few external citations from other research pyramids.

Consequently, publication citation graphs are highly unlikely to face structural changes within an already constructed research pyramid because (i) citations do not disappear like web links, (ii) once two papers are published, no new links between them are added, (iii) new citations to old paper are less likely to occur, and (iv) indirect citations to a publication are of lesser effect on its PageRank score (Desikan et al., 2005). Structural changes affect only the developing (i.e., recent) research pyramids. Thus, popularity (or PageRank scores) of publications are expected to converge over time to a steady-state value, which is the essence of the popularity growth model (Cho et al., 2005).

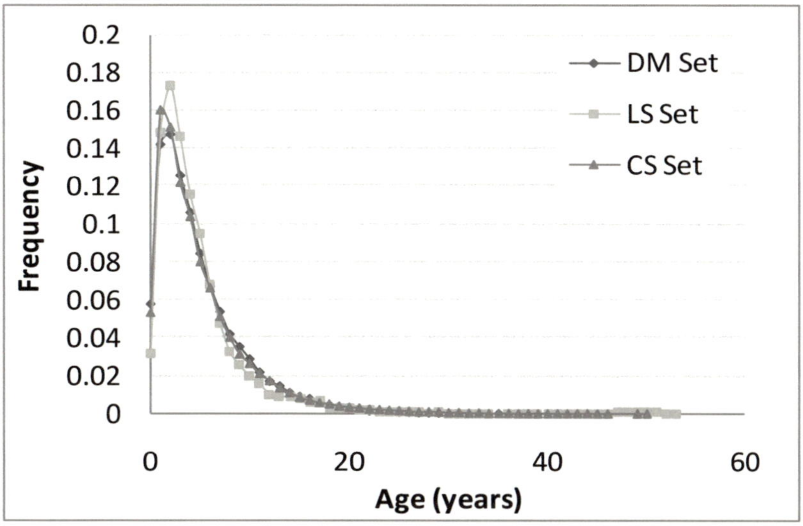

Fig. 13. Empirical citation-age probability distribution curves (i.e., citation age vs frequency of citations with that age) of publications in three datasets (i) Data management (2) life sciences and (iii) computer science.

4.4 The user citation behavior model

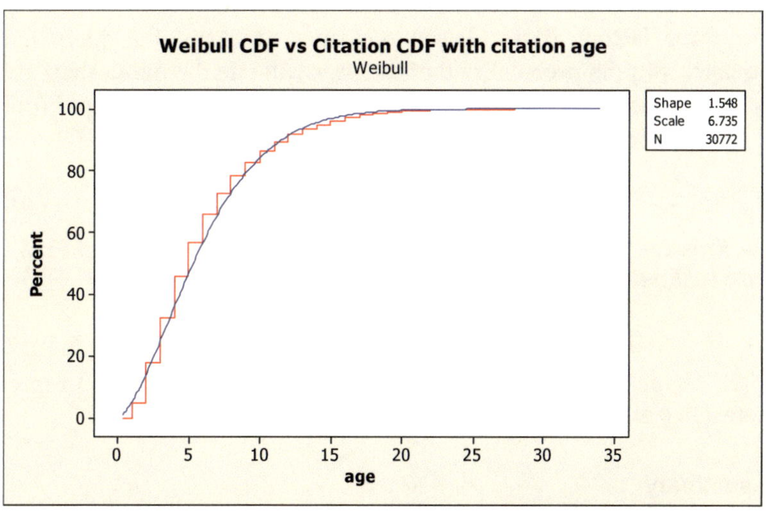

Fig. 14. (a) Age vs frequency of citations of publications. (b) Weibull distribution CDF

Figure 13 shows that user interest in citing a particular paper significantly decays over time. The best probabilistic distribution that fits the citation-age PDFs of figure 13 is the Weibull distribution (Mathworks, 2008). Figure 14 contains the cumulative distribution function (CDF) of the Weibull distribution, and the empirical CDF of the citation-age distribution for the data-management dataset. The two CDF curves show a high match. Using Minitab, 2008 software (Minitab, 2008), we have observed that the citation age curve (figure 14) conforms to the Weibull distribution with the estimated parameters shape (γ)=1.548 and Scale (α)=6.735. Thus, the probability $P(u \rightarrow v)$ of the citation from u to v to occur, is computed as

$$P(u \rightarrow v) = f_{weibull}(|age(u,v)|;\ \gamma, \alpha) \tag{3}$$

where $|age(u,v)|$ is the absolute time difference (in years) between the publication years of u and v. The probability density function of Weibull distribution is given by

$$f_{weibull}(x;\ \gamma, \alpha) = \frac{\gamma}{\alpha} . (x/\alpha)^{\gamma-1} e^{-(\frac{x}{\alpha})^{\gamma}} \tag{4}$$

assuming that $f_{weibull}(x;\ \gamma, \alpha) = 0$ for $x < 0$ (which is true in our case as a publication will not receive any citation if it is not published). In section 5.5, we use this formula in estimating the publication quality considering the aging factor.

4.5 Publication quality with aging factor

Assume that a user issues a search query at time t. Viewing the user as a potential author of an upcoming publication, the user will probably follow the Weibull distribution in his/her citations. i.e., the user cites a relevant publication v with probability equal to $f_{weibull}(t - t_{Year}(v))$ where $t_{Year}(v)$ is the publication year of v.

Thus, we argue that considering both the publication quality and the aging factor together leads to a better search output ranking. One possible way to order user search query results is to consider three factors: (i) text-based relevancy of v and the query terms, (ii) the publication quality, (iii) the probability that the user will cite the publication given the ages of relevant publications. Thus, for a given search query term w, and output (publication) v, one possible form of combining the three factors is as follows

$$final_{score(v)} = Sim(w,v) * \widehat{\boldsymbol{P}}(p,t) \tag{5}$$

where $Sim(w,v)$ is the text-based similarity between w and v, and $\widehat{\boldsymbol{P}}(p,t)$ is the *temporal popularity of the publication* at time t which is computed as

$$\widehat{\boldsymbol{P}}(p,t) = f_{weibull}(t - t_{Year}(v);\ \gamma, \alpha) * \boldsymbol{P}(p,t)$$

Definition: The ***temporal popularity*** of a publication p at time t, $\widehat{\boldsymbol{P}}(p,t)$ represents users' expected interest in p at t.

4.7 Section summary

In this section, we have (i) experimentally validated the popularity growth phase of publications (Cho et al., 2005), (ii) proposed a probabilistic model for domain-specific publication citation behavior, and (iii) extended *the popularity growth phase* to capture publication popularity decay phase.

5. Chapter summary and future research directions

5.1 Chapter summary

In this chapter, we have introduced a number of recent techniques for ranking the search results of online digital libraries.

Evaluating citation-based score measures of publications.

In section 2 of this chapter, we compared and evaluated several publication score functions; including PageRank (Brin & Page, 1998), Authorities (Kleinberg, 1998) and citation-count scores (Chakrabarti, 2003). We observed the separability problem with all of these functions, which is defined as the scoring functions producing scores that do not distribute well over a given scale, e.g., [0, 1]. Instead, distributions of the existing publication score functions are highly skewed, and decay very fast (Render, 2004), resulting in a much less useful comparative publication assessment capability for users. This lack of separability is caused by the "rich gets richer" phenomena (Render, 2004; Li & Chen, 2003), i.e., a very small number of publications with relatively high numbers of in-citations have even higher chances of receiving new citations. Yet, these scoring functions are still not very accurate, probably due to topic diffusion in search outputs (Haveliwala, 2002).

Improved publication scores via research-pyramids

In section 3, we observed that (a) the complete publication citation graph (of AnthP) is highly clustered, (b) each cluster of the complete publication set has a pyramid-like structure in terms of the citation graph of the cluster, and (c) each cluster represents a highly specific research topic. These three observations validated the research pyramid model proposed by (Aya et al., 2005).

We also found that topic similarities decay over both citation ages and citation paths. We used two topic similarity decay curves to guide the research-pyramid construction, and proposed and validated two algorithms to identify research pyramid structures in citation graphs.

Within research-pyramid citation graphs, we noticed that the average number of in-citations per paper varies, pointing to the importance of comparative publication scores within research pyramids. We then observed that normalizing publication scores within research-pyramids produces accurate and nearly normally distributed scores of publications.

Popularity Growth and Decay of Publications

In section 4, we proposed new definitions for popularity growth and decay for publications by coupling Cho et. al.'s model of popularity growth with our probabilistic publication citation behavior model, which we referred to as *the publication quality with aging factor*. In detail, we (i) experimentally validated the popularity of publications change over time and follow the logistic growth equation (Cho et al., 2005), (ii) proposed an empirical model for one aspect of researchers' citation behavior in technology-driven fields of study such as computer science (this model captures researchers' tendency not to cite old publications), and (iii) extended the popularity growth model (Cho et al., 2005) to capture publication popularity decay. Our major findings were as follows: **(a)** empirically, the probability of citing any publication conforms to the Weibull distribution (Mathworks, 2008) over the age of that publication. However, the shape and scale parameters of the distribution changes with the quality of publication venues, **(b)** we showed that the derivative of the popularity growth function accurately represents (i.e., directly proportional to) the temporal publication popularity at any time, **(c)** we observed that our definition of *publication quality with aging factor* matches the derivative of the popularity growth curve. This provides an analytical foundation for our growth and decay model of publication popularity.

5.2 Future research directions

Advanced Search Interface via Research Pyramids

As future work, one may work on the problem of automatically annotating research pyramids with keywords representing fine-grained research topics. Also, by using the identified research pyramids, we may work on visualization, namely, building a hierarchical structure that places research pyramids into a hierarchical structure. Using RP annotations and the hierarchical structure of RPs, building an advanced query interface that involves pruned searches becomes possible.

Accurate Identification of Research Pyramids

The two RP-identification algorithms proposed in section 2 are very basic, and form the first attempts. As future work, one may find more accurate techniques to identify cornerstone publications within research pyramids. Also, more accurate techniques to identify members of each RP need to be developed.

Publication-venue Specific User Citation Behavior

As future work, one can work on identifying the correlation between the impact of the publication venue on user's citation behavior and publications that appear in prestigious conferences. More specifically, one may attempt to model users' citation behavior for prestigious publication venues. Our hypothesis is that, by understanding users' citation behavior, one can provide users of online digital libraries with higher quality of services.

6. References

ACM Digital Library (2008), http://portal.acm.org/dl.cfm. Viewed in March 2008.

ACM SIGMOD Anthology (2003), http://www.acm.org/sigmod/dblp/db/anthology.html. Viewed in 2003.

Ahmed, T.; Johnson, B.; Oppenheim, C. & Peck, C. (2004). Highly cited old papers and the reasons why they continue to be cited, Part II., The 1953 Watson and Crick article on the structure of DNA, Scientometrics, 61:147-156, 2004.

Aya, S.; Lagoze, C.; & Joachims, T. (2005). Citation Classification and its Applications, International Conference on Knowledge Management.

Bani-Ahmad*, S.; Cakmak A.; Ozsoyoglu, G. & Al-Hamdani, Abdullah (2005). Evaluating Score and Publication Similarity Functions in Digital Libraries. ICADL, 2005.

Bani-Ahmad, S. & Ozsoyoglu, G. (2007). Improved Publication Scores for Online Digital Libraries via Research Pyramids. ECDL 2007.

Bani-Ahmad, S.; Cakmak, A.; Ozsoyoglu, G. & Al-Hamdani A. (2005). Evaluating Publication Similarity Measures, IEEE Data Eng. Bull. 28(4): 21-28, 2005

Brin, S. & Page, L. (1998), The anatomy of a large-scale hypertextual web search engine, Computer Networks and ISDN Systems.

Cakmak, A. (2003). HITS- and PageRank-based Importance Score Computations for ACM Anthology Papers, Tech. report, EECS Dept, CWRU, 2003.

Case, D. O. & Higgins, D. M. (2000). How can we investigate citation behavior? A study of reasons for citing literature in communication, Jour. Of American Society of Information Science, 51(7):635-645, 2000.

Chakrabarti, S. (2003), Mining the Web, Morgan-Kauffman, 2003.

Cho, J.; Roy, S. & Adams, R. (2005). Page Quality: In Search of an Unbiased Web Ranking, ACM SIGMOD.

CiteSeer (2008), www.citeseer.com. Viewed in March 2008.

CiteSeer-Lists (2008). List of Most cited articles in Computer Science, http://citeseer.ist.psu.edu/articles.html. viewed on March 2008.

DBLP (2003). The DBLP Computer Science Bibliography. http://www.informatik.uni-trier.de/~ley/db. Viewed in April 2003.

Desikan, P.; Pathak, N.; Srivastava, J. & Kumar, V. (2005). Incremental page rank computation on evolving graphs. In the proceedings of WWW conference 2005.

Google Scholar (2008), http://scholar.google.com/scholar. Viewed in March 2008.

Haveliwala, T. H. (2002). Topic-sensitive PageRank, WWW Conference, Hawaii, 2002.

IEEE Xplore (2008), http://ieeexplore.ieee.org. Viewed in March 2008.

Jeh G. & Widom, J. (2002). SimRank A measure of structural-context similarity, ACM SIGKDD International Conference on Knowledge Discovery and Data Mining, 2002.

Kleinberg, J. (1998). Authoritative sources in hyperlinked environments, The 9th ACM-SIAM Symposium on Discrete Mathematics (SODA) Conference, 1998.

Li, X. & Chen, G. (2003). A local-world evolving network model, Physica A 328 (2003) 274 - 286

Mathworks (2008), http://www.mathworks.com/. Viewed in April 2008.

Minitab (2008). Minitab Statistical Software, http://www.minitab.com/. Viewed in April 2008.

Ntoulas, A.; Cho, J. & Olston, C. (2004). What's new on the web?: the evolution of the web from a search engine perspective. WWW '04.

Pan, F. (2006). Comparative Evaluation of Publication Characteristics in Computer Science and Life Sciences, MS Thesis, EECS, Case Western Reserve University, 2006.

PubMed (2008). http://www.ncbi.nlm.nih.gov/entrez/query.fcgi. Viewed in March 2008.

Ratprasartporn, N. & Ozsoyoglu, G. (2007). Finding Related Papers in Literature Digital Libraries, ECDL 2007.

Ratprasartporn, N., Po, J., Cakmak, A., Bani-Ahmad, S., Ozsoyoglu, G., On Context-Based Publication Search Paradigm: Gene-Ontology-Specific Contexts for Searching PubMed Effectively. Technical Report, CWRU 2006.

Ratprasartporn, N.; Po, J.; Cakmak, A.; Bani-Ahmad, S. & Ozsoyoglu, G (2007). Evaluating utility of different ranking functions in context-based environment, DBRank Workshop, Istanbul, Turkey, April 2007.

Redner, S. (2004). Citation statistics from more than a century of physical review. Physics 0407137, 2004.

ScienceDirect (2008). www.sciencedirect.info. Viewed in March 2008.
Wasserman, S. & Faust, K. (1994). Social Network Analysis, Cambridge U. Press, Cambridge, 1994

6

Exploring Digital Libraries through Visual Interfaces

Beomjin Kim[1], Jon Scott[1] and SeungEun Kim[2]
[1]*Department of Computer Science, Indiana University-Purdue University Fort Wayne*
[2]*Department of Multimedia Engineering, Seoul Women's University*
[1]*USA*
[2]*South Korea*

1. Introduction

Libraries are long standing institutions, providing an important service of making information widely available. So it is with Digital Libraries (DL), but this evolution into a computerized format does not come without its own unique challenges. The variety and quantity of information available in the digital space is truly astounding. However, as this growth continues, traditional methods for searching are becoming less effective to support the needs of users to find information quickly and easily.

The conventional library book search system provides several attributes associated with books as a response to the users' inquiry. This includes title, author, publication year, ISBN, page total, and similar information. While considering the increasing volume of data, the current text-based approach to result presentation is not an ideal solution for the modern digital environment. Particularly in the case of comparing a lengthy list of search results, this approach is ill-suited, as it is inefficient and non-intuitive (Good et al., 2005). Assistance, such as ranked results, can aid in such problems but the user will still be relied on to investigate the top results individually (Veerasamy & Heikes, 1997; Dushay, 2004). Additionally, the current popular approach of presenting a summary of content may not accurately reflect what is of value to the user.

The advancements and trends that allow for the rapid growth of DL also permit more elaborate interfaces with which to access them (Bertini et al., 2005). Information Visualization is one such avenue, which has proven to be an effective approach in acquiring information from a large compilation of data. By making use of users' perceptual cognition for navigating extensive digital workspaces, their ability to understand, and speed with which they review the information space is improved (Card et al., 1999). Previous studies have proven the significance of visualization in the users' information forage (Veerasamy & Heikes, 1997; Hawkins, 1999; Kim et al., 2002).

One common approach to assist users' search activities uses visualization techniques combined with information filtering. The users' interaction defines the attributes of interest that easily filter out unrelated data. The following visualization procedure transforms the remaining data into graphical illustrations. FilmFinder and HomeFinder are interactive visual interfaces which assist the user to narrow down the search scope and easily compare results using the visualization (Ahlberg & Shneiderman, 1994; Williamson & Shneiderman, 1992). Another common approach focuses on presenting the underlying information through visualization. A novel text visualization interface, TileBars, shows the distribution behavior of a set of query terms (Hearst, 1995). This presentation allows users to compare multiple documents compactly and concurrently. Other visualization techniques in this category concentrate on showing a portion of the information at a great level of detail while maintaining the overall structure of the information (Lamping et al., 1995). Information clustering is another method for supporting navigation of a large data collection. Related documents are clustered together, whose notable characteristics are visualized using a mixture of attributes (Shneiderman et al., 2000; Au et al., 2000; Nowell et al., 1996). Visualization methodologies, such as those mentioned here, have shown that the illustration of data has contributed to improving the user's ability to comprehend information quickly. This, in turn, leads to increased speed and accuracy in finding desired information (Card et al., 1999; Kim, 2004).

We can apply these kinds of visual abstractions to enhance searches on different types of data domains. By presenting information in such a way, a large amount of content can be displayed in a format which is more intuitive. This has the benefit of allowing the user to analyze data more effectively, increasing the user's ability to comprehend results and make better content selections. Periscope, for example, is a visualization system targeted at web search results. It provides a series of different visualizations which users can utilize to analyze and explore the result set. A holistic interface can be used to organize documents into various categories, such as language and format, or web related attributes such as DNS domains. An analytical interface allows for up to seven attributes to be relayed at a time, through use of X, Y, Z axes, color, size, shape, and animation (Wiza et al., 2004).

The search based on the underlying content will increase the accuracy in finding targeted information from the available resources. Think for a moment how one might search a physical book for a topic of interest. The logical place to start would be the index. Indexes are valuable resources for referencing major terms which appear in a book. The categorical and hierarchical layout of terms in the index allows us to identify associated topics easily, along with their relationships without reading the underlying contents. The page numbers coupled with each entry makes it possible to estimate the amount information relating to a particular subject. The index will represent the overall layout of entire book contents. Due to a lack of readily available sources, this valuable information has been under utilized. The current trend of digitizing books in recent years allows us to exploit content in searches, instead of just depending on superficial book attributes. The visualization techniques utilizing this information will further enhances the user's search on the DL system.

The main objective of this book chapter is on the utilization of visualization techniques for exploring the DL system. The following chapter will survey and summarize various visualization approaches which applied to DL. We will introduce a visual interface which presents general book information through iconic representations. This chapter also proposes a novel visualization which utilizes the book index for mimicking the content analysis. It will allow for detailed comparison of index-based information between selected works. Two different visualizations for this detail view are implemented, each with different strengths. The procedure and analysis of results for a usability test follow, along with discussion and future possibilities, and final conclusions.

2. Related works

The efficacy of visualization in searching a large information space has been proven in many previous studies (Veerasamy & Heikes, 1997; Kim et al., 2002). DL are one promising area that should exploit visualization techniques in searching on various forms of archived information, such as text, imagery, multimedia, citations, and even computer mediated communication (Abbasi & Chen, 2007). The 3D Vase Museum is one example applying visualizations for browsing photographs in a digital library collection (Shiaw et al., 2004). A Focus+Context type visualization displays a set of Greek vases in the Perseus digital library in a simulated 3D virtual museum. By moving around the virtual space, users can appreciate vases with accompanying text data. Christel and Martin introduced visualization techniques for browsing and navigating another type of multimedia, video documents (Christel & Martin, 1998). Meanwhile, Chen proposed a novel approach utilizing a different side view of information in accessing the digital library (Chen, 1999). It visualizes semantic structures and co-citation networks extracted from a collection of documents. This method displayed the author co-citation networks in a 3D virtual space attempting to reveal the structure of a field of hyperlinks with co-citation patterns of authors.

Borner and Chen explained that there are three common usage requirements for visual interfaces to the DL: First, to support the identification of the composition of retrieval result. Second is to understand the interrelation of retrieved documents to one another. Lastly, to refine a search, gain an overview of the coverage of a DL and to visualize user interaction data in relation to available documents. The goal would be to evaluate and improve DL usage (Borner & Chen, 2002).

Clarkson et al. developed a visual interface emphasizing on the hierarchy of the repository in presenting the DL search results. They used the hierarchical representation in digital repositories for developing an interface for enhancing query-based search engines. A treemap, a well-known technique, is used to organize results in a space-efficient hierarchical display (Bederson et al., 2002). The system, known as ResultMap, maps each document in the hierarchical tree structures to a treemap where items matched with given query are highlighted. ResultMap presents the full contents of a hierarchical dataset while providing a view of underlying levels. The experimental results from two controlled lab studies showed that participants expressed preferences to use ResultMap system and produced comparable performance to a text-only engine (Clarkson et al., 2009).

When using physical books, people tend to view multiple at once. This is to better compare and review information across multiple sources, and to have a better overall understanding of the domain. In their study, Good et al, identify this to be a major weakness in current DL displays (Good et al., 2005). To address related issues, researchers have conducted studies applying visualization techniques for book searches and presenting various forms of search results for easy comparison (Shen et al., 2006; Silva et al., 2003). Envision is a visual interface presenting book search results in a rigid matrix (Nowell et al., 1997). The search results are presented as icons in a 2D grid where the visual attributes represent the characteristics of returned documents. Envision allows the user to organize the visualized output interactively based on their information needs.

The Graphical Interface for DL (GRIDL) and ActiveGraph adopted a similar approach in presenting search results. The GRIDL displays a hierarchical cluster of the relevant data to a query on two-dimensional display (Shneiderman et al., 2000). This system provides an interactive grid layout, the axes of which are selectable from a variety of different attributes.

Results were displayed within each cell as a collection of different size icons, color coded by document type. ActiveGraph presented search results based on scatter plots (Marks et al., 1996). ActiveGraph also provides similar functionalities to specify shape, color, and size of nodes representing various forms of digital resources. Because ActiveGraph system results in much more node clustering and overlap, a logarithmic transformation is provided, along with the ability to filter out unwanted items.

Many studies mainly focus on aiding the user in comparing the search results effectively by presenting book properties such as book title, author, publication, year, through various visual attributes, but they don't express in detail the amount of content related to user interest. Citiviz is a visual interface tool kit combining text mining and information visualization (Kampanya et al., 2004). In order to present the insight of similarity among documents as well as traditional document attributes, this system used two visualization techniques: an animated 2D scatter plot to represent document attributes and a dynamic hyperbolic tree to show hierarchical relationships among documents. By allowing users to manipulate the manner in which data is displayed, these visualizations provided a better chance to find patterns within the data that may not typically be apparent.

Lin proposed another approach through a graphical table of contents (GTOC) that tries to exploit a different perspective of underling information by utilizing the table of contents of the book. GTOC showed the dimension of items in the table of contents based on Kohonen's self organizing feature map algorithm (Lin, 1996). The paper introduces how documents can be organized and then visualized to allow the user easy access of underlying contents. The GTOC prototype describes various interactive tools to assist the user exploring document contents and analyzing relationships among terms in the table of contents.

Both the attributes associated with documents and its underlying contents are valuable resources finding the relevant information of the users' interest. The increasing computing power and performance of graphics devices make it possible to exercise these information in presenting search results. The following section introduces a newly developed visualization system that will assist the user's search while utilizing the book index, which has been underutilized as a visualization resource.

3. Method

The Visual Interface for Digital Library Search (VIDLS) system utilizes an Overview+Detail approach for presenting book search results. This is a visualization technique that uses multiple images to display the entire data space, as well as show an up-close, detailed view of the data (Baudich et al., 2002; Shneiderman, 1996). Similar to traditional library searches, the overview will present outline of the book search results through graphical illustration. The user interactively selects a subset of visualized icons that will allow them to execute content level exploration. When a user provides search terms of interests, the Detail view presents a visualization which relates, in depth, the information presented by the index. For our pilot study, we developed two possible visualizations for this view of the index, each with its own strengths. One emphasizes space utilization, whereas the other is designed to focus on clearly presenting term relationships.

3.1 Overview visualization

The Overview allows the user to perform a general search on the data space, similar to traditional library tools. This visualization utilizes a tabular layout which offers a familiar spread-sheet style organization of book search results. The attribute of each axis can be independently selected by the user, allowing for a more targeted display and increasing the users' comprehension of the data set (Shneiderman et al., 2000). This functionality will assist the user in customizing the search based on their own judgment of which attributes are more important. In the Overview, each book is represented as a circular node, located in the appropriate cell based on the axes. To deliver the estimated amount of content, node size is determined by the normalized page count of the book compared to the rest. Books with a greater number of pages naturally map to the largest nodes. This will allow users to quickly identify the amount and distribution of content available.

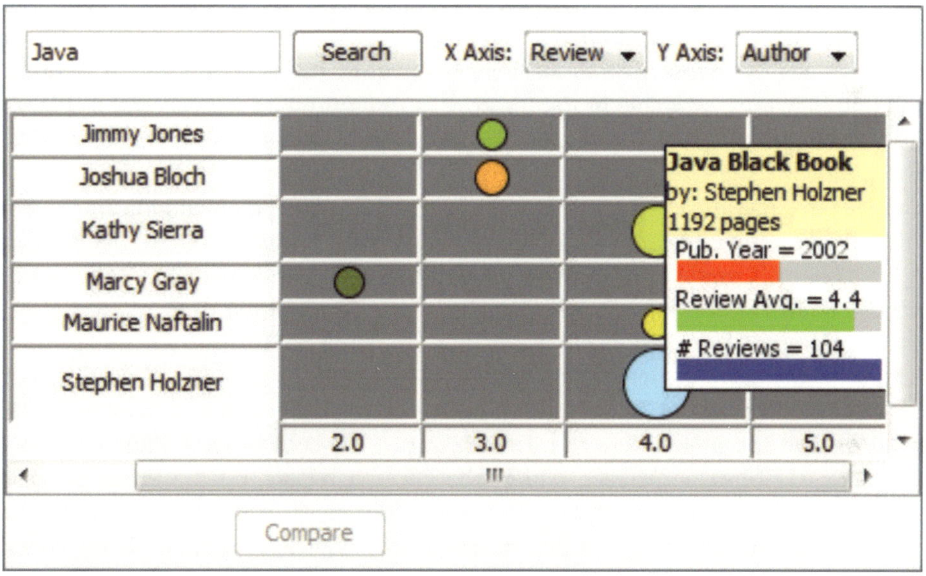

Fig. 1. Overview interface displaying search results with tool-tip

The system presents other book attributes through a color coding scheme. The green component is derived through collaborative filtering. This is a content-filtering technique based upon the opinion of users whom have already evaluated the item in question (Resnick et al., 1994). This will be a valuable piece of information to know regarding the quality of the book. In the case of VIDLS, collaborative filtering would be done by collecting user reviews, much like you found find at a merchant website. Higher intensity of the green component would indicate a more positive response from reviews.

The accuracy of the content-filtering is highly correlated with the number of evaluators and their preferences. As an example: the mean score of a book which has a low number of reviews could potentially be misleading and unreliable (Allen, 1990). To account for this, the Overview associates the blue component with the number of unique evaluations given to a book. The publication year is a valuable attribute to find the most up to date information. This metric has been represented through the red component. With the utilization of the RGB color scheme, the larger more recent books with a solid review will be closer to white in intensity, while older, smaller, poorly reviewed works tend toward black. If the user needs to know more precise information for the components, or other detailed information of the work, the system provides this via a tooltip interface (figure 1).

3.2 Detailed visualization

Once a user makes a set of selections from the Overview, the system will provide a detailed view of those items. This display is tasked with presenting visualized index data for each book, allowing the user to perform more refined queries, and compare and contrast each work in detail. Two visualizations were implemented on a data model to present the same information while emphasizing different attributes: one a radial graph, and the other a sunburst-like display (Stasko et al., 2000).

3.2.1 Data model

The underlying model for the detailed visualizations relies on several important characteristics associated with a term in the index. These are: number of pages, number of occurrences, content density, and location relative to the parent term. Although this information is readily available in the index, it is unintuitive in a text format. Presenting these attributes via graphical illustration, the user should gain greater understanding of the content, and make more informed choices of which books to choose.

The number of pages associated with a term by the index is a potential indicator as to how much coverage a topic receives in a book. A work with a greater number of pages on a subject is intuitively going to have more potential value than one with less. Naturally, this attribute is represented by size in the visualizations. To assist the user in quickly making general comparison between each book, this attribute is further expanded to be a cumulative page total of the term along with its sub-terms.

The number of occurrences and content density are related through a color code. This is intended to give the user a better understanding of the comparative value of each term being displayed. Term occurrence within the book is related by the green component. Although one work may have more information referenced in a single index entry for a topic, that does not necessarily make it the better choice. If another book contained references of a particular term in many different locations within the index, that may be an indication of a greater breadth or complexity of coverage on that topic. The number of term occurrences are normalized across the display, with the instances of greatest coverage mapping to the highest green intensity, and the one with the fewest having no green intensity.

Although two books may have the same total of pages for a particular topic, this should not be taken to mean they have equal value. Consider the situation in which one index allocates ten pages for a topic, but they are separate and not listed as a single range of pages. Another index containing the same topic, but listed as a single range of ten pages, such as 152-161 may be more valuable to the user. The first may have fragmented references of the topic, but no detailed coverage, whereas the second may have a full section or chapter dedicated to the subject. To relate this information to the user, the content density is mapped to the blue color component. The value is given by calculating the ratio of page continuity to the total number of pages for a term. This is shown by equation 1, where C_{ib} is the blue intensity for term i, $\sum_{j=0}^{n} P_j^c$ is the number of individual page ranges for i, T_i is the total number of pages for the term i, and I_{max} is the brightest intensity of blue possible on the machine. This gives terms with more concentrated information a stronger representation in the visualization.

$$C_{ib} = \left(1 - \left(\frac{\sum_{j=0}^{n} P_j^c}{T_i}\right)\right) * I_{max} \quad (1)$$

The last attribute represents the relationship between a sub-term and its parent. Similar to the previous attribute, a sub-term which is located close to its parent within the book could be an indication of cohesive coverage of the topic. A user may regard such a case with more value than one where the sub-term is more removed from the parent's location. The value of this attribute is calculated by equation 2.

$$D_j = ABS\left(\frac{NORM\left(\sum_{k=0}^{n}(P_j^k - \overline{Root_i})\right)}{N}\right) \quad (2)$$

D_j is a normalized distance between the root node and associated sub-node j; P_j^k is the page number contains sub-term j; $\overline{Root_i}$ is the mean page number having the root word i; and *NORM* and *ABS* are a normalization and absolute function respectively.

3.2.2 Visualizations

The two visualizations share several aspects, in addition to the attributes described previously. Each displays the matching term of the search prominently in the center, with the sub-terms radiating outward. Since each term is sized based on the cumulative page count of itself and sub-terms, the root node will give users a quick guidance as to which book has more content. Additionally, each graph has a context side-bar that indicates which term is currently moused-over, along with a histogram displaying its color components. The similarities end here for the two visualizations.

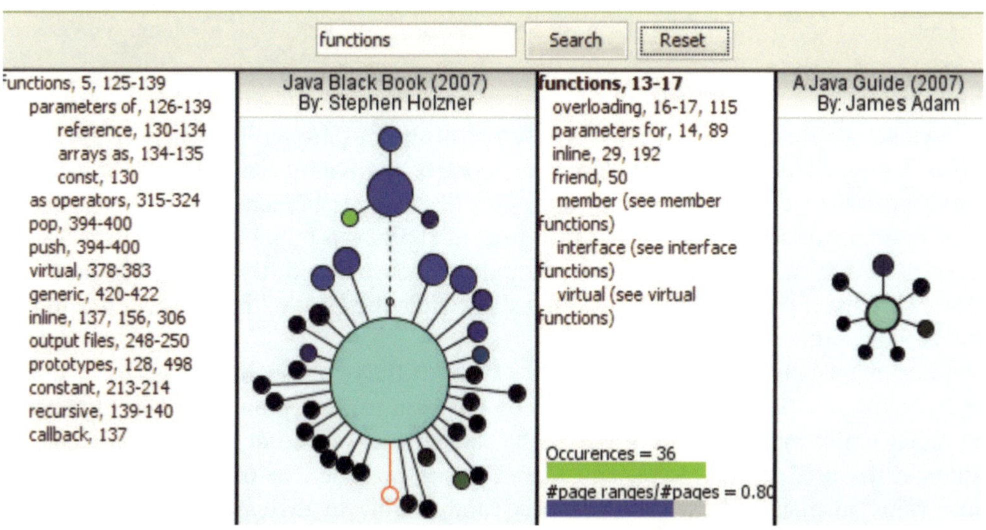

Fig. 2. Diagram shows two books being compared in the Detail View. The left shows expanded sub-terms and an overflow node. The right has context highlighting of text list (bold-face font) and bar display from user interaction

The first visualization approach employs a radial graph layout; with each term presented as a circular node branching off the parent. Sub-terms are sized in the same way as the root, with node size directly correlated to the total number of pages. The largest sub-terms start from the top toward the bottom of the visualization. This is done to prevent over-crowding of the display. Terms with the fewest pages are considered less important, and are collapsed into a single node, indicated by a red outline, if not enough space is available. Another way in which space is conserved is by displaying only the first level of sub-terms. A node with hidden sub-terms has a ridged outline. These along with the red 'overflow' node can be clicked show the hidden terms (figure 2).
In contrast, the second visualization follows a sunburst-like design. Sub-terms are displayed in concentric sections around the center, extending from their parent term. Each sub-term 'slice' is sized as a percentage of its page allocation from the parent's. This has the benefit that all terms can be displayed compactly without hiding any. No additional user interaction would be required to explore the full term hierarchy. One potential downside of this design, compared to the previous one, is that terms are crowded together. This may cause difficulty in picking them out from their neighbors.

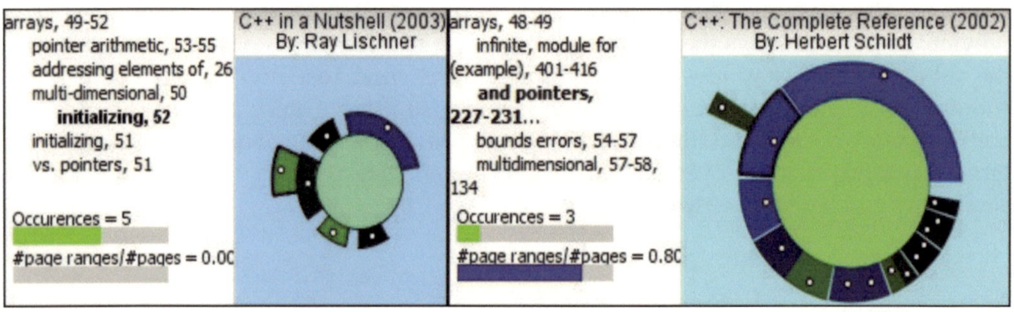

Fig. 3. Alternate sunburst detailed view

In the radial graph, the relation between a sub-term and its parent is indicated by the branch length. Terms which appear on pages near those of the parent naturally are drawn with shorter branches. Since the sunburst approach has forgone branches to conserve space, a different analogue is required. Each slice instead contains a bubble, which will relate this information (figure 3). As the closeness to parent is normalized, the term with the closest relationship has a bubble at the base of the slice, while the term with the most distant has a bubble on the outer edge of its slice.
As was previously noted, the chief difference between the two visualizations is their concern for space conservation. With its emphasis on the term relation branch, and distinct nodes, the radial graph may have more clarity, but at the cost of poorer space utilization. This results in the need to hide terms considered less important. The other visualization puts more value in making better use of space, and is able to display all terms efficiently. However, when many terms are displayed at once, the resultant crowding could make smaller slices difficult to see. The addition of the bubble overlay to each slice can add to this difficulty.

4. Experiment

To measure the effectiveness of VIDLS, a series of usability tests were performed to compare it to more traditional text-based interfaces. In this set of experiments the VIDLS system, using the radial graph detailed layout, was used in conjunction with a text-only interface for the same information.

Each usability test consisted of a small group of three to five students, comfortable in the use of computers, whom had no prior experience with VIDLS. Each group was given a brief orientation presentation, and then allowed to acclimate to the functionality of both applications for a few minutes. The tests then began, with each user asked to search for books and information with the text-only application and then with the visualization based approach. Once the test concluded, participants then filled out a survey to measure their quantitative and qualitative feedback of VIDLS in comparison to the text-based format.

The questionnaire has 14 questions which utilize a 5 point Likert scale; 5 indicating the highest level of satisfaction, and 1 the lowest. Table 1 shows the survey results that summarizes the user's feedback to VIDLS over a text-based library search system. Participants overall found the VIDLS system to be satisfactory, with some comments highlighting that unfamiliarity with the visualizations led to preference of the text-based design.

The Overview visualization was well received, with 82% of testers responding that it improved their ability to quickly identify desirable books. This was supported through the exploratory aspects of the system, which participants indicated positively as giving meaningful result displays, and facilitating better understanding of the information.

The radial graph visualization of index level information was also seen in a positive light, as 65% found it to be a useful representation, and only 11% preferring the familiar text-only listing of results. As with the Overview, testers considered the Detail View to also be useful in expressing the concentration of information, and improving selection among the results. Table 1 shows a summary of survey results.

Question	Pos.	Neut.	Neg.
VIDLS overall was preferable to a text-based search	53%	35%	12%
The Overview improved identification of desirable books	82%	6%	12%
Use of the selectable axis facilitated a better understanding of a set of books.	71%	24%	5%
The Overview helped in selecting a subset of books.	65%	29%	6%
It was easy to discern book attributes based on node color	53%	18%	29%
The Detailed view was preferable to a text approach	65%	24%	11%
It was easy to discern term attributes based on node color	47%	24%	29%
The Detail view made relevant book selection easier	88%	12%	0%
The relation between a term and it's child was understandable	65%	35%	0%
The Detail view helped identify terms related to the search	94%	6%	0%

Table 1. Post experiment survey results

5. Discussion and future work

Overall, feedback was positive toward the VIDLS system. Users indicated it was a helpful and effective alternative to more traditional search utilities. Among the responses, familiarity with text-based result displays was a common explanation for favoring it over a new approach. It is promising that the majority of participants still showed preference for the visualized prototype.

One of the chief strengths of VIDLS highlighted by the usability tests is its exploratory nature. The customization afforded by the selectable axes in the overview, and the interactive nature of the detailed view greatly enhanced users search activity. Many felt that their understanding of the information was improved by these traits. This aspect of the system is also important, in that it may help lead users to other terminology related to their goal, but exempt from their initial search vocabulary.

Although most were comfortable with it, the color-coded attributes proved to be the main area of difficulty for users. The primary issue highlighted by the experiment is user difficulty with interpreting the color codes of both views. Although around half in both instances were comfortable with this aspect of the system, around 30% had trouble with it. The post-experiment interviews provided two main causes for the diverging opinions. First, the RBG color model was not familiar to some. These users cited heavy exposure to the RYB (primary color pigments) model as being a source of confusion when interpreting the displays. The increased unfamiliarity left those individuals feeling more comfortable using a text-based search.

The other difficulty reported by users was in determining the relative value of one result with another. This could be, in part, a result of the human eye being more sensitive to some colors rather than others. For example, green-yellow colors have the strongest reception, which could mislead a user into considering a result with this color to have more overall value than another when that may not be the case (Foley et al., 1996). Researching and examining alternate color models will be one of the challenging task for future work on the VIDLS system.

While users found the graph approach to be effective, it has plenty of room for improvement. The issue of overlapping prevents showing all information at once. If possible, it would be preferable to avoid that situation, as it may reduce the effectiveness of the visualization. As stated earlier, the layout does give the graph design more clarity and makes it easy to pick out individual items; however some users found it difficult to compare two nodes which aren't adjacent to each other.

The sunburst layout could improve upon these points. The compact design greatly reduces the need to hide information for typical indexes without extensive hierarchies. It may also cut down on unnecessary competing visual information created by the empty space seen in the graph layout. Another possibility is that the slice shape of sub-term nodes is more distinct, and may afford more visual context when making comparisons.

Though small in size, the experiment supported the viability of VIDLS as a search utility. Still, larger experiments will need to be planned in order to better understand how the prototype compares against existing search methodologies. Testing will also need to be done to confirm how the sunburst and radial visualizations differ in effectiveness. These will be key topics as future work on VIDLS continues.

Other areas for future work include investigating content analysis. Although indexes proved to be a useful foundation for visualization, these are limited to books. Other media lack such precompiled information. VIDLS would need to integrate methods to examine document content in order to extract the information it presents. This is a very ambitious topic, but could expose additional attributes for expressing to the user, as well as allowing for a more universal application of the system. Similarly, enhancing VIDLS to have thesaurus-like capability to identify similar topics would be another valuable addition. Grouping such items together would further improve a users understanding of which work has more comprehensive coverage on a topic.

6. Conclusion

The emergence of the Digital Library provides an interesting dichotomy: effortless access to a large compilation of data, but increased challenges in finding a few specific works of interest. Having effective mechanisms for exploring this space is both an important and also demanding research topic. Information visualization can be one possible solution in addressing these difficulties presented by digital library systems. This chapter surveyed existing approaches, applying a range of visualization techniques for querying information in the digital library system with a focus toward books. The developed interfaces presents multiple attributes associated with books through visual icons on a table. This simple graphical illustration assists the user to compare and contrast search results intuitively. The chapter also introduces a novel method that utilizes book indexes for enhancing searches. The exploitation of indexes will further enhance search activities, making them more efficient and effective. The conducted survey-based usability tests that compared the proposed system over traditional text-based approaches showed the efficacy of the visual interfaces as a search supporting tool on digital libraries. This chapter concludes with the belief that visualizations will be a promising approach to address current issues in the digital library system suffering from the complexity and volume of its sources.

7. References

Abbasi, A. & Chen, H. (2007). Categorization and Analysis of Text in Computer Mediated Communication Archives Using Visualization, *Proceedings of the 7th ACM/IEEE-CS Joint Conference on Digital Libraries*, pp.11-18

Ahlberg, C. & Shneiderman, B. (1994). Visual information seeking using the FilmFinder, *Proceedings of the ACM Conference on Human Factors in Computing Systems*, pp.433-434

Allen, R. (1990). User Models: Theory, Method, and Practice, *International Journal of Man-Machine Studies*, Vol. 32, pp. 511-543

Au, P.; Cary, M.; Sewraz, S.; Guo, Y. & Rüger, S. (2000). New Paradigms in Information Visualization, *Proceedings of the 23rd Annual International ACM SIGIR Conference on Research and Development in Information Retrieval*, pp. 307-309

Baudich, P.; Good, N.; Bellotti, V. & Schraedley, P. (2002). Keeping Things in Context: A Comparative Evaluation of Focus Plus Context Screens, Overviews and Zooming, *Proceedings of the SIGCHI Conference on Human Factors in Computing Systems,* pp. 259-266

Bederson, B.; Shneiderman, B. & Wattenberg, M. (2002). Ordered and Quantum Treemaps: Making Effective Use of 2D Space to Display Hierarchies, *ACM Transactions on Graphics,* Vol. 21, No. 4, pp. 833-854

Bertini, E.; Catarci, T.; Di Bello, L. & Kimani, S. (2005). Visualization in Digital Libraries, *Lecture Notes in Computer Science,* Vol. 3379, pp. 183-169, Springer-Verlag, Berlin

Borner, K. & Chen, C. (2002). Visual Interfaces to Digital Libraries: Motivation, Utilization, and Socio-technical Challenges, *Lectures Notes in Computer Science,* Vol. 2539, pp. 1-9 Springer-Verlag, Berlin Heidelberg New York

Card, S.; Mackinlay, J. & Shneiderman, B. (1999). *Readings in Information Visualization Using Vision to Think,* Morgan Kaufman

Chen, C. (1999). Visualizing Semantic Spaces and Author Co-citation Networks in Digital Libraries, *Information Processing and Management: an International Journal,* Vol. 35, No. 3, pp. 401-420

Christel, M. & Martin, D (1998). Information Visualization Within a Digital Video Library, *Journal of Intelligent Information Systems,* Vol. 11, No. 3, pp. 235-257

Clarkson, E.; Desai, K. & Foley, J. (2009). ResultMaps: Visualization for Search Interfaces, *IEEE Transactions on Visualization and Computer Graphics,* Vol. 15, No. 6, pp. 1057-1064

Dushay, N. (2004). Visualizing Bibliographic Metadata - A Virtual (Book) Spine Viewer. *D-Lib Magazine,* Vol.10, No. 10

Good, L.; Popat, A.; Janssen, W. & Bier, E. (2005). Fluid Interface for Personal Digital Libraries, *Proceedings of the 9th European Conference on Research and Advanced Technology for Digital Libraries,* pp. 162-173

Hawkins, D. (1999). Information Visualization: Don't Tell Me, Show Me!, *Online,* Vol. 23, No. 1, pp. 88-90

Hearst, M.A. (1995). Tilebars: Visualization of term distribution information in full text information access. *Proceedings of the ACM Conference on Human Factors in Computing Systems,* pp. 59-66

Kampanya, N.; Shen, R.; Kim, S.; North, C. & Fox, E. (2004). Citiviz: A Visual User Interface to the CITIDEL System, *Lecture Notes in Computer Science,* Vol. 3232, pp. 122-133, Springer-Verlag, Berlin

Kim, B.; Johnson, P. & Huarng, A. (2002). Colored-sketch of Text Information, *Journal of Informing Science,* Vol. 5, No. 4, pp. 163-173

Kim, B. (2004). Visual Interface for Evaluating Internet Search Results, *Lecture Notes in Computer Science,* Vol. 2973, pp. 533-542, Springer-Verlag, Berlin

Lamping, J.; Rao, R. & Pirolli, P. (1995). A Focus+Context Technique Based on Hyperbolic Geometry for Visualizing Large Hierarchies, *Proceedings of the ACM Conference on Human Factors in Computing Systems,* pp. 401-408

Lin, X (1996). Graphical Table of Contents, *Proceedings of the 1st ACM International Conference on Digital Libraries*, pp.45-53

Marks, L.; Hussel, J.; McMahon, T. & Luce, R. (1996). ActiveGraph: A Digital Library Visualization Tool, *International Journal on Digital Libraries*, Vol. 5, No. 1, pp. 57-69

Nowell, L.; France, R.; Hix, D.; Heath, L. & Fox, E. (1996). Visualizing Search Results: Some Alternatives to Query-Document Similarity, *Proceedings of the 19th Annual International ACM SIGIR Conference on Research and Development in Information Retrieval*, pp. 67-75

Nowell, L.; France, R. & Hix, D. (1997). Exploring Search Results with Envision, *Proceedings of the ACM SIGCHI*, pp. 14-15

Resnick, P.; Iacovou, N.; Suchak, M.; Bergstrom, P. & Riedl, J. (1994). GroupLens: An Open Architecture for Collaborative Filtering of Netnews, *Proceedings of the ACM Conference on Computer Supported Cooperative Work*, pp. 175-186

Shen, R.; Vemuri, N.; Fan, W.; Torres, R. & Fox, E. (2006). Exploring Digital Libraries: Integrating Browsing, Searching, and Visualization, *Proceedings of the 6th ACM/IEEE-CS Joint Conference on Digital Libraries*, pp. 1-10

Shiaw, H.; Jacob, R. & Crane, G. (2004). The 3D Vase Museum: A New Approach to Context in a Digital Library, *Proceedings of the 4th ACM/IEEE-CS Joint Conference on Digital Libraries*, pp. 125-134

Shneiderman, B (1996). The Eyes Have It: A Task by Data Type Taxonomy for Information Visualizations, *Proceedings of the IEEE Symposium on Visual Languages*, pp.336-343

Shneiderman, B.; Feldman, D.; Rose, A. & Grau, X. (2000). Visualizing Digital Library Search Results with Categorical and Hierarchical Axes, *Proceedings of the 5th ACM Conference on Digital Libraries*, pp. 57-66

Silva, N.; Sánchez, A.; Proal, C. & Redbollar, C. (2003). Visual Exploration of Large Collections in Digital Libraries, *Proceedings of the Latin American Conference on Human-Computer Interaction*, pp.147-157

Stasko, J.; Catrambone, R.; Guzdial, M. & McDonald, K. (2000). An Evaluation of Space-Filling Information Visualizations for Depicting Hierarchical Structures, *International Journal of Human-Computer Studies*, Vol. 53, No. 5, pp. 663-694

Foley, J.; Van Dam, A.; Feiner, S. & Hughes, J. (1996) *Computer Graphics: Principles and Practice*, 2nd ed. Addison-Wesley Publishing Company

Veerasamy, A. & Heikes, R. (1997). Effectiveness of a Graphical Display of Retrieval Results, *Proceedings of the 20th Annual International ACM SIGIR Conference on Research and Development in Information Retrieval*, pp. 236-245

Williamson, C. & Shneiderman, B. (1992). The dynamic HomeFinder: evaluating dynamic queries in a real-estate information exploration system, *Proceedings of the 15th Annual International ACM SIGIR Conference on Research and Development in Information Retrieval*, pp. 338-346

Wiza, W.; Walczak, K. & Cellary, W. (2004). Periscope: A System for Adaptive 3D Visualization of Search Results, *Proceedings of the ninth international conference on 3D Web technology, pp. 29-40*

7

Automating the Maintenance of Greenstone Collections

Wendy Osborn[1], Steve Fox[1], David Bainbridge[2] and Ian H.Witten[2]
[1]*University of Lethbridge*
[2]*University of Waikato*
[1]*Canada*
[2]*New Zealand*

1. Introduction

Many applications generate multimedia documents, such as images and video, on a daily basis. For example, many municipalities have a photo-radar system to catch vehicles that violate traffic laws such as speeding or ignoring red lights. Many pictures of vehicle license plates are created every day. If these images are organized into a digital library, the collection would need to be updated regularly to incorporate new images. Another example is a traveller who wants to update a digital library of trip photos with new pictures of her travels while traveling around the world.

When documents and metadata are added to a digital library collection on a regular basis, such as hourly, daily or weekly, an automated and scheduled approach to collection maintenance is preferred over having to manually update the collection. In addition, an automated approach should be simple to use, therefore making time available for other important tasks.

Digital library software such as Greenstone (Witten et al., 2009), DSpace (Tansley et al., 2006) and Fedora (Lagoze et al., 2006) require that items be added manually to the collection. In Fedora, data is retrieved at the time of viewing. However, a location needs to be manually configured. Further, although Fedora and DSpace do provide application programming interfaces (APIs) to extend functionality, programming knowledge is required for using an API and for setting up tools based on it.

We present a solution for automating and scheduling updates that occur on a regular basis. Our solution is implemented in the Greenstone digital library software system (Witten et al., 2009), and comes in two parts. The first part of our approach is a command-line scheduling module. The Scheduler both automates the construction and modification of a collection, and schedules the construction to occur at specific intervals, such as hourly, daily or weekly. In addition, the owner of a collection can update the collection manually, without affecting the scheduled collection builds. Further, the Scheduler interacts with the existing task scheduling mechanism on the host system, which keeps the Scheduler minimal, yet powerful. The second part of our approach involves incorporating the Scheduler into the Greenstone Librarian Interface (GLI) (Witten, 2004). This will allow users who are more comfortable with managing collections through a graphical user interface to take advantage

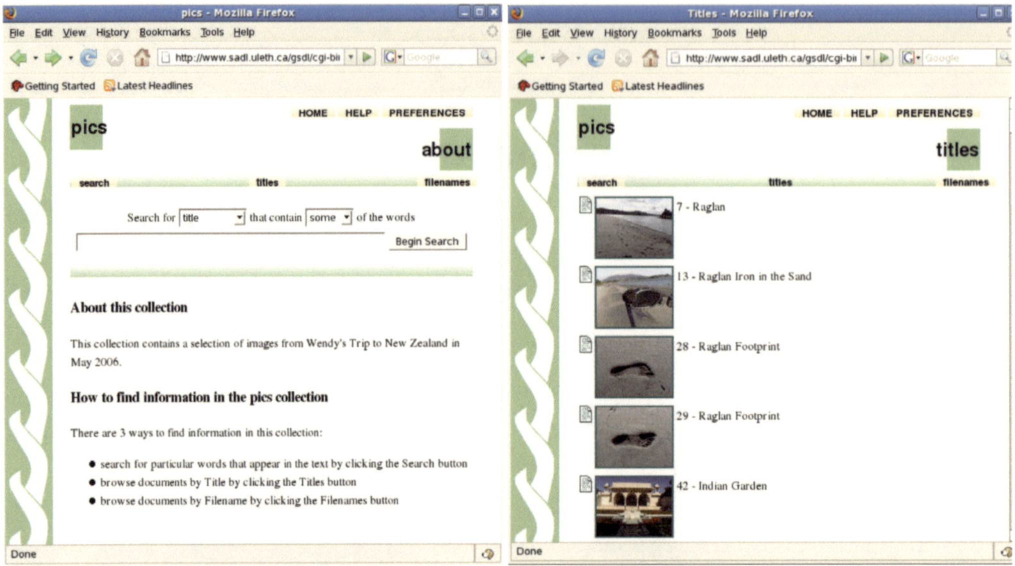

(a) Front Page of pics Collection (b) Viewing pics Collection

Fig. 1. pics Collection in Greenstone

of the functionality of the Scheduler. In addition, this allows us to handle certain tasks associated with scheduling in a uniform and flexible manner.

This chapter proceeds as follows. Sections 2, 3 and 4 present background information on Greenstone, the Librarian Interface, and Cron. Section 5 presents the Scheduler, the command-line tool for scheduling automatic builds of Greenstone collections. Section 6 presents an evaluation of the Scheduler. Section 7 presents the extensions to the Librarian Interface required to support the Scheduler. Section 8 presents a scenario that overviews the use of the Scheduler from the Librarian Interface. Finally, Section 9 concludes the chapter and provides some future directions of research.

2. Greenstone

Greenstone (Witten et al., 2009) is a suite of software for creating digital library collections and making them available locally or via the Internet. A collection can contain documents of different formats, including images, PostScript and PDF files, audio, formatted and unformatted text, and many others. A collection built using Greenstone can be customized in many ways. For example, a collection owner can customize the types of documents that can appear in the collection, the appearance of the interface to the collection, and how the collection will be accessed by other users. In addition, Greenstone is extensible. For example, functionality to support other data formats that are not provided with Greenstone can easily be added to a collection.

There are two types of accessors in Greenstone. The first is an index that provides support for searching. The second is a classifier that provides support for browsing. A collection can be configured for browsing by any metadata that is specified by the collection owner or extracted by Greenstone. Furthermore, a collection can be configured for searching on the same metadata fields, as well as full text.

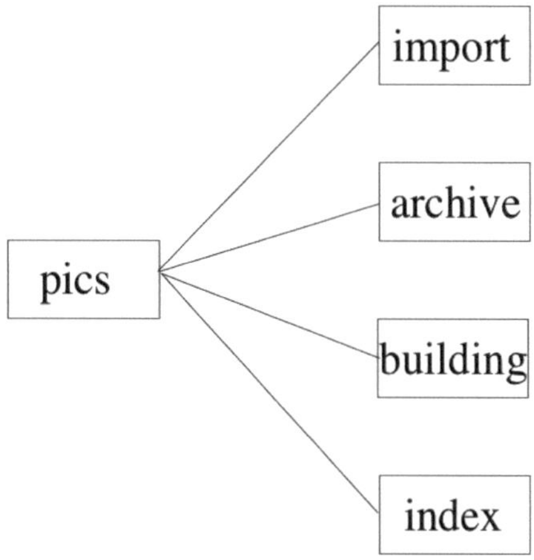

Fig. 2. Internal Representation of a Greenstone Collection

Figures 1(a) and 1(b) depict a Greenstone collection called *pics*. The *pics* collection is configured to accept images only. Figure 1(a) shows the front page of the collection, which provides general information on the collection. In addition, the collection is configured for both browsing and searching by either Title or Filename. Figure 1(b) shows a display of some images from the pics collection. In this view, the collection is being browsed by Title. The user can click on any image to obtain a larger image for viewing.

Figure 2 depicts the internal representation of a Greenstone collection. Here, the four main directories of a collection – *import, archives, building, and index* – are displayed. The purpose of each is described below:

- *import*. The *import* directory contains all documents that are to be added to the collection. If desired, the documents can be organized in a hierarchical directory structure within the *import* directory.
- *archives*. The *archives* directory stores all documents that have been processed from the import folder and added to the collection. All documents in the *archives* directory are represented in a canonical XML format.
- *building*. The *building* directory is a working directory for creating all indices and classifiers that are specified for the collection.
- *index*. The *index* directory contains the indices and classifiers after they are created.

A Greenstone collection is created or modified by the following four steps (Witten et al., 2009): document addition, document importation, accessor creation, and collection activation. Each step is described in detail below:

1. *document addition*. New documents that will be added to a collection are placed into the *import* directory for the collection.
2. *document importation*. Each document in the import directory is processed for inclusion by creating a canonical XML representation for it. This is accomplished by specifying an *import* command. Different importing options can be specified by the user. For example, documents in the *import* directory can be added to an existing collection by using a -*keepold* option. Alternatively, all documents in the *import* directory—new and existing—can be used to create a new instance of the collection by using a -*removeold* option. All imported documents are placed in the *archives* directory.

3. *accessor creation*. After the documents in the *import* directory are added to the collection, indices and classifiers are set up by processing the canonical XML representations of all documents. This is accomplished by specifying a *build* command. New indices and classifiers can be built by specifying a *-removeold* option. Alternatively, existing indices and classifiers can be modified by specifying a *-keepold* or *-incremental* option. The resulting indices and classifiers are located in the *building* directory.
4. *collection activation*. Finally, the collection is activated by moving the indices and classifiers from the *building* directory to the *index* directory. The collection is now viewable online.

The command for each step can be executed in a terminal or command window, or via the Greenstone Librarian Interface.

3. Greenstone Librarian Interface

The Greenstone Librarian Interface (GLI) (Witten, 2004) is a graphical user interface that provides a user-friendly method to build and configure Greenstone collections. It incorporates the four steps above. The only steps that are required by the user are to place documents to the import directory via the Gather panel, and to add the documents to the collection via the Create panel. In addition, the Librarian Interface allows a user to create new collections, select metadata sets, configure which document types to allow, and select *import* and *build* command options. Figure 3 shows the Librarian Interface.

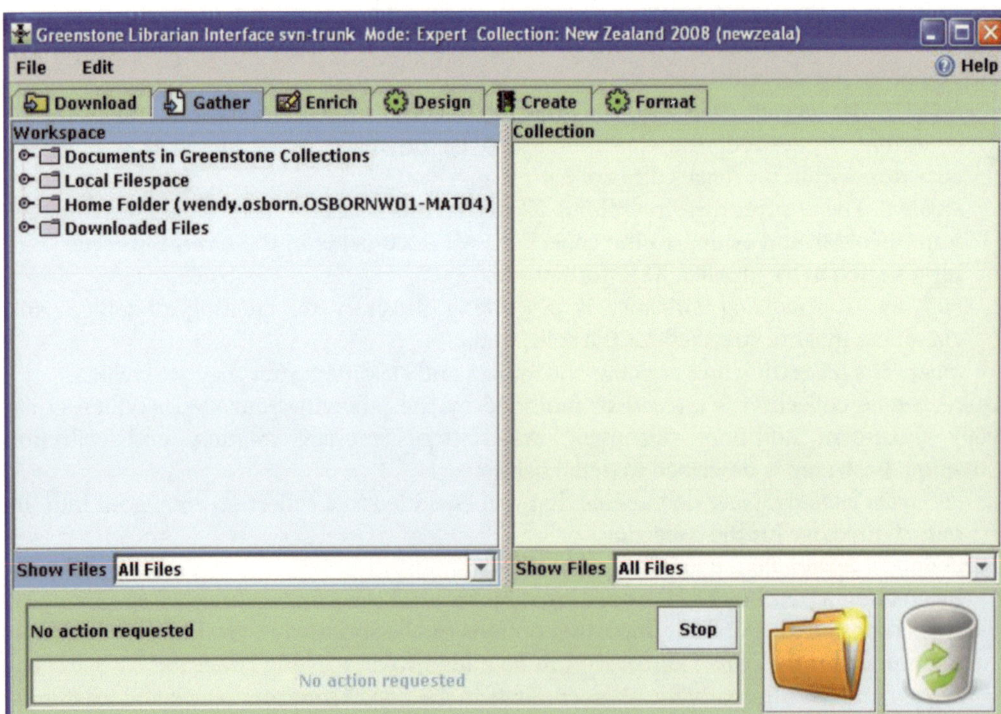

Fig. 3. The Greenstone Librarian Interface

4. Cron

Cron (Nemeth et al., 2007) is a program for users to schedule tasks that will run automatically at a specified time. A task can be one command, or a script containing several commands that are executed in sequence. Initially, Cron was implemented for Unix and Linux platforms, with most systems running Vixie Cron (Vixie, 1994). Mac OS X also runs Vixie Cron. In addition, versions of Cron now exist for Windows platforms, such as Pycron (Schapira, 2004). We summarize the general ideas behind all implementations of Cron that are applicable to our work.

Cron runs continuously in the background of the operating system. Every minute, Cron reads several task configuration files. Each such file is called a crontab file. A crontab file contains a record for every task that is scheduled for execution. Cron locates and runs all tasks that are scheduled at the current time.

The format of a crontab record is (*min hr dom moy dow user task*), where *min, hr, dom, moy,* and *dow* are the minute, hour, day of month, month of year and day of week, respectively, *user* is the username that the command will run under, and *task* is the command or script that is executed at the specified time. A task can be scheduled to run hourly, daily, weekly, monthly, or yearly:

- *hourly.* An hourly scheduled task executes every hour at a specified minute.
- *daily.* A task that is scheduled daily executes at a specific hour, which is required, and a specific minute. If no minute is specified, execution will occur every minute during the specified hour.
- *weekly.* A weekly scheduled task runs on a specified day, which is required, and at a specified hour and minute. If no hour is specified, execution will occur every hour during the specified day.
- *monthly.* A monthly scheduled task runs on a specified day (between the 1st and last day of the month).
- *yearly.* A yearly scheduled task runs on a specified month.

Any unspecified values are replaced with an asterisk in the crontab record.

Systems that use Vixie Cron support two types of crontab files - system crontab and user crontab. The system crontab files are primarily for system administration and maintenance tasks. Also, even if all tasks have a specified low-level username, root privileges are required for modifying a system crontab file. User crontab files, on the other hand, can be set up by any user on the system to execute tasks under their own username. Assuming the user has permission to execute the task, no root permissions are required. In addition, Pycron only supports user crontab files. Therefore, the Scheduler will employ a user crontab file.

Figure 4 displays a sample user crontab file. It contains 4 tasks that are scheduled for specific times. The first task, /collect/pics/gsdl.pl, is scheduled to be run at 30 minutes past every hour. The second task, /usr/bin/cleanup.bash, is scheduled for execution daily at 11:59pm.

```
30  *  *  *  * /collect/pics/gsdl.pl
59 23  *  *  * /usr/bin/cleanup.bash
00  6  *  *  7 /home/someuser/alarm
00  0  1  1  * echo "Happy New Year!"
```

Fig. 4. Sample Crontab File

The third task, home/someuser/alarm, is scheduled every Sunday at 6:00am. Finally, the fourth task, which echoes "Happy New Year!", is schedule for execution every January first at 12:00 AM.

5. The Scheduler

We first present our design for the Scheduler command-line module in Greenstone. The Scheduler is written in Perl and runs on Linux, Windows and Mac OS X. It also utilizes the Cron scheduling service (Nemeth et al., 2007) for scheduling collection re-building. We chose Perl because a Perl script can be executed across different platforms without the need to recompile. Similarly, we chose Cron because it is available for Linux and Mac OS X (Vixie, 1994), as well as Windows (Schapira, 2004). Therefore, we can maintain the the cross-platform requirement of Greenstone.

The Scheduler requires the following parameters from the user as input:

1. the collection to be rebuilt,
2. the full *import* command that is required to import documents into the collection,
3. the full *build* command required to construct the indices and classifiers for the collection, and
4. a specification of either an hourly, daily, or weekly build.

For example, if the user wants the collection *pics* to be scheduled for construction on a daily basis, the parameters would look something like this:

schedule.pl pics "import.pl –removeold pics"
"buildcol.pl –removeold pics" daily

where *pics* is the name of the collection, *"import.pl –removeold pics"* is the Greenstone command for importing documents into the collection *pics*, *"buildcol.pl –removeold pics"* is the Greenstone command for creating the required indices and classifiers for *pics*, and *daily* indicates that the collection will be scheduled for construction on a daily basis.

Using the arguments provided by the user, the Scheduler performs two main tasks: 1) create a script that automates the building of the collection (i.e. build script), and 2) create a crontab record that schedules the execution of the build script at specified intervals.

5.1 Automation script generation

The Scheduler generates a build script for any *import* and *build* command, and for the Linux, Windows or Mac OS X platforms. The build script contains all instructions that are required for building the specified collection. The commands include those for setting the Greenstone environment variables required for the collection building process, the *import* command and the *build* command.

Figure 5 shows a sample build script for Linux that contains the instructions for building the collection *pics*, as specified in the *schedule.pl* command above. The first four instructions set the environment variable that are required for the *import.pl* and *buildcol.pl* commands. The next two instructions are the specified *import* and *build* commands. The remaining instructions handle cleanup in order to activate the collection. Similarly, Figure 6 shows a sample build script for Windows that is generated for the same *schedule.pl* command above.

```
#!/usr/bin/perl

$ENV{'GSDLHOME'}="/gsdl";
$ENV{'GSDLOS'}="linux";
$ENV{'GSDLLANG'}="EN";
$ENV{'PATH'}="/usr/local/gsdl/bin/script:/usr/local/gsdl/bin/linux";
system("import.pl -removeold pics");
system("buildcol.pl -removeold pics");
system("\\rm -r /gsdl/collect/pics/index/*");
system("mv /gsdl/collect/pics/building/*
            /gsdl/collect/pics/index/");
system("chmod -R 755 /gsdl/collect/pics/index/*");
```

Fig. 5. Sample Automation Script for Linux

```
#!/usr/bin/perl

$ENV{'GSDLHOME'}="C:\\gsdl";
$ENV{'GSDLOS'}="windows";
$ENV{'GSDLLANG'}="en";
$ENV{'PATH'}="C:\\gsdl\\bin\\windows\\perl\\bin;C:\\gsdl\\bin\\windows;
C:\\gsdl\\bin\\script;C:\\Perl\\bin\\;
C:\\WINDOWS\\system32;C:\\WINDOWS;
system("import.pl pics");
system("buildcol.pl pics");
system("rd \/S \/Q \"C:\\gsdl\\collect\\pics\\index\"");
system("md \"C:\\gsdl\\collect\\pics\\index\"");
system("xcopy \/E \/Y \"C:\\gsdl\\collect\\pics\\building\\*\"
\"C:\\gsdl\\collect\\pics\\index\\\"");
```

Fig. 6. Sample Automation Script for Windows

5.2 Crontab generation

A crontab record is created to execute the automation script at a specified interval. The user has the option of specifying an hourly, daily or weekly build. An hourly build is scheduled for the beginning of the hour, a daily build is scheduled for midnight, and a weekly build is scheduled for Sunday morning at midnight. After creating the crontab record, it is added to the crontab file or replaces an existing crontab record. Figure 7 depicts the daily crontab record for the automation script in Figure 5, while Figure 8 depicts the crontab record corresponding to the automation script in Figure 6.

```
00 0 * * * /gsdl/collect/pics/gsdl.pl
```

Fig. 7. Crontab Record for Linux

```
00 0 * * * c:\gsdl\collect\pics\gsdl.pl
```

Fig. 8. Crontab Record for Windows

6. Evaluation

In this section, we discuss the performance of the Scheduler. The focus of our experiments is to evaluate the Scheduler for correct execution in specific situations. For correct execution, we looked at the following:

- *Crontab*. Does the Scheduler generate a correct crontab record? A crontab record is correct if: 1) it is accepted by the crontab program (Linux and Mac OS X only), and it causes Cron to execute the automation script at the proper time.
- *Automation Script*. In addition, does the scheduler generate the correct automation script to build a collection. An automation script is generated correctly if the collection it is created for is rebuilt correctly given the parameters that are specified when the script is created.

We conducted three experiments. The first is an hourly build of one collection. The second is an hourly build of two collections. The third is a daily build of one collection. All three experiments were performed on both Linux and Windows. These tests were not performed extensively on Mac OS X. However, the scheduler was executed many times on this platform to ensure that it does work.

6.1 Hourly build of one collection

The focus of this experiment is to ensure that the Scheduler produced a correct crontab record and automation script to re-build a collection of images every hour for 24 hours. To determine that each execution of the automation script was successful, we looked at the following. For Linux, Cron was configured to send an email message containing the output of the automation script. The email message for each of the 24 builds contains an output for a successful Greenstone build. For Windows, Pycron maintains a log that contains two records for each automation script execution – one record indicating the start of execution, and one record indicating the end of execution and a return code. The terminating records for all 24 builds have a return code of zero, which indicates a successful execution of the automation script.

In both cases, a visual inspection of the collection was also performed periodically to verify the success of the Scheduler.

6.2 Hourly build of two collections

The focus of this experiment is to ensure that if multiple collections are scheduled to be rebuilt at the same time, they are successfully rebuilt. We scheduled the building of two collections on hourly intervals for 24 hours. A perusal of email messages (for Linux) and the log (for Windows) verify that both collections were rebuilt successfully.

6.3 Daily build of one collection

The focus of this experiment is twofold. The first is to ensure correct daily execution of an automation script generated by the Scheduler. The second is to simulate a situation of a collection that has images added to it on a daily basis. We schedule one collection to be built daily for seven days. The collection starts with 10 images, and 10 images are added daily. In addition to the successful daily build, the collection did reflect the addition of the new images that arrived daily.

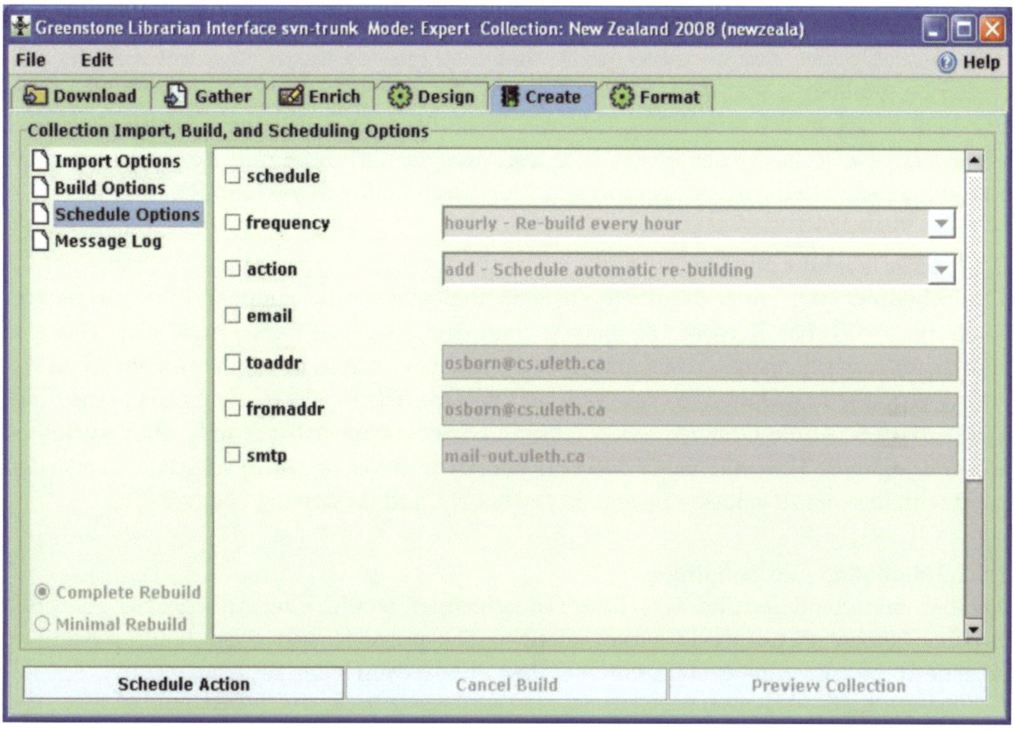

Fig. 9. The Schedule Options Panel

7. Scheduling in the Librarian Interface

The Scheduler is a minimal, yet powerful tool for maintaining Greenstone collections. It hides the details concerning the collection building process, and also the details for scheduling a Cron task. However, the Scheduler has two main limitations. The first is that the user is still required to know the syntax and command-line parameters for both the *import* and *build* commands in order to perform scheduling. The second is that, currently, notification of collection building success—or failure—is still dependent on the version of Cron (and indirectly, the operating system it is running on) that is used.

The Librarian Interface provides a user-friendly tool for building collections, including configuring the *import* and *build* commands. Therefore, it is ideal to extend the Librarian Interface to allow the configuration of the Scheduler as well. Figure 9 depicts the Librarian Interface extension to support the scheduling of collection builds. Currently, the Create panel is displaying most of the parameters (i.e. Schedule Options) for the Scheduler.

Notice that no explicit options exist for the *import* and *build* commands. This is because the *import* and *build* commands are created based on the arguments selected from the Import Options and Build Options panels. Therefore, the user no longer needs to know the exact syntax of the *import* and *build* commands.

7.1 User modes

The Librarian Interface has four modes of use— Library Assistant, Librarian, Library Systems Specialist, and Expert—stepwise increasing the functionality available to the user

(Witten, 2004). It was important to determine which modes would have access to the Scheduling Options, and for those modes that were granted access, how much access each would be granted. It was decided that Library Systems Specialists and Experts would be provided access to the Scheduling Options. In addition to determining which options to make available to each user mode, it is also necessary to determine how the Scheduler would interact with the existing *import* and *build* functionality in the Librarian Interface.

7.1.1 Mode level for options

The Scheduler was first modified so that the passing of command-line arguments conformed with that of other Greenstone commands, such as *import* and *build*. This also allowed us to easily specify which user mode could have access to each argument when it is added as a Schedule Option in the Librarian Interface. The Expert user mode is granted full access to all Schedule Options, while Librarian Systems Specialist is only granted limited access to options. This user mode can only specify whether or not to schedule a collection build with the default values—a frequency of hourly, and no sending of email.

7.1.2 Scheduling and building

Another important decision was how the Scheduler would interact with the collection building functionality of the Librarian Interface. The question asked was, should scheduling be done at the same time as collection building, or be a completely separate task?
For Expert mode, the functionality for Scheduling is separate from that of collection building. This is because an expert user may want to configure and manually re-build their collection before scheduling an automatic re-build of it. For Library System Specialist mode, the Scheduling functionality is done at the same time as collection building. If the specialist chooses to schedule, a new scheduled build is created. If the specialist chooses not to schedule, any existing scheduled builds are deleted.

7.2 Cron event logs

It is important to maintain logs that keep track of the outcome of a scheduled collection build. Both Vixie Cron and Pycron maintain a log that keeps track of the attempted execution of all scheduled tasks. Neither scheduling service keeps track of the success or failure of a scheduled task, nor do they keep track of the output of a task. In addition, to view logs created by Vixie Cron, the user must have root access.
Another desirable feature of maintaining logs is the ability to be able to only record output that is considered important, and to disregard all other task output. For example, if the output from the input and build commands of Greenstone is required, but the output from moving indices and classifiers is not considered important, the log should reflect this.
Therefore, the Scheduler is modified in two ways to handle the logging of building script output. The first is to create a custom log for each execution of the automation script. The automation script creates a unique filename every time it is executed by using a timestamp. The second is to specify in the automation script which actions will have its output redirected to the logfile. The actions whose output is to be ignored will have its output redirected to the 'bit bucket' (e.g. /dev/null/ in Linux).

7.3 Email notification

It is also important than an email notification service be provided, which will inform users of the outcome of their scheduled collection build. We handle email notification from the Scheduler and Librarian Interface for the following reasons:

1. *User notification.* Whether Cron notifies users about the outcome of a scheduled task depends on the its implementation. For Vixie Cron, the outcome of a task (i.e. output from either successful task completion, or error output) is emailed to the owner of the task. Pycron does not send email notification.
2. *Flexibility of Notification.* In Vixie Cron it is possible to suppress email notification, either by setting an environment variable to null, or by redirecting all output to a file or the 'bit bucket'. However, this is normally an all-or-nothing event—either all output, or none, is sent by email. Similar to logging, a desirable feature would be to send email that contains only the most important parts of the building process, and ignores other parts of the building process.
3. *Greenstone Email Support.* Greenstone comes with a Perl email script, that is a wrapper for the Perl sendmail command. The email script is platform-independent. Therefore, it is ideal to use it to provide a uniform way to send email concerning the execution of a scheduled task. In addition, the script does not require the piping of build output directly to it, but instead can send the contents of a file.

Therefore, both the Librarian Interface and the Scheduler are modified so that email notification is handled in a uniform and user-friendly manner across all operating systems.

First, options have been added to the Scheduler that are required for the Perl email script—specifically, a flag to specify that email will be sent (*-email*), the sender (*-fromaddr*), receiver (*-toaddr*) and the email server that will be used to send the email (*-smtp*). Also, the corresponding fields exist in the Schedule Options pane of the Librarian Interface. In order to assist users in using the email features of scheduling, the Librarian Interface attempts to populate the fields *-toaddr*, *-fromaddr*, and *-smtp* in the Schedule Options pane by consulting the configurations for the Librarian Interface and Greenstone. If suitable values are available from these sources, they are assigned to the appropriate fields.

Second, the output from the building script must be captured and re-directed to the Perl email script. The capturing of output already takes place, in the event log. This serves as the file that the email script will send to the user. Also, since it contains only the output that is considered important, this will be reflected in the email message as well.

Finally, the Scheduler is modified so that, if specified, the automation script will send an email message containing the contents of the log to the specified recipient. An added bonus is that if email is not specified, the log can still be consulted by the user if required.

7.4 Scheduled building in isolation

An important modification to the Scheduler is to ensure that a scheduled build is completed in its entirety without interference from another scheduled build. A build may take a significant amount of time depending on the size of the collection—from seconds for a small one to 33 hours for a collection containing 20 GB of raw text and 50 GB of metadata (Boddie et al., 2008).

To handle this, the automation script for the collection checks for a lock file, which indicates that a collection build is underway. If the file exists, the collection owner is notified via email and information is placed in the event log. Otherwise, a lock file is created before the scheduled build begins, and is removed when the build finishes. This ensures that multiples builds do not occur concurrently.

8. Example: collecting pictures while traveling

In this section, we present a simple application of scheduling from the Librarian Interface. In this scenario, we have a traveler who wants to post pictures of their trip in a Greenstone collection for her friends to view. Instead of waiting until the end of the trip, the traveler wants to post her pictures from each day, incrementally adding to the collection on a daily basis. The traveler does not want to worry about obtaining the Librarian Interface to rebuild the collection while traveling. Instead, she simply wants to upload the pictures to the *import* directory of her collection, and have her collection rebuilt automatically and on a daily basis. This can be accomplished by setting up a scheduled, automatic rebuild of the collection of travel photos from the Librarian Interface.

First, before departing, the traveler runs the Librarian Interface and creates a new collection. Then, the user selects the Create tab to display the collection creation pane. From here, clicking on Schedule Options will display the available options for setting up a scheduled, automatic collection build of the collection of travel pictures. Figure 10(a) depicts the available scheduling options, which are displayed with default and derived values as appropriate. Here, the traveler selects schedule, which indicates that she wants to set up a scheduled, automatic build. Also, she selects a frequency of hourly and an action of add (or, to create a new scheduled build).

Next, the traveler clicks on Schedule Build. This will set up the building script for the collection of travel pics, as well as the *crontab* record that will indicate to Cron that the collection is to be rebuilt daily. The collection is now ready to be re-built while the traveler is away.

At the end of the first day of travel, she uploads three pictures, which are added to the collection when the collection is re-built automatically overnight. The updated collection is depicted in Figure 10(b). The next day, the traveler uploads three more pictures. When the collection is re-built overnight, these pictures are added to the existing collection. Figure 10(c) depicts the updated collection with the new pictures.

Although not shown here, the user can switch to the Import Options and Build Options and select any options that are required for collection importing and building. These options are incorporated into the automatic building script that is created for the collection. In addition, the user can manually build and configure their collection as many times as necessary to confirm the right sequence is being performed, before setting up a scheduled, automatic build.

9. Conclusion and future work

In this paper, we present our solution to automated and scheduled collection maintenance in Greenstone. First, we propose the Scheduler, which provides support for an automatic rebuild of a collection at specific intervals by specifying a few simple parameters. The Scheduler interacts with a resident task scheduler on the local operating system, which results in a minimal but powerful tool. Several experiments are performed to show the correct execution of the Scheduler for different build times and for different numbers of collections.

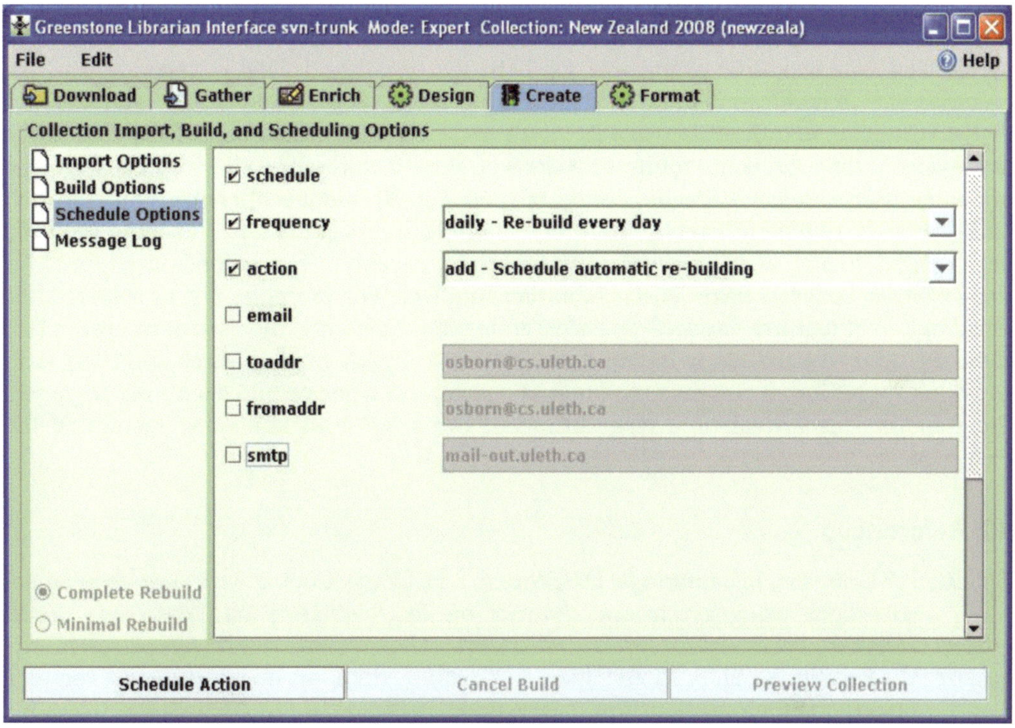

(a) Schedule Options Panel

(b) Build - First Day

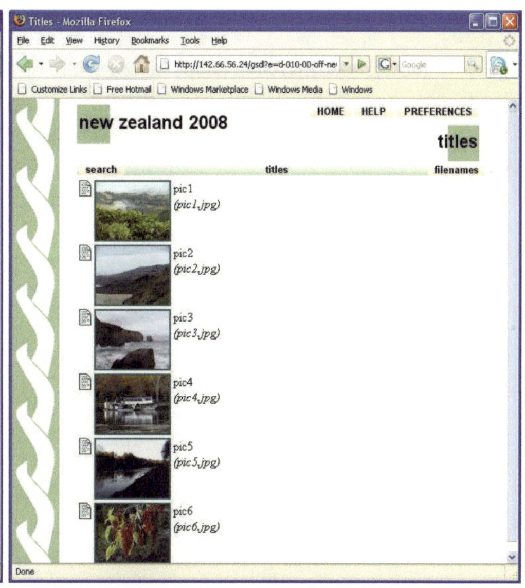

(c) Build - Second Day

Fig. 10. Collection Build Scheduling

In addition, we propose the incorporation of the Greenstone Scheduler into the Librarian Interface. This overcomes two limitations of the Schedule—the requirement to know the syntax and command-line arguments for both the *import* and *build* commands, and the inconsistency of notification of collection building success or failure. Providing an interface to the Scheduler improves its usability and provide further abstraction of the scheduling process from the user. Some future directions of work include the following. The first is to allow the user to select a specific period of time (e.g. 20 minutes after the hour) for their collection to be re-built. Currently, collection building occurs at the top of the hour (hourly), at midnight (daily) and on Sunday at midnight (weekly). The second is support for dependencies between fields in the Librarian Interface. For example, if a user selects the email option, it requires -*toaddr*, -*fromaddr*, and -*smtp*. Currently, the user must ensure that these are also selected, as it is not done automatically. A final research direction is to provide support for an automatic re-build of a collection when certain events are triggered. For example, the arrival of a new document can trigger an automatic rebuild of the collection.

10. References

Boddie, S., Thompson, J., Bainbridge, D. &Witten, I. H. (2008). Coping with very large digital collections using greenstone, *Proc. of the ECDLWorkshop on Very Large Digital Libraries*.

Lagoze, C., Payette, S., Shin, E. &Wilper, C. (2006). Fedora: an architecture for complex objects and their relationships, *International Journal on Digital Libraries* 6(2): 124–138.

Nemeth, E., Snyder, G. & Hein, T. R. (2007). *Linux Administration Handbook*, Prentice-Hall.

Schapira, E. (2004). Python cron - great cron for windows. Website. Last visited June 2010. http://sourceforge.net/projects/pycron.

Tansley, R., Bass, M. & Smith, M. (2006). Dspace as an open archival information system: Status and future directions, *Proc. of the 10th European Conference on Digital Libraries*.

Vixie, P. (1994). Vixie cron for FreeBSD. Website. Last visited June 2010. http://www.freebsd .org/cgi/cvsweb.cgi/src/usr.sbin/cron/.

Witten, I. H. (2004). Creating and customizing collections with the Greenstone Librarian Interface, *Proc. of the Int'l Symp. on Digital Libraries and Knowledge Communities in Networked Information Society*.

Witten, I. H., Bainbridge, D. & Nichols, D. (2009). *How to Build a Digital Library*, Morgan Kaufmann.

8

Security and Digital Libraries

Edward Fox and Noha ElSherbiny
Virginia Tech
USA

1. Introduction

Security is an important issue in digital library design. Security weaknesses in digital libraries, coupled with attacks or other types of failures, can lead to confidential information being inappropriately accessed, or loss of integrity of the data stored. These in turn can have a damaging effect on the trust of publishers or other content providers, can cause embarrassment or even economic loss to digital library owners, and can even lead to pain and suffering or other serious problems if urgently needed information is unavailable (Tyrväinen, 2005).

There are many security requirements to consider because of the variety of different actors working with a digital library. Each of these actors has different security needs (Chowdhury & Chowdhury, 2003). Thus, a digital library content provider might be concerned with protecting intellectual property rights and the terms of use of content, while a digital library user might be concerned with reliable access to content stored in the digital library. Requirements based on these needs sometimes are in conflict, which can make the security architecture of a digital library even more complex.

The design of the security architecture of a digital library must go beyond simply adding one or a few modules to a previously designed system. This is because there may be security holes in pre-existing modules, and because difficulties can arise when attempting to integrate the modules. The security architecture of a digital library must be designed so that security concerns are handled holistically. A security system designer must view the whole architecture and consider all of the applicable security factors when designing a secure digital library. The nature of a security attack may differ according to the architecture of the digital library; a distributed digital library has more security weaknesses than a centralized digital library.

Security attacks can be categorized as physical attacks and logical attacks (Stallings, 2006). A physical attack involves hardware security where keys, locks, cards, and visitor monitoring is used. A logical attack involves an attack on the content or digital library system. We focus on the logical attacks and software security of digital libraries.

2. Security issues with digital libraries

According to the DELOS Reference Model (Candela et al., 2007) there are 6 main concepts in a digital library universe: content, user, functionality, architecture, quality, and policy. Each of these concepts has security issues that affect it.

2.1 Content

The content of a digital library includes the information objects that a digital library provides to the users. Some of the security issues involved are integrity and access control. Integrity requires that each object/resource has not been altered or changed by an unauthorized person. Access control encompasses two security requirements. The first is authentication where the user must log into the system while the second is confidentiality, which means that the content of an object is inaccessible by a person unless they have authorization. Not all digital libraries are free; often content is provided to digital library users for a certain fee, whereupon access control is needed to protect the content. Further, some content is inappropriate for some users, or targeted to particular user groups; there are a whole host of such other reasons for access control.

Logical attacks such as hacking and message tampering can affect the integrity and confidentiality of the content. Improved information access in digital libraries has raised many issues that affect the management of digital libraries. Content Management, or more specifically Digital Rights Management, refers to the protection of content from the different logical security attacks and issues relating to intellectual property rights and authenticity.

2.1.1 Digital rights management

DRM provides content protection by encrypting the content and associating it with a digital license (Tyrväinen, 2005). The license identifies the user allowed to view the content, lists the content of the product, and states the rights the user has to the resource in a computer readable format using a digital rights expression language (DREL) or extensible Rights Markup Language (XrML) that also describes constraints and conditions.

There are 7 technologies used to provide DRM (Fetscherin & Schmid, 2003). Table 1 summarizes the DRM components and supporting technology.

Each of these components involves mechanisms used to provide DRM:

- **Encryption**: Encryption techniques such as symmetric and asymmetric ciphers can be used to provide access control; public-key encryption is used in payment systems that control how and by whom the content is used.

  Symmetric ciphers using DES, 3DES, AES, and RC4 algorithms require the use of a shared secret key to encrypt data before it is sent. At the receiver's end the cipher text is decrypted using the same secret key. Symmetric ciphers depend on both the sender and receiver knowing the shared key.

  Asymmetric ciphers use a pair of keys, public and private, for each of the sender and the receiver. The public keys of both the sender and the receiver are known but the private key is kept secret. If encryption is performed using the public key then only the private key can be used for decryption and vice versa.
- **Passwords**: Stored strings must be matched by users desiring access.
- **Watermarking**: Characters or images are added to reflect ownership. Steganography is used to conceal data inside audio, video, or images (Johnson & Jajodia, 1998). Different watermarking techniques have different aims; some watermarks might be visible while others invisible. Some watermarks are reversible (Mintzer et al., 1997); it depends on the desired use of the watermark and what is being protected.
- **Digital signature**: Asymmetric encryption can be used. Likewise, hash algorithms such as MD5 and SHA can be used to create a signature (Stallings, 2006).

Component	Protection Technology
Access and usage control	Encryption (e.g., symmetric, asymmetric), passwords
Protection of authenticity and integrity	Watermarks, digital signatures, digital fingerprints
Identification by metadata	Allows description of an object in suitable categories, covering the digital content, rights owner, and conditions.
Specific hardware and software	Includes all hardware and software used by the end-device through which the digital content is being played, viewed, or printed.
Copy detection systems	Search engines, which search the network for illegal copies and use watermarking.
Payment systems	Can be seen as a certain type of protection technology as it requires user registration, or credit card authentication, which also require a trust relationship between the content provider and the customer.
Integrated e-commerce systems	DRMS must include systems which support contract negotiation, accounting information, and usage rules.

Table 1. DRM Components and Protection Technologies, adapted (Fetscherin & Schmid, 2003)

- **Digital fingerprint**: Digital fingerprints are a more powerful technique involving digital signatures and watermarking. The creator of the content creates a unique copy of the content marked for each user; the marks are user-specific hence called fingerprints. Should a user illegally distribute the content, the creator can use search robots to find those copies (Schonberg & Kirovski, 2004).
- **Copy detection systems:** Search engines also can help locate such copied objects. Copy-detecting browsers can protect digital content too.
- **Payment systems:** Users must divulge personal information to pay for content. Installing payment systems can help protect digital content.

There is no standard mechanism for providing DRM, mainly due to the lack of regulations (Chowdhury & Chowdhury, 2003), however there are various systems and protocols introduced to provide content management and support fair usage policies.
There is a tradeoff between security and performance. Nadeem and Javed use a Pentium-4, 2.4 GHz machine running Microsoft Windows XP operating system, encrypt 20527 bytes to 2323398 bytes of data using DES, 3DES, and AES. For 20527 bytes of data it took 2 seconds to encrypt using the DES algorithm and 4 seconds to encrypt using the AES algorithm (Nadeem & Javed, 2005). It can be seen that the more complex the encryption algorithm the longer it takes to encrypt the data. In another study, encrypting data with the RSA algorithm using a key size of 1024 took 0.08 milliseconds/operation on an Intel Core 2 1.83 GHz processor under Windows Vista in 32-bit mode, while using a key size of 2048 took 0.16 milliseconds/operation (Dai, 2009).

2.2 User

The User in a digital library refers to "the various actors (whether human or machine) entitled to interact with digital libraries" (Candela et al., 2007). Digital libraries connect the different actors with the information they have and allow the users to consume old or generate new information. Security issues relating to the users of a digital library intersect with content issues discussed above. A main logical security issue relating to users and content is access control. Different access control requirements arise for distributed systems (Tolone et al., 2005) to ensure both confidentiality and authentication:

- Access control must be applied and enforced at a distributed platform level, so should be scalable and available at various levels of granularity.
- Access control models should allow a varied definition of access rights depending on different information and must be dynamic where changes to policies are easily made and easy to manage.
- "Access control models must allow high-level specification of access rights."(Tolone et al., 2005)

Digital library users may need to be authenticated before they can access content. Global/universal identification may not suffice. A service provider that provides content based on a non-identity based criteria like age will not benefit from global identification because there is no way to verify the authenticated user's personal information. Usernames and passwords are not efficient ways to provide authentication.
One of the most widely used authentication protocols is Kerberos. It (Neuman & Ts'o, 1994) is a client-server model, which secures communication with servers on a local network. Developed at MIT in the 1980s to provide security across a large campus network, it is based on the Needham-Schroeder protocol and has now been standardized and included in many operating systems such as UNIX, Linux, Windows 2000, NT, XP, etc.
Kerberos is used as an authentication protocol in cases where attackers monitor network traffic to intercept passwords. It secures communication, provides single sign on and mutual authentication, and does not send a user's password in the clear on an insecure network.
An alternative solution suitable for digital libraries (Winslett et al., 1997), is to represent information about an individual using credentials. Credentials are "abstract objects which contain statements expressing knowledge or information from a definite context." Credentials do not specify direct information about a client and their attributes, they

describe the local environment and context in which the requests originate (Ching et al., 1996).

Digital credentials can be used as a means of authentication in providing DL access control (Winslett et al., 1997). Two agents can be used to assist in the management: a personal security assistant and a server security assistant, to manage digital credentials using a client/server model. The server must notify the client of the credentials required for the current request. The client then sends its credentials for authentication. The client must have some trust of the server to give its credentials, which raises privacy issues.

The personal security assistant is used to obtain credentials on behalf of the client, store the credentials, parse and interpret the required credentials, and manage the acceptance policies (Winslett et al., 1997). A server security assistant is available to specify the credential acceptance policies and their usage.

There is a tradeoff between flexibility and security that must be considered when choosing an access control model, as is discussed below.

2.2.1 Access matrix model

This conceptual model specifies the rights that each subject possesses for each object (Tolone et al., 2005). Actions on objects are allowed or denied based on the access rights specified. There are 2 implementations of the AMM:

- An Access Control List provides a direct mapping of each object the subjects are allowed to access, and their usage rights (owner, read, or write).
- A Capability List defines the objects each subject is allowed to access and the usage rights.

Access control lists and capability lists are not suitable for distributed systems. Their limitations lead to multiple problems (Nagaraj, 2001). ACL provides limited expressibility of policies. Any change in the policies will propagate in the system/application. Authentication in a system that uses ACL solely is a problem because using username & password in a distributed system is not practical. In a distributed system, administration of the system should be decentralized by delegation to reduce the overhead. The owner of the object specifies a policy in ACL. If an overall policy is specified by an entity higher than the object owner, then conflicts may occur in the access rights. The number of administrative entities in a distributed system can be very large. Not all the administrators may have trust amongst themselves, resulting in incorrectly defined policies. For example, admin A may trust B but not C, however B may trust C. If A were to define policy for B then it would be implicitly applicable to C, causing problems.

2.2.2 Role-based access control

Role-based access control involves policies that regulate information access based on the activities the users perform. Such policies require the definition of roles in the system: "a set of actions and responsibilities associated with a particular working activity" (Sandhu & Samarati, 1994). Permissions are assigned to roles instead of individual users. Specifying user authorization involves 2 steps: first assigning the user to a role, second defining the access control that the role has over certain objects.

RBAC is easier to manage and is more extensible than ACL. However RBAC doesn't flexibly handle constraints, where a user with a specific role may need specific permission on an object. An example of RBAC architecture addressing key limitations is OASIS (Bacon et al., 2003), for use in distributed systems. Role management in OASIS is decentralized and service specific. OASIS is integrated with an event-based middleware that notifies applications of any environmental changes. Roles are parameterized by applications and services to define their client roles, and to enforce policies for role activation and service invocation within each session. Role membership certificates (RMC) are returned to each user on successful login, to be used as a credential to activate other roles (Bacon et al., 2003).

RBAC is suitable for use with digital libraries because it supports decentralized architectures and varying roles, however RBAC doesn't allow for the definition of different roles in a collaborative group.

2.2.3 Task based access control

The Task based access control model extends subject/object access control by allowing the definition of domains by task-based contextual information (Tolone et al., 2005). Steps required to perform the task are used to define access control; the steps are associated with a protection state containing a set of permissions for each state, which change according to the task. TBAC uses dynamic management of permissions.

TBAC systems are limited to defining contexts in relation to activities, tasks, or workflow progress. Since it is implemented by recording usage and validity of permissions, therefore, TBAC requires a central access control module to manage permissions activation and deactivation in a just-in-time fashion.

2.2.4 Team based access control

RBAC doesn't address cases where group members of different roles want to collaborate in a single group. The TMAC model defines collaboration by user context and object context. "User context provides a way of identifying specific users playing a role on a team at any given moment" (Tolone et al., 2005) while object context defines the objects required.

TMAC offers the advantages of RBAC along with ability to specify fine-grained control on users and on object instances. A scalable access control data structure can be used with large collections, applying concepts of team based access control, focusing mainly on the access control data structure, and employing an access control framework called Document Access Control Method (DACM) with a Document Storage System (DocSS) (Gladney, 1997). DACM allows the decentralized administration of privileges, the definition of different rule sets to control a single collection, and different delegation patterns as models.

Current object access control policies use an array of rules to record the privileges each subject is allowed to each object. This is impractical to manage in the large data collections found in digital libraries. DACM solves this problem by finding symmetries in a permission function to allow a brief expression without losing important distinctions.

2.2.5 Content based access control

Another approach to access control models involves defining models according to content. This approach is applicable in digital libraries and distributed systems (Adam et al., 2002), where the access rights to the user are dynamic and may change with each login. Content

based access control policies are very well suited for digital libraries and distributed systems. Recent research has proposed different models; most use digital credentials for authentication, but vary in the definition/storage of the policy.
An important content based access control model (Ferrari et al., 2002), introduces a content-based access control system, Digital Library Authorization System, that utilizes the Digital Library Authorization Model (DLAM). Subject, object, and privilege sets can't be used to define policies in digital libraries mainly because DLs are dynamic with large collections of data and subjects. It defines access control policies based on subject qualifications and characteristics. DLAM provides a means to specify the qualifications and characteristics of subjects. It uses content dependant and independent access control and allows the definition of policies with varied granularity.

2.3 Functionality

The concept of functionality encompasses the services that a Digital Library offers to its users (Gonçalves et al., 2008). The minimum functions of a Digital Library include adding new objects to the library or searching and browsing the library and other functions relating to DL management. A security attack that can affect the functionality of the Digital Library is a Denial of Service attack, which can affect the performance of the system and prevent users from accessing the system.

2.4 Architecture

Digital libraries are complex forms of information systems, interoperable across different libraries and so require an architectural framework mapping content and functionality onto software and hardware components (Candela et al., 2007). There are various models for architecture, e.g., client-server, peer-to-peer, and distributed. All these require the protection of the communication channels between 2 parties, where sensitive data might be transferred (Kohl et al., 1998). Securing the connections involves different layers - Internet, transport, or application layer - depending on the architecture of the system.
The distributed model is scalable and flexible. It is useful when building a digital library with changing content from different sources and offers potential for increased reliability. The security requirements for a distributed digital library are challenging, since the content and operations are decentralized. Fault tolerance and error recovery are issues that affect a distributed system. Replication is used to increase the availability of the system. While this approach solves problems with denial of service attacks, it complicates the protection of the content because a replica of the content exists.
The client-server model doesn't have the same security problems as a general distributed model, however, it presents a major security weakness, the server being a single point of failure. Attacks are concentrated on one server rather than on the multiple replicas of a distributed model.

2.5 Quality

The content and behavior of a Digital Library is characterized and evaluated by quality parameters. Quality is (Gonçalves et al., 2007) a concept not only used to classify functionality and content, but also used with objects and services. Some of the parameters are automatically measured and are objective while others are considered subjective; some are measured through user evaluations.

2.6 Policy

Policy is the concept that represents the different regulations and conditions that govern the interaction between the Digital Library and users. Policy supports both extrinsic and intrinsic interactions (Candela et al., 2007) and their definition and modification.

Examples of security issues relating to policies include providing digital rights management, privacy, and confidentiality of the content and users, defining user behavior, and collection delivery.

3. Summary

Digital libraries should be secure. This is an important quality that affects all aspects, as has been shown above using the DL characterization of the DELOS Reference Model (Candela et al., 2007). We also can summarize and elaborate upon this point using another framework for DLs (Goncalves et al., 2004).

The 5S framework supports Societies and their needs, covering all aspects mentioned above about Users and related Policies, as well as Quality (Gonçalves et al., 2007). Since Societies cover software actors, agents, components, modules, etc., this also encompasses related Architectural issues. Thus, security with regard to Societies covers issues like client/server, commerce, identity, peer-to-peer, privacy, rights, roles, teams, and trust.

Scenarios cover functions, operations, requirements, services, and tasks. Examples (Gonçalves et al., 2008) include access, access control, authentication, browsing, copying, denial of service attacks, encryption, payment, recovery, searching, usage, and watermarking.

Spaces cover distributed aspects, as well as representations related to 1D, 2D, 3D, and higher dimensional spaces. These include feature, measure, metric, probability, vector, and topological spaces – used throughout computer and human systems.

Structures cover all types of organization, including data structures and databases, with lists (e.g., access control or capability), graphs, and networks. Structures are overlaid on other constructs in the 5S framework, especially on Streams. Thus, documents are structured streams, while protocols involve scenarios applied to structured communication streams. Structures and Streams cover all types of content, and the many security issues related, including digital rights management, fingerprints, and watermarks.

Clearly, DL security support can be complicated, but the above discussion should help readers organize their thinking and make sure that DL systems meet security requirements.

4. References

Adam, N. R., Atluri, V., Bertino, E. & Ferrari, E. (2002). "A Content-Based Authorization Model for Digital Libraries." *IEEE Transactions on Knowledge and Data Engineering* 14(2) : 296-315.

Athanasopoulos, G., Fox, E., Ioannidis, Y., Kakaletris, G., Manola, N., Meghini, C., Rauber, A. & Soergel, D. (2010). A Functionality Perspective on Digital Library

Interoperability. *Research and Advanced Technology for Digital Libraries, Proc. 14th European Conference, ECDL2010, Sept. 6-10.* Glasgow: 405-408

Bacon, J., Moody, K. & Yao, W. (2003). "Access control and trust in the use of widely distributed services." *Software Practice & Experience (Middleware)* 33(4): 375 - 394.

Candela, L., Castelli, D., Ferro, N., Ioannidis, Y., Koutrika, G., Meghini, C., Pagano, P., Ross, S., Soergel, D., Agosti, M., Dobreva, M., Katifori, V. & Schuldt, H. (2007). The DELOS Digital Library Reference Model. http://www.delos.info/index.php?option=com_content&task=view&id=345

Ching, N., Jones, V. & Winslett, M. (1996). Authorization in the Digital Library: Secure Access to Services across Enterprise Boundaries. *Third International Forum on Research and Technology Advances in Digital Librarie.* Washington, DC, IEEE: 110 - 119

Chowdhury, G. & Chowdhury, S. (2003). *Introduction to Digital Libraries,* Facet Publishing.

Dai, W. (2009). "Speed Comparison of Popular Crypto Algorithms." Accessed in 2010, from http://www.cryptopp.com/benchmarks.html.

Ferrari, E., Adam, N. R., Atluri, V., Bertino, E. & Capuozzo, U. (2002). "An Authorization System for Digital Libraries." *The VLDB Journal* 11(1): 58 - 67.

Fetscherin, M. & Schmid, M. (2003). Comparing the Usage of Digital Rights Management Systems in the music, film, and print industry. *Proceedings of the 5th International Conference on Electronic Commerce.* Pittsburgh, Pennsylvania, ACM

Gladney, H. M. (1997). "Access Control for Large Collections." *ACM Transactions on Information Systems (TOIS)* 15(2): 154 - 194.

Gonçalves, M. A., Fox, E. A., & Watson, L. T. (2008). "Towards a Digital Library Theory: A Formal Digital Library Ontology." *Int. J. Digital Libraries* 8(2): 91-114

Goncalves, M., Fox, E., Watson, L. & Kipp, N. (2004). "Streams, Structures, Spaces, Scenarios, Societies (5S): A Formal Model for Digital Libraries." *ACM Transactions on Information Systems (TOIS)* 22(2): 270 - 312.

Gonçalves, M. A., Moreira, B. L., Fox, E. A., & Watson, L. T. (2007). ""What is a good digital library?" - A quality model for digital libraries." *Information Processing and Management* 43(5): 1416-1437

Johnson, N. F. & Jajodia, S. (1998). " Exploring Steganography: Seeing the Unseen." *IEEE Computer* 31(2): 26-34.

Kohl, U., Lotspiech, J. & Nusser, S. (1998). Security for the Digital Library - Protecting Documents Rather than Channels. *Ninth Workshop on Database and Expert Systems.* Vienna, Austria: 316 - 321

Mintzer, F., Lotspiech, J. & Morimoto, N. (1997) "Safeguarding Digital Library Contents and Users." *D-Lib Magazine* 3(7/8), July/August 1997, http://www.dlib.org/dlib/december97/ibm/12lotspiech.html.

Nadeem, A. & Javed, M. Y. (2005). A Performance Comparison of Data Encryption Algorithms. *1st International Conference on Information and Communication Technologies.* Karachi, Pakistan, IEEE: 84 - 89

Nagaraj, S. V. (2001). Access Control in Distributed Object Systems: Problems with Access Control Lists. *Tenth IEEE International Workshops on Enabling Technologies: Infrastructure for Collaborative Enterprises.* Cambridge, MA, IEEE: 163 - 164

Neuman, C. & Ts'o, T. (1994). Kerberos: An Authentication Service for Computer Networks. *IEEE Communications Magazine,* IEEE. 32: 33 - 38

Sandhu, R. S. & Samarati, P. (1994). Access Control: Principle and Practice. *IEEE Communications Magazine,* IEEE. 32: 40 - 48

Schonberg, D. & Kirovski, D. (2004). Fingerprinting and Forensic Analysis of Mutimedia. *Media Management.* New York, USA, ACM

Stallings, W. (2006). *Cryptography and Network Security,* Pearson Prentice Hall.

Tolone, W., Ahn, G.-J., Pai, T. & Hong, S.-P. (2005). "Access Control in Collaborative Systems." *ACM Computing Surveys* 37(1): 29 - 41.

Tyrväinen, P. (2005) "Concepts and a Design for Fair Use and Privacy in DRM." *D-Lib Magazine* 11(2), February 2005, http://www.dlib.org/dlib/february05/tyrvainen/02tyrvainen.html.

Winslett, M., Ching, N., Jones, V. & Slepchin, I. (1997). Assuring Security and Privacy for Digital Library Transactions on the Web: Client and Server Security Policies. *IEEE International Forum on Research and Technology Advances in Digital Libraries (ADL).* Washington, DC, IEEE: 140 - 151

Part 3

Promotion and Evaluation

9

Institutional Repositories: Facilitating Structure, Collaborations, Scholarly Communications, and Institutional Visibility

Liauw Toong Tjiek (Aditya Nugraha)
Petra Christian University
Indonesia

1. Introduction

The advancement of information and communication technology (ICT) - Internet in particular - has caused enormous changes in the world we are living today. Many things are not what they used to be decades, or even years ago. Imagine how we communicated and shared information in the fifties, when computers were still 'archaic' and the Internet was still in its inception stage. Compare that to the numerous communication gadgets and the information overload that we have today. All those changes happened in only a little over fifty years.

Libraries as information providers have also undergone massive changes due to their close association to the way people communicate, collect, manage, use, and share information. Any advancement in ICT will have direct and indirect impacts on the ways libraries provide their collections and services to their user communities and society in general. Some advancements might be welcome by libraries. Others might be perceived as threats to the existence of (traditional) libraries since they are perceived as 'things' that would cause (traditional) libraries to become obsolete, or at least redundant, amidst the new emerging technologies. Some have also caused mixed reactions among librarians, who might 'love' and 'hate' them at the same time. Librarians usually love advancements in ICT since they can help tremendously in the librarians' efforts to fulfill the information needs of their users. However librarians might also notice that many (or most?) of their traditional roles as librarians have been, or will be, taken away from them by those advancements.

Digital libraries (DLs), which include all of its variants such as institutional repositories (IRs), is one of the most important changes in libraries triggered by advancements in ICT. DLs have caused fundamental changes in the way libraries operate. It has also challenged the traditional roles of libraries and compelled them to redefine their roles in this new environment. It is in this context that discussions in this chapter will proceed.

Discussions in this chapter are the results of the expansions and 'conversations' from several of my previous journal articles on IRs. However they will take into account as much as possible and where appropriate, recent developments and discussions about IRs. The discussions will also use Desa Informasi (Information Village) - an institutional repositories project at Petra Christian University (PCU) Library in Surabaya, Indonesia - as a study case. The project is not intended to serve as an example of a success in IRs implementation. In fact, it is still far from an ideal implementation of IRs. It is being used solely for the purpose of sharing experiences gained from its execution. Naturally, perspectives raised in the discussion will be of an academic librarian in a developing country. The environment, where the project is being carried out - a medium-sized private university with mostly undergraduate students - will certainly offers certain influences into the discussions as well.

2. ICT Advancements and the future of libraries

The rapid developments of ICT since the birth of computers and the Internet has contributed so much in changing the way we live our daily life. They affect the way we do things, which includes the way we do our jobs. They even affect the way we relate to one another in terms of personal relationships, as well as professional ones. Almost everything we do in daily basis has something to do with ICT. It ranges from simple stand-alone applications to collaborative and networked systems. Nowadays it's almost unimaginable to write an article without the help of a word processor application, online dictionary or thesaurus, reference management application, and online journal databases. All these advancements have offered invaluable help for people from any professions in terms of working more effectively and productively.

Some ICT advancements however can cause fundamental changes in the traditional roles and functions of certain professions. They fundamentally alter the ways in which people or institutions provide products and services. Libraries - especially academic libraries - and their librarians have been living through these inevitable, yet often subtle, transformations. Nowadays most librarians are familiar with - or at least aware of - approval plans, selector services, new acquisitions of library materials with embedded electronic bibliographic records, copy cataloging, self-check-in/out, Internet search engines, virtual reference services, etc. All these roles and/or functions (acquisition, cataloging, reference, etc.) were traditionally the domains of (local) librarians. Local librarians used to have the authority over or in charge of performing these roles and/or functions. However the new environment affected or created by ICT advancements has created new 'arrangements', where these basic roles and/or functions are gradually being taken over by ICT, or at least transferred to other institutions outside the libraries (Liauw, 2006b). In short, traditional roles and/or functions of librarians are being challenged by the rapid technological changes, which usually also leads to social changes.

Librarians need to 'redefine' their roles and/or functions in the new landscape of the future information society. Davenport stated something that I believe is a good response to the challenge. She suggested that librarians should have "expanded, more collaborative roles in the creation and dissemination of knowledge," which will empower (academic) libraries to assume new role and/or function as learning space instead of information storehouse (Davenport, 2006). It is now up to librarians on how to assume this 'new' role and/or function in the new landscape.

Digital libraries (DLs) and/or institutional repositories (IRs) offer opportunities for librarians and libraries to re-assert their influence in the creation and dissemination of knowledge. DLs/IRs is a strategic move for libraries to maintain their relevance in the new landscape of ICT-savvy society. However before going into any further discussions, we need to be on the same page on what we call digital libraries (DLs) and/or institutional repositories (IRs).

3. Institutional repositories and desa informasi

IRs is one of the relatively new terms generated by advancements in ICT, one that needs to be defined to enable us to proceed with our discussion. One of the pioneers in IRs - Clifford Lynch - gave one of the most fundamental definitions of IRs:

> *"a university-based institutional repository is a set of services that a university offers to the members of its community for the management and dissemination of digital materials created by the institution and its community members. It is most essentially an organizational commitment to the stewardship of these digital materials, including long-term preservation where appropriate, as well as organization and access or distribution." (Lynch, 2003)*

It is worth to mention specifically that Lynch defined IRs as "a set of services" instead of merely digital contents. Lynch also sees "institutional repositories as a species of digital library than a publishing platform," (Poynder, 2006) which is a sufficient ground for me to conclude that "the terms IRs and DLs ... [are] interchangeable" (Liauw, 2006a). Lynch's definition - "a set of services" - suggests his far reaching look into the future. However for the sake of flow of discussion, let's talk first about (digital) contents of IRs.

There are several different views on what IRs should contain. These different views don't necessarily contradict one another. They rather define IRs contents from different scopes and perspectives, which in my opinion can complement one another. McDowell gave a more technical classification of IRs contents by stating:

> *"IR contents were classified into the following types: ETDs; e-prints (pre- or post- print articles); working papers and technical reports; conference proceedings and presentations; e-journals and e-books; learning objects; multimedia files (digital audio/video); datasets; pictures (images); digitized archival documents and university records (historical texts and primary sources); non-scholarly institutional publications; undergraduate student work; graduate student work (non-ETD); and course content (syllabi, assignments, lectures)." (McDowell, 2007)*

Crow defined IRs contents more concisely as "scholarly; produced, submitted, or sponsored by an institution's faculty (and, optionally, students), or other authorized agents; non-ephemeral; and licensable in perpetuity" (Crow, 2002a). In terms of contents of IRs, Lynch suggested that:

> *"a mature and fully realized institutional repository will contain the intellectual works of faculty and students – both research and teaching materials – and also documentation of the activities of the institution itself in the form of records of events and performance and of the ongoing intellectual life of the institution." (Lynch, 2003)*

It is interesting to notice that Lynch's definition above doesn't limit IRs contents to "the intellectual *works* of faculty and students - both research and teaching materials" (emphasis added) only. Instead it also encompasses "documentation of the *activities* of the institution itself in the form of records of *events* and *performance* and of the ongoing intellectual *life* of the institution" (emphasis added).

Desa Informasi (DI) adopts Lynch's definition for IRs contents and assumes that Crow's and McDowell's definitions as "subsets of Lynch's" (Liauw, 2006a) and summarizes them into the characteristic of "locally-produced" contents. Desa Informasi then expands the definition to also include contents that have "features of local entities" (Liauw, 2006b). Using parallel terminologies from the traditional (hardcopy) collections, the "locally-produced" contents are the equivalence of "grey literature", while contents with "features of local entities" are the equivalence of "local collections" (see "Harrod's librarians' glossary and reference book"). The term "local content" is a familiar term among Indonesian librarians in defining both characteristics, and it will be used in this chapter to refer to contents with both characteristics.

DI started off as a limited-in-scope of theses digitization project to address the physical space limitation of PCU Library, which then evolved into an institutional repositories project. DI utilizes a custom-made web-based application called iSPEKTRA to manage digital objects using modified Dublin Core metadata set (http://dewey.petra.ac.id/dgt_directory.php). Although "interoperability on a metadata level has clearly been the most active area in digital repositories ... [and] spurred by the Open Access movement, numerous repositories exposed their metadata through standard protocols," (Aschenbrenner et al., 2008) iSPEKTRA has not yet addressed the interoperability issues in terms of compliance to Open Archives Initiatives - Protocol for Metadata Harvesting (OAI-PMH). It is a crucial issue that is being addressed along with the development of the new version of iSPEKTRA.

DI divides its collections into Themes instead of one big collection in order to create 'added value' to the collections. The main consideration is that "having several smaller thematic collections of interest to the communities is far better than having one big collection consisting of just about anything people can throw into the collection without any defining 'character' that binds them together" (Liauw, 2006a). The current DI collections are as follows: (Liauw, 2005)

- *Digital Theses: Petra Christian University students' theses collection in digital format; mostly PDF documents. There are also an increasing number of multimedia resources generated by the students of Faculty of Art and Design.*
- *eDIMENSI: digital version of articles from DIMENSI, scientific journals published by various academic departments of Petra Christian University.*
- *Petra@rt Gallery: works of art by campus communities (mostly students' works) or works of art that are exhibited/displayed at Petra Christian University campus; mostly photographs and digitized-images. The collection contains wonderful visual resources, capturing and immortalizing the intrinsic knowledge and values of art in the works documented. Some of the wonderful themes are the Visual Poetry, Café Décor, Chairs of Indonesia, Destination Branded, Nusantara Bersatu (United Archipelago), etc.*
- *Petra iPoster: posters (with visual design elements) of events or issues related to Petra Christian University.*
- *Petra Chronicle: historical documents related to Petra Christian University.*

Fig. 1. An old photo from *Surabaya Memory*

The collection themes above clearly represent the "locally-produced" definition of DI contents. One other collection that represents the definition of "features of local entities" is the Surabaya Memory collection. It contains digital heritage resources on Surabaya city. Another newly-planned collection will be the "Chinese in Indonesia" digital collection, which is intended to supplement the special collection of the same name (in physical/ hardcopy format). This latest collection (still in planning stage as of the time of this book's publication) is created as support system for the newly-established Center for Chinese Indonesian Studies at Petra Christian Universities.

4. Facilitating structure amidst information overload and chaos

As with most IRs, "student work accounts for the largest percentage of items" in DI. Digital Theses is the largest collection in DI so far. This phenomenon happens in many institutions implementing IRs since "ETDs [Electronic Theses and Dissertations] are simply the lowest hanging fruit, and new submission batches can generally be counted on each semester" (McDowell, 2007). ETDs are also the 'preferred' contents since they "raise the profiles of the students who author them, the faculty and departments who foster them, and the institutions that provide them to the world" (Lippincott, 2006). The following tables will give readers a glimpse of DI collections.

Collection Name/Theme	# of Records	# of Digital Objects	Total Size (bytes)
Digital Theses	12,618	134,268	170,284,316,475
eDIMENSI	809	809	282,689,311
Petra iPoster	120	244	365.416.831
Petra@rt Gallery	261	854	4,132,526,401
Surabaya Memory	258	657	402,415,694
Petra Chronicle	180	559	2,489,567,862
TOTAL	**14,246**	**137,391**	**177,956,932,574**

Table 1. Breakdown of Desa Informasi's Digital Collections by Themes (as of Aug 31, 2010). Source: Petra Christian University Library - 2009/2010 Annual Report

Collection Name	# of Digital Objects				
	Text	Image	Moving Image/Video	Animation	Audio, etc.
Digital Theses	115,830	18,228	119	24	67
eDIMENSI	809	0	0	0	0
Petra iPoster	0	244	0	0	0
Petra@rt Gallery	57	797	0	0	0
Surabaya Memory	25	632	0	0	0
Petra Chronicle	160	399	0	0	0
TOTAL	116,881	20,300	119	24	67

Table 2. Breakdown of Desa Informasi's Digital Collections by Types of Document (as of Aug 31, 2010). Source: Petra Christian University Library - 2009/2010 Annual Report

In their article titled "Size isn't everything: Sustainable repositories as evidenced by sustainable deposit profiles," Carr & Brody stipulated that "sustained deposits" is a more accurate measurement than merely the size of IRs, since it reflects "community engagement." They stated that "one of the measures of repository success should therefore be the university community's take-up of these services" (Carr & Brody, 2007). They warned against using the size of IRs as the only indication of 'healthy' IRs. Referring to Davis and Connolly's 2007 article titled Institutional repositories: Evaluating the reasons for non-use of Cornell University's installation of DSpace, they noticed that "a repository can exhibit respectable overall growth that is attributable mainly to special-case batch imports" (Carr & Brody, 2007). Along this line of thinking, we should then analyze the deposit profile of DI to see any indication of its 'health.' Table 3 shows the growth of digital resources in DI from 2005 up to 2010. Carr & Brody used *daily* deposit profile in their survey of IRs by utilizing ROAR registry of Institutional Repositories. However since such data is not available for DI, Table 3 uses *annual* deposit profile instead.

	2005/2006	2006/2007	2007/2008	2008/2009	2009/2010
# of Records	3,178	5,025	7,697	10,857	14,246
Growth from Previous Year	N/A	1,847	2,672	3,160	3,389
# of Digital Objects	N/A	39,438	68,510	98,092	137,391
Growth from Previous Year	N/A	N/A	29,072	29,582	39,299

Table 3. Growth of Desa Informasi's Digital Collections (2005 - 2010).
Source: Petra Christian University Library - 2005/2006 to 2009/2010 Annual Reports

We can conclude from Table 3 that DI has a 'healthy' deposit profile since the growth of its contents is sustainable. Table 3 shows a steady growth in # of Records and Digital Objects every year. It is an indication of community engagement in supplying resources for DI.

We can also conclude from our discussion so far that higher education institutions produced intellectual works in numerous subjects and formats besides the obvious scholarly works (theses and dissertations, journal articles, and research reports). Student works usually comprise the bulk of the works.

Unfortunately most lecturers and academic departments don't have the 'sensitivity' or the expertise needed to identify these student works as intellectual outputs that can be re-used as learning resources. They don't know how to collect, organize, manage, and re-use/serve these digital objects as learning resources. Davenport observed that "[academic departments in universities] lack the organization and structures that would allow campus departments to easily share such information" (Davenport, 2006). Based on my observations, most faculties only keep the digital version of the resources on CD Roms and stack them in cabinets. This practice will consequently make the resources hard to be found and re-used. It's as if faculties are lost amidst the chaotic and unstructured information overload.

Academic libraries could and should jump into the scene to introduce some sense of structure into the seemingly chaotic information resources produced by students (and faculties). IRs can be introduced as an elegant solution for the academic departments' need for organizing these works and re-use them as learning resources. JISC (Joint Information Systems Committee) suggested this approach when it reported that IRs "are increasingly expected to act as corporate information management tools (records management and content management systems) and data sharing platforms (e.g. for the re-use of research data and learning objects)" (Poynder, 2006). This is one of the variations of IRs implementations (Furlough, 2010) and a common approach in Indonesian higher education libraries. However libraries should not just offer the IRs platform as a solution and then leave the academic departments, faculties, and students on their own to figure out how to self-archive (uploading their works into the IRs) and help them organize those resources. Based on an article by Erickson, Rutherford, & Elliott (2008), Salo warned against this approach when she reminded the readers that "the term 'self-archiving' has been taken too literal, abandoning faculty to their uncertainties and incapacities" (Salo, 2008).

Librarians should actively assume their 'new' role as IRs managers to increase the probability of a successful implementation of IRs by providing needed assistance to students and (especially) faculties in populating IRs. Libraries should do extra efforts to assist the academic departments, faculties, and students to get their works into IRs. However in their efforts to populate IRs, it is of a strategic importance for libraries to always present the issue as the academic departments and lecturers' interests, not merely the libraries' (Liauw, 2006a).

Mediated-deposit services was the method of choice for content acquisition for DI since it was formally launched in 2005. Local conditions required it and the fact that librarians would be the ones in charge of managing the contents - including the metadata - sounded more promising in the long run. The approach also asserts the role of librarians in providing some sense of structure into the whole collections. This choice turns out to be the right one since it works so far, while the alternative doesn't look too promising. In her article Salo stated that "the notion that faculty members [(and students for that matter)] will actually push buttons and type metadata in order to deposit materials into IRs is an *article of faith* among repository-software developers. In practice, however, most deposits are third-party mediated, many by librarians, some by support staff or IT personnel" (Salo, 2008, emphasis added). Salo's assertions and experience in DI prove that although mediated-deposit services might sound more 'expensive' and labor-intensive, it does offer more sustainability for IRs and more visibility to the role of librarians in the overall landscape of university-wide information management/organization.

Fig. 2. Batik pattern in *PetraArt Gallery*

Content acquisition strategy is different from one collection to the others, based on the nature of the contents. For example, the content acquisition for Digital Theses is pretty straight forward since it 'piggybacks' on the university-wide theses deposit policy, which mandates all graduating students to deposit their theses to the Library in hardcopy and softcopy format. Contents for Petra@rt Gallery on the other hand are much harder to acquire since they are produced sporadically without any fixed-patterns. However it is crucial that content acquisition process establishes some kind of connections to the "administrative systems of the university or the local communities it serves" as Liauw suggested, since "otherwise the collection [(acquisition)] process will be too massive to manage sporadically and the sustainability of the flow of resources from the communities into the IRs will depend largely on fluctuating individual interests" (Liauw, 2006a). Contents for eDIMENSI are acquired through formal cooperation with the university's research center, which acts as the publisher for DIMENSI journals. This approach ensures 100% incorporation of all articles published by the center into DI. Petra iPoster provides valuable lessons in its content acquisition effort and deserves a longer description. It is a common practice in Indonesian universities for the Public Relations office to be in charge for approving posters that will be posted on campus premises. We would have thought that a formal cooperation with the Public Relations office would guarantee 100% acquisition of posters at PCU by requiring poster-issuing units to provide the digital version of the submitted posters. However experience showed that it isn't as simple as that initial assumption. User behaviors play critical roles in this matter. Poster-issuing units usually don't have the digital version since they outsource the design and printing process to outside vendors. It requires extra time and effort to get them from the vendors. Other reasons might simply be the reluctance of the poster-issuing unit to spend more time preparing the digital copy to be submitted to the Public Relations office, especially when people are usually under a tight deadline to put the posters up. A request to provide an extra hardcopy poster as an alternative, instead of the digital version, was not successful either. We then noticed that another unit - the Campus Facility Management unit - is in charge for taking down 'expired' posters all across campus based on the expiry date stamped on each poster by the Public Relations office. We saw it as an opportunity to collect the posters for inclusion into Petra iPoster. So, instead of discarding the posters we merely ask the Campus Facility Management unit to send the posters to the Library. This never-thought-of-before approach proves to work well since it does not require any - or at least too much - disruption in the unit's daily operations. Aschenbrenner et al. suggested this approach by saying that "repositories [should] become a natural part of the user's daily work environment" (Aschenbrenner et al., 2008). The authors

Fig. 3. Sample Poster from *Petra iPoster*

were referring to the overall aspects of IRs but the principal can be applied in a narrower scope to content acquisitions in IRs. We don't encounter too many difficulties in acquiring contents for Petra Chronicle since most historical materials related to PCU will be deposited to the Library. The Library has had supports from various parties in developing Petra Chronicle and Petra iPoster since the personal nature of the resources, which have certain appeals to the nostalgic aspects of various stakeholders. The support only increases with the upcoming 50th Anniversary of PCU in 2011.

Fig. 4. Surabaya Memory Exhibition in A Mall (2007)

In acquiring contents for IRs, librarians should actively come to the academic departments, lecturers, and students as someone who is offering an information/resources management system to address their needs for organizing faculty and student works. IRs can be offered as the solution that will help in introducing and facilitating structure amidst the bulk and numerous different types of faculty and (especially) student works. Librarians will then be able to re-assert their role as information managers for their campus communities.

Surabaya Memory (SM) presents another challenge in its content acquisition due to the nature of its contents that features "local entities," which translates into public participation in the content development. Unlike contents for other collections in DI that are locally produced, contents for SM is developed by involving the campus communities as well as general public. There has been some level of public participation from individuals and organizations that lent their personal or institutional collections relating to the heritage and history of Surabaya city. However the current level of public participation is still not as well as expected. Liauw observed that the two main reasons for this lack of participation are "the lack of information-sharing culture and the sentimental/personal [or even financial] values of heritage-related resources to their owners or copyright holders." Bluntly put, "some people have been making money out of selling duplicates of old photographs and manuscripts" (Liauw, 2010). On the other side, some individuals have been spending a lot of money to acquire old photographs and manuscripts into their personal collections. The money spent in acquiring those resources has become a big obstacle to share the resources - not even their digitized version - with the society. It's also a common knowledge that "big collectors tend to collect for their *own* enjoyment" (Liauw, 2010, emphasis added). Facing such challenges, Liauw suggested two strategies to help alleviate the problem. The first strategy is to collaborate with big collectors to hold exhibitions. When we have gained their trust it usually (but not always) is easier to solicit their participations by contributing some of their collections to SM. The second strategy is to "network with other heritage-based organizations to identify individuals with possession of cultural heritage materials" (Liauw, 2010). I would like to also add that it is very important to show to stakeholders (especially those big collectors) that the shared resources will benefit the society.

Although content acquisition itself has posed many challenges, it is essential that we do not view any IRs projects only as a matter of populating it with the desired contents. McDowell offered another perspective on IRs. He offered a definition from functional point of view, which defines IRs as: (McDowell, 2007)

1. *"an institution-wide service. Faculty members of every academic unit must be able to submit, regardless of departmental affiliation [no use or subject limitations].*
2. *intended to collect, preserve, and provide access to, among other things, faculty scholarly output in multiple formats.*
3. *must be actively taking submissions."*

Although DI does fulfill the above definition and has managed to reach some level of sustainability in content acquisition, it still falls short in providing services and interactions/ collaborations to its users, capitalizing on the acquired contents. Regarding future directions for IRs, Furlough suggested that IRs (contents) should be "integrated into instruction, reference and collection development" (Furlough, 2010).

Based on the discussions above IRs, such as DI, has managed to fulfill its role to "serve as tangible indicators of a university's quality and to demonstrate the scientific, societal, and economic relevance of its research activities." Let's now examine the successfulness of IRs in fulfilling its other role to "provide a critical component in reforming the system of scholarly communication ... [and to] reasserts control over scholarship by the academy, increases competition and reduces the monopoly power of journals" (Crow, 2002b).

5. Facilitating scholarly communications

Although reforming scholarly communication system has been one of the "two strategic issues" (Crow, 2002b) that IRs try to address, McDowell concluded that "IR has been relatively unsuccessful in fulfilling [that] 'original' role." This assertion was supported by his survey, which found that "the percentage of peer-reviewed works - pre- and post-prints, e-journal articles, and e-books - is considerably [small], around 13%" (McDowell, 2007). It is obvious IRs has been facing serious challenges in the scholarly communication arena.

There are several reasons why IRs is not the preferred choice for disseminating researches. Aschenbrenner et al. observed that "journal publication patterns are already well in place and they are often (rightly or wrongly) considered the most reliable route to scientific credit" (Aschenbrenner et al., 2008). Foster added to that observation by identifying the current established system that "rewards faculty members with tenure and promotion based on their success at getting published in respected scholarly journals" as the main reason why "professors do not have much incentive to put their material in an experimental online archive" (Foster, 2004). There are also some faculties "who believe that self-archiving [in

IRs] may threaten their rights over their work, their relationship with their favorite publishers, or their status in their disciplinary communities." This trend has led Salo to assert that "libraries whose support for repositories rests purely on hopes of collecting peer-reviewed literature would be well-advised not to bother with them" (Salo, 2008).

Another challenge in the scholarly communication arena comes from the fact that most IRs are functioning only as digital resources management system, without "the more complex services on which users [authors or faculties] depend" (Chavez, et al., 2007). IRs might be useful and/or powerful for organizing and managing digital resources, but "[authors] want something that will support the authoring process, not just the finished product" (Foster, 2004). IRs also needs to strive to "become a natural part of the user's [or authors'] daily work environment" (Aschenbrenner et al., 2008). This might explain why IRs can achieve relative successes in acquiring contents from students, but not from faculties or peer-reviewed publication authors. Salo noticed that slight exceptions might apply for "younger scholars [or faculties, who] may [still] be attracted to self-archiving as a way to game a prestige system otherwise stacked against them" (Salo, 2008).

Besides all the shortcomings of IRs in the scholarly communication arena, I believe IRs has managed to reduce the total monopoly of conventional journal publishers. Many journal publishers have revised their publishing and copyright policies to allow authors to self-archive in institutional or subject repositories. The new policies wouldn't have had materialized had it not been because of open access movement (or spirit) embodied in IRs. There are currently open access (book and journal) publishers offering alternatives to conventional publishers. More and more universities and research institutions are jumping into the open access (and IRs) bandwagon by instituting Open Access Mandates in their institutions. Although in its current state IRs might not achieve big success in (radically) reforming scholarly communication, I believe that IRs has contributed - to certain extent - the efforts in "advancing the positive transformation of scholarly communication *over the long term*" (Crow, 2002b, emphasis added).

The same challenge is faced by DI in acquiring journal articles from faculties. DI - as an IRs system - has not yet accommodated any authoring or collaborative process. In its current state, DI acquires contents for eDIMENSI (scientific journal articles) collections through a formal cooperation with the Research Center at PCU. The Research Center is the formal agency at PCU that manages the review, editorial, and publication processes of DIMENSI journals using the Open Journal System (OJS). The cooperation allows the Library to batch download the newly published articles and feed them into DI. It might be the future direction to merge the two systems into a single platform, which will streamline much of the processes involved in both entities (Research Center and Library) and open up opportunities to create new collaborative features in the future.

6. Facilitating collaborations

An important aspect of IRs that is often overlooked is its potential as a collaborative platform for the campus communities. If we agree that IRs is, as Lynch stated, "a set of services that a university [library] offers to the members of its *community* for the management and dissemination of digital materials created by the *institution* and its *community* members" (Lynch, 2003, emphasis added) then academic libraries have an invaluable asset in their hands. This asset has a functions and/or roles that span traditional boundaries of campus communities, units, and academic disciplines. Due to this nature, academic libraries that implement and manage IRs will soon discover themselves introduced to a rich variety of local contents produced by different campus communities covering a wide range of academic disciplines.

Fig. 5. A Thematic Onsite Exhibition Featuring Photography Documentary of Sedulur Sikep Ethnic Group in Central Java, Indonesia (2006)

Cross-pollination or cross-fertilization of knowledge is a natural consequence of exposures to such rich and diverse local contents. Contents produced by a campus community can be re-used as learning resources by other campus communities. Marketing or promotional efforts can be conducted by academic libraries to introduce these local contents to all academic departments and provide insights on possibilities of their uses for each department. Libraries can also expand features in their IRs to be able to link to e-learning systems (such as Moodle) used on campus. The linking will enable students and faculties to access our local contents directly from the e-learning systems that they are using for teaching and learning, thus increasing exposures of the contents to various campus communities. These efforts will expose local contents from a specific campus community to a wider audience.

Thematic exhibitions will also provide rich exposures for students, who otherwise would have been 'confined' to their particular field of studies. The experience will enrich students' learning experience. Thematic exhibitions of local contents can sometimes create unique opportunities for inter-disciplinary conversations. Liauw told of an interesting story as an example of how thematic exhibitions can create such conversations. A thematic onsite exhibition featuring photography documentary of Sedulur Sikep - an ethnic minority in Central Java, Indonesia - was held in 2006, displaying works of a student from Visual Communication Design Department. The exhibition sparked interests from other academic disciplines to conduct other researches on the ethnic minority. An English Department faculty was interested to conduct further study on the linguistic aspects of the ethnic minority. Another faculty from Interior Design Department expressed interests in doing further studies on the ornamental design on the ethnic's settlements (Liauw, 2006b). This example shows that academic libraries should treat their local contents and exhibition spaces as assets to be used to facilitate collaborations and conversations across academic disciplines.

Fig. 6. School Children Playing Information Scavenger Game at Surabaya Memory Exhibition (2007)

Fig. 7. Surabaya Memory Heritage Walk (2007)

Wider collaborations among different campus units and academic departments can be facilitated when academic libraries capitalize on their local contents in IRs to reach out to the society. Academic libraries can create and carry out various programs and activities jointly with other campus communities. Surabaya Memory (SM) provided a good example on this aspect. Digital resources in SM have been used as part of the teaching and learning process by Architecture Department, Tourism and Leisure Management Department, and Hotel Management Department. However SM has also become a collaborative platform for PCU Library and other campus units to reach out to the society in Surabaya city. Every May (anniversary of Surabaya) SM conducts thematic exhibitions in a mall in Surabaya. During the exhibition, which usually lasts four to ten days, various competitions, cultural performances, and heritage walks are held to celebrate the city's anniversary. All these programs and activities have been made possible by the collaborations between the Library and various academic departments. The Event Management course at Hotel Management Department has been using SM as real world projects for its students. The students are assigned to help the Library in preparing and supervising the exhibition, looking for sponsors, creating events and performances during the exhibition, etc. The Cultural Tourism course at Tourism and Leisure Management Department has also been using SM as real world projects for its students by conducting heritage walks throughout the year for campus communities as well as the general public. IRs can also serve as collaborative platform to build networks with various parties outside the university boundaries. SM has been functioning as a networking tool for PCU. Various co-operations and collaborations have been initiated between PCU communities and outside parties through SM. Furthermore SM has served as a common platform for campus communities at PCU to reach out to the society.

It is obvious from the discussions above that IRs can facilitate collaborations if academic libraries are willing to go beyond merely populating their IRs with digital contents. Collaborations with various campus communities will strengthen the libraries' roles on campus and help libraries tremendously in advocating their services to the campus communities. Libraries can even increase the institutional visibility of the whole institution with their IRs projects.

7. Facilitating institutional visibility

Academic libraries have always contributed to the institutional visibility of their host institutions. They have unconsciously played 'silent' marketing role, promoting their host institutions in the process. Their unique nature as public spaces has allowed them to be visited by various members of the community, inside and outside of campus boundaries. Libraries are the very few institutions in the world where ordinary people would feel comfortable to visit even though they don't have any membership or institutional affiliation. Academic libraries should capitalize on this aspect to facilitate institutional visibility. Before the advent of the Internet and DLs/IRs, this would mean providing their traditional collections and services, and physical spaces to the campus communities and the society.

The Internet, open access movement, and DLs/IRs have provided new opportunities for academic libraries to raise their contributions to the facilitating of institutional visibility of their host institutions. Digital contents in IRs should be provided freely to enable a wider dissemination to the global audience, which in turn will translate into a significant increase in institutional visibility. There is no longer any physical barrier that limits the scope of the dissemination of the IRs' contents as in physical library collections. This is also the experience of DI. Table 4 shows the web access profile for "petra.ac.id" domain (accessed on September 30, 2010 from http://www.alexa.com). The table shows that http://digilib.petra.ac.id (the server that stores the digital local content of DI) and

Where Visitors Go on Petra.ac.id

Subdomain	Percent of Site Traffic
digilib.petra.ac.id	59.6%
dewey.petra.ac.id	20.5%
petra.ac.id	5.1%
genesis.petra.ac.id	4.3%
careercenter.petra.ac.id	4.3%
puslit2.petra.ac.id	1.8%
faculty.petra.ac.id	1.1%
fportfolio.petra.ac.id	1.1%
it.petra.ac.id	0.7%
puslit.petra.ac.id	0.7%
communication.petra.ac.id	0.4%
john.petra.ac.id	0.4%

Table 4. Domain Profile for "petra.ac.id" from Alexa
Source: http://www.alexa.com/siteinfo/petra.ac.id

http://dewey.petra.ac.id (the online catalog of PCU Library that store the metadata of the digital resources stored in DI) are the two top sub-domains that generate 80.1% of the traffic to "petra.ac.id" domain. (years) age range and mostly browse the Internet from school or home. This is a very significant contribution that PCU Library - through DI - has made to the overall 'Internet marketing' of the university. The access statistics from Alexa is confirmed by the weblog of the DI server (http://digilib.petra.ac.id) as shown in Table 5.

More opportunities to facilitate institutional visibility can be gained when we share metadata of our digital contents with other IRs. This can be achieved by utilizing the OAI-PMH or even a 'low-tech' approach by exporting the metadata and exchange them using spreadsheet application such as Microsoft Excel. This approach is being utilized by DI while an upgrade to an OAI-PMH compliant system is still in progress. The Indonesian Ministry of National Education under its Directorate General of Higher Education has launched a collaborative program to create a 'union catalog' of metadata for local contents from higher education institutions across Indonesia called Garuda (http://garuda.dikti.go.id). Networking opportunities like this provide increased visibility of our IRs and host institution.

Rankings by independent organizations that measure websites and online resources provide additional incentives for developing IRs. One of them is the Ranking Web of World Universities (http://www.webometrics.info) that measures world universities' commitment to open access by looking at digital contents on their websites. Using certain methodology it has managed to rank world universities based on several parameters. DI opens up its digital contents to be indexed by Google, which has enabled Webometrics to measure the "Size" and "Rich Files" (see http://www.webometrics.info/methodology.html) stored in DI.

Month	Unique Visitors	Number of Visits	Pages	Hits	Bandwidth
Sep-09	160,097	355,177	3,125,802	6,686,167	191.36 GB
Oct 2009	224,082	607,877	5,305,997	11,296,525	315.91 GB
Nov 2009	215,583	563,184	5,005,537	10,664,877	325.83 GB
Dec 2009	201,370	510,646	4,581,746	9,751,878	283.93 GB
Jan-10	212,415	538,796	4,538,643	9,769,348	295.05 GB
Feb-10	197,727	450,327	4,293,240	8,789,435	360.64 GB
Mar-10	247,483	615,001	5,058,876	10,573,688	431.89 GB
Apr-10	237,076	577,638	4,845,910	10,138,585	454.83 GB
May 2010	207,424	484,272	4,225,088	8,831,741	436.39 GB
Jun-10	199,156	454,782	3,975,456	8,281,444	496.72 GB
Jul-10	174,474	360,614	3,175,481	6,503,735	398.71 GB
Aug 2010	157,810	317,685	2,804,185	5,897,145	338.25 GB
	2,434,697	5,835,999	50,935,961	107,184,568	4,329,51 GB

Table 5. Web Access Statistics of Desa Informasi (Sep 2009 - Aug 2010)
Source: http://digilib.petra.ac.id/awstats/awstats.pl

Webometrics rankings are important for us in Indonesia since they are being used by Directorate General of Higher Education as one of several metrics to measure performances of Indonesian higher education institutions. PCU has been ranked #5 along with big state universities in Indonesia. A good rank will surely contribute to the increased visibility of the host institutions. This fact strengthens the assertion that IRs serve as one of "meaningful indicators of an institution's academic quality … thus increasing the institution's visibility, status, and public value" (Crow, 2002b).

8. Conclusion

Advancement in ICT has reshaped the landscape of the future for many professions. Librarian as a profession and libraries as institutions are not immune to changes brought by ICT. Many of their traditional functions and/or roles have been altered or even taken away from them by technology, thus librarians and libraries –especially academic libraries - need to 'redefine' their functions and/or roles to stay relevant in the new landscape of the future.

Institutional repositories (IRs) - as a species of digital libraries (DLs) - provides opportunities for academic libraries to re-assert their roles in the communities they serve. Through IRs academic libraries can strengthen their roles as managers of institutional information assets and re-use them as learning resources for the benefits of the campus communities.

In their efforts to populate IRs, academic libraries should not leave faculties on their own. Besides providing an IRs application to manage digital contents, libraries should also assist faculties and campus communities in identifying, collecting, and re-using those contents. By doing all these efforts libraries introduce structure into the myriads of digital contents available in or produced by campus communities.

Although in the scholarly communications arena IRs has not yet achieved substantial successes, IRs has managed to at least reduce the total domination of conventional journal publishers. With extra efforts libraries can utilize IRs to facilitate scholarly 'conversations' across different academic disciplines on campus.

By setting goals beyond merely populating IRs, libraries will be able to capitalize on IRs' contents to create various programs and activities that will facilitate and foster collaborations among different campus communities, and between campus communities and the society. IRs can even develop into a common platform for campus communities to reach out to the society.

Amidst the ups and downs of IRs projects in academic libraries across the globe I would like to echo the optimism voiced by Aschenbrenner et al.:

> *"Digital repositories have rapidly become an integral part of higher education and other digital environments. Setbacks with regard to user adoption, and technological dead ends of insular efforts, have not induced a significant dip in the growth of the community. Instead, they have added new perspectives on how repositories can be embedded into their organizational and social contexts." (Aschenbrenner et al., 2008)*

More fundamentally, amidst technological changes and the changing landscape of our profession, I would like to close our discussion by citing one of the fundamental principles of our profession:

> *Underlying the special character of librarianship is not its techniques, but its fundamental values. The significance of librarianship lies not in mastery of sources, organizational skills, or technological competence, but in why librarians perform the functions they do.* (Rubin, 2004, p. 468)

9. References

Aschenbrenner, Andreas et al. (2008). The future of repositories? Patterns for (cross-) repository architectures. *D-Lib Magazine*, 14 (11/12), November/December 2008. Retrieved September 03, 2010 from http://www.dlib.org/dlib/november08/aschenbrenner/11aschenbrenner.html

Carr, Leslie & Brody, Tim. (2007). Size isn't everything: Sustainable repositories as evidenced by sustainable deposit profiles. *D-Lib Magazine*, 13 (7/8), July/August 2007. Retrieved September 03, 2010 from http://www.dlib.org/dlib/july07/carr/07carr.html

Chavez, Robert et al. (2007). Services make the repository. *Journal of Digital Information*, 8(2). Retrieved on September 03, 2010 from http://journals.tdl.org/jodi/article/view/195/179

Crow, Raym. (2002a). *SPARC institutional repository checklist & resource guide.* Washington, D.C.: The Scholarly Publishing & Academic Resources Coalition. Retrieved September 03, 2010, from http://www.arl.org/sparc/bm~doc/IR_Guide_&_Checklist_v1.pdf

Crow, Raym. (2002b) *The Case for Institutional Repositories: A SPARC Position Paper.* Washington, D.C. The Scholarly Publishing & Academic Resources Coalition. Retrieved September 03, 2010 from http:// www.arl.org/sparc/bm~doc/ir_final_release_102.pdf

Davenport, Nancy. (2006). Place as Library? *EDUCAUSE, January/February 2006*. Retrieved September 03, 2010, from http://www.educause.edu/ir/library/pdf/erm0616.pdf

Erickson, J., Rutherford, J., & Elliott, D. (2008) The future of the institutional repository: Making it personal. In *Third International Conference on Open Repositories 2008*. Retrieved April 10, 2008, from http://pubs.or08.ecs.soton.ac.uk/125/

Foster, Andrea L. (2004). *Papers wanted: Online Archives Run by Universities Struggle to Attract Material*. Chronicle of Higher Education, 50 (42), pp. A37-A38.

Furlough, Michael. (2010). *Sepulchres*. Personal blog. Retrieved September 03, 2010, from http://www.personal.psu.edu/mjf25/blogs/on_furlough/2010/05/sepulchres.ht ml

Liauw, Toong Tjiek. (2005). Desa Informasi: Local Content Global Reach. *Proceeding of the 2005 Seminar of the International Council on Archives, Section on University and Research Institution Archives*. Michigan State University, East Lansing, MI - U.S.A. (Sep 6-9, 2005).

Liauw, Toong Tjiek. (2006a). Desa Informasi - The Role of Digital Libraries in the Preservation and Dissemination of Indigenous Knowledge. *International Information and Library Review*, 38(3), pp. 123-131.

Liauw, Toong Tjiek. (2006b). Desa Informasi: A virtual village of 'new' information resources and services. *Program: Electronic Library and Information System*, 41 (3), pp. 276-290.

Liauw, Toong Tjiek. (2010). Surabaya Memory: Opportunities and challenges of open access e-heritage repositories. In *IFLA Satellite Pre-conference*. Mediterranean Agronomic Institute of Chania, Crete - Greece (Aug 6-8, 2010).

Lippincott, Joan K. (2006). Institutional Strategies and Policies for Electronic Theses and Dissertations. *EDUCAUSE Center for Applied Research, 2006(13)*. Retrieved Septermber 03, 2010 from http://www.educause.edu/ir/library/pdf/ERB0613.pdf.

Lynch, Clifford A. (2003). Institutional Repositories: Essential Infrastructure for Scholarship in the Digital Age. *ARL Bimonthly Report*, 226. Mar 26, 2004. Retrieved September 03, 2010 from http:// www.arl.org/bm~doc/br226ir.pdf

McDowell, C. (2007). Evaluating institutional repository deployment in American academe since early 2005: Repositories by the numbers, part 2. *D-Lib Magazine*, 13(9/10). Retrieved September 03, 2010, from http://www.dlib.org/dlib/september07/mcdowell/09mcdowell.html

Poynder, Richard. (2006). *Clear Blue Water*. September 03, 2010. http://dialspace.dial.pipex.com/town/parade/df04/BlueWaterMain.pdf

Rubin, Richard E. (2004). *Foundations of Library and Information Science (2nd Editiion)*. New York: N.Y.

Salo, Dorothea. (2008). Innkeeper at the Roach Motel. *Library Trends*. University of Illinois at Urbana-Champaign. Retrieved September 03, 2010 from HighBeam Research: http://www.highbeam.com/doc/1P3-1661837451.html

10

Developing and Using a Guide to Assess Learning Resource Quality in Educational Digital Libraries

Heather Leary[1], Sarah Giersch[2], Andrew Walker[1] and Mimi Recker[1]
[1]Utah State University,
[2]Columbia University
United States of America

1. Introduction

The democratization of content creation via ubiquitous Internet tools and infrastructure (Anderson, 2006) has fueled an explosion of user-generated digital content in the commercial and educational markets. Federal agencies in the United States, such as the National Science Foundation, are actively seeking ways to integrate teachers and learners into the *education cyber-infrastructure* (Computing Research Association, 2005; Pea et al., 2008). The overall purpose of this education cyberinfrastructure is to connect people with information and with web-based tools to improve productivity, teaching, and learning. By connecting teachers and learners with tools, they become co-creators of educational content.

Educational digital libraries, part of this cyberinfrastructure, have been created as places to deposit and disseminate educational content, which often takes the form of online learning resources of varying levels of granularity. Digital library content can be created easily and deposited rapidly, placing it outside the peer review processes typically employed by publishers and professional societies, but it is unclear whether teachers are using high quality online learning resources in the classroom. To date, educational digital library developers, catalogers, teachers and school administrators have depended on one or a combination of the following proxies to establish an imprimatur of content quality: the reputation and oversight of a funding organization (e.g., the National Science Foundation), the credentials of the content creator (e.g., the National Science Teachers Association), or the collection development policies of specific digital libraries (e.g., the National Science Digital Library or the Digital Library for Earth System Education). However, the definition of "quality"for organizations like those listed above often reflects internal policies and goals, resulting in reviews or judgments that are not comparable across institutions.

Further blurring the boundaries between creator-reviewer, teacher-learner and publisher-consumer, many sites employing user ratings and comment tools, such as YouTube (http://www.youtube.com/), Flickr (http://www.flickr.com/), iTunesU (http://www.apple.com/education/itunes-u/), and ccMixter (http://ccmixter.org/) provide an alternative to the evolving education cyber-infrastructure, creating a rich and diverse environment for disseminating user-generated educational content. Most educational digital libraries do not rely on even a quasi-review for assessing the quality of the content created for, or by, their users as the above sites do. However, in the omnipresent climate of accountability within the U.S. K-12 education system at the federal, state and local levels, education digital libraries are being challenged to prove their value. For these reasons, it is useful, if not necessary, to develop a method to review the quality of online education resources. And, since social networking tools make sharing a by-product of content creation, it is necessary to develop a standardized set of measures that can be employed across a range of education digital library environments while leveraging existing and emerging social and technical networks to enrich, facilitate, and automate the review process.

This chapter describes the development of a guide to assess the quality of educational learning resources within the context of the Instructional Architect (http://ia.usu.edu), a web-based content-authoring tool for K-12 teachers in the United States. We describe the motivation for developing this Quality Guide, the process for creating it by synthesizing the rubrics of other education digital libraries, and the results of testing and using the Guide with K-12 teachers in the context of professional development workshops. Analyses of its usability and reliability indicate that the Quality Guide influences how teachers design instructional activities using online learning resources. But, defining "quality" remains a difficult task since the perception of quality is dependent on a reviewer's, or user's, purpose for the learning resources and context of their use.

2. Background

Over the past 10-15 years, as part of the many global initiatives created to provide access to online educational resources, educational digital libraries in the United States have been developed for K-12 and higher education audiences with support from state and federal agencies: (e.g., the Department of Education; the National Science Foundation), from private foundations (e.g., the William and Flora Hewlett Foundation; the George Lucas Education Foundation), and from universities (e.g. MIT). These institutions funded projects create, or provide access to, curricula that integrates online educational resources and training programs to empower teachers to incorporate learning technologies into their daily preparation and practice and, ultimately, to design their own learning resources. Educational digital library developers have gathered online learning resources of varying levels of granularity (e.g., from images to entire lessons) and of varying sources of authorship (e.g., grant-funded subject matter experts; K-12 teachers; graduate students) into central online portals to enable discovery and re-use by other educators.

While traditional libraries use collection development plans to guide acquisitions that are based on knowledge of their users, educational digital libraries acquire resources created as a result of projects with museums, practicing teachers, researchers and from Internet users. The challenge is to balance collecting and providing access to many online learning resources while maintaining a level of resource quality, cataloging, and curation that distinguishes educational digital libraries from generic Internet search engines and non-educational social software.

However, it is often as difficult for teachers and learners to define quality as it is for the courts to define pornography. As U.S. Supreme Court Justice Potter Steward once noted, "I know it [pornography] when I see it." The problem (or the solution?) lies in the perspective of users who are confronted with a variety of resources of indeterminate origin. For school administrators, teachers, and learners, a high quality resource could consist of an entire lesson that meets several state standards; a web-based animation that accurately depicts a science concept; or, an essay that provides an answer in a quiz.

Grappling with the idea of "quality", several education digital libraries have already created rubrics to assess their content. As we tried to apply these criteria to the content in the Instructional Architect, as described below, we observed that portions of each rubric were applicable in different settings, and other portions were specific to each digital library with little room for re-use outside of the original context (Martin, 2004). As such, our goals were 1) to synthesize the various dimensions of existing rubrics in order to identify a standardized set of criteria that could potentially be used by any digital library with online educational resources (Giersch, Leary, Palmer & Recker, 2008a), and 2) to create a guide that could be used to assess the quality of materials in the Instructional Architect projects (http://ia.usu.edu). This chapter briefly describes our process for developing the standardized set of assessment criteria; evaluating its utility and usability with middle school science and math teachers; developing a Quality Guide for use with Instructional Architect projects; testing its reliability; and, exploring how the Guide could foster teachers' skills in designing learning resources.

3. Previous research

Many education digital library builders have developed rubrics to help assess the quality of online educational resources generated by teachers, faculty and learners. However, the motivations and methods for implementing the rubrics vary as do the implied assumptions about the value of the results for each education digital library.

Established publishing houses and professional societies institute peer review processes to maintain a reputation for producing quality publications thereby increasing subscriptions and membership. For newly-funded education digital libraries, under pressure to prove their value, rubrics and a process to measure quality, were created to first *establish* a reputation with users (Robertshaw, Leary, Walker, Bloxham, Recker, 2009). Similarly, other education digital libraries used rubrics to support access to high quality resources in a digital library or repository (Liu & Ward, 2007; McMartin, 2004) because use of a collection development policy for inclusion of quality resources adds value and buy-in from peer reviewers and users (Sumner et al, 2003). Still other sites developed a rubric to guide authors in creating high quality online resources by gathering feedback from target users (McMartin, 2004).

The methods by which education digital libraries collected data using rubrics and how they used that information also varied. Muramatsu and Agogino (1999) used a rubric to gather feedback from *targeted users* to inform collection development, while Recker, Walker, and Lawless (2003) gathered data through automated mechanisms to provide teachers with suggestions based on resources they had previously viewed and used. Establishing peer-review panels and processes was not a *de facto* choice for every education digital library (Fitzgerald, Lovin, & Branch, 2003; ORC, McMartin, 2004). Enlisting users-as-builders, or reviewers-as-builders, is a characteristic of the grass-roots environment in which many education digital libraries evolved over the last decade in the U.S. However, many digital library developers found that gathering reviews from users was difficult, though providing incentives, in the form of awards (Muramatsu & Agogino, 1999) or other methods (McMartin, 2004), was one way to increase acceptance and adoption of the rubric and review process and of the education digital library in general.

The process of creating and testing an assessment rubric can be time consuming. Many rubric creators believe it is important to map out stakeholders and end-users, review previous work by other digital libraries (Knox et al, 1999), and learn how to gather data (Recker, Walker, Lawless, 2003; Sumner et al., 2003). Testing a rubric with users, for formative evaluation, further refines the rubric, yielding usability information (Fitzgerald, Lovin, & Branch, 2003) as well as real time feedback from target users (Recker, Walker, Lawless, 2003; Sumner et al., 2003), which ultimately assists with the process of implementing the rubric with a larger group of users.

4. Context

4.1 The Instructional Architect

The Instructional Architect is a simple, web-based authoring tool designed to help K-12 teachers find, design, and use online learning resources in their classrooms (Recker, 2006). When using the Instructional Architect, teachers search for and save links to online learning resources from the Web and educational digital libraries such as the National Science Digital Library (http://nsdl.org). Resources that can be linked include online content, RSS feeds and podcasts. Once resources are gathered users then create 'Instructional Architect projects' (in the form of web pages) that contain instructional objectives, activities, and assessments. The resources are either embedded into the project or link out to web-based resources. In this way, teachers create Instructional Architect projects that customize resources to their local context. Figure 1 shows an Instructional Architect project and an accompanying resource.

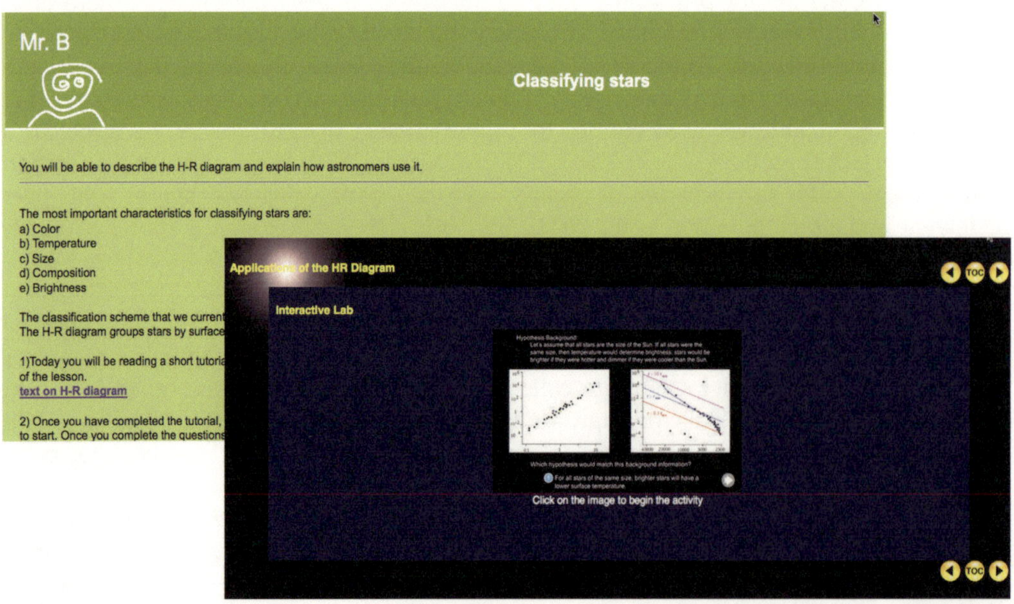

Fig. 1. Example of an Instructional Architect project created by Mr. B and related resource.

Initially the majority of users were K-12 teachers in the U.S. who participated in professional development workshops from 2005-2009. Recently, the Instructional Architect system has garnered more widespread usage and spread 'virally' to teachers not directly attending these workshops. Table 1 shows statistics on Instructional Architect usage and growth in the number of Instructional Architect projects and resources over the last 12 months.

Data	N	*12-month growth*
Registered users	5,300	23%
Instructional Architect projects created	11,500	37%
Online learning resources used	52,100	67%
Visits to Instructional Architect project (since 8/2006)	1 million	64%

Table 1. Instructional Architect usage data (to August 2010).

Before any of the abundant Instructional Architect projects created by users can be ingested into educational digital libraries, like the National Science Digital Library, to become part of the education cyberinfrastructure, they need to be evaluated for quality. To support this outcome, the Instructional Architect projects must be reviewed with a rubric that is reliable across multiple sites, a process that is scalable across the thousands of IA projects, and that has useful results for end-users, reviewers, and digital library developers.

5. Method

5.1 Synthesizing existing rubrics & creating the Quality Guide

Following the recommendations above for establishing a rubric to assess content (Knox et al, 1999; Recker, Walker, Lawless, 2003; Sumner et al., 2003), we began with a literature review in the disciplines of computer science, library and information science, education (specifically online learning objects), and digital libraries. We selected only articles that included or referenced rubrics used to review online educational resources. The literature review yielded articles with descriptions of 12 rubrics (Liu, & Ward, 2007; Fitzgerald, Lovin, & Branch, 2003; Nesbit, Belfer, Leacock, 2003; Ohio Resource Center; Knox et al., 1999; Recker, Walker, & Lawless, 2003; Sumner, Khoo, Recker, & Marlino, 2003; Custard & Sumner, 2005; Kastens, DeFelice, Devaul, DiLeonardo, Ginger, Larsen, et al., 2005; McMartin, 2004; Muramatsu & Agogino, 1999).

In keeping with our first goal (to synthesize the various dimensions of existing digital library rubrics in order to identify a standardized set of criteria that could potentially be used by any digital library with online educational resources), our initial plan was to identify review criteria at the most granular level and then do a frequency analysis to identify broad topics that applied across criteria (e.g., pedagogy or usability). These would then become the foundational criteria. Accordingly, we un-bundled the rubrics and identified over 200 review criteria, some of which included only one or two words and sometimes no definition. However, when conducting our frequency analysis, we found it difficult to group similar review criteria because:

- None of the rubrics used a standard vocabulary for their review criteria;
- The definitions for criteria contained multiple concepts that defied easy categorization; and,

- Some criteria (with and without definitions) were so contextualized to their site that they became virtually meaningless when viewed out of context from the whole rubric.

These factors also made it difficult to create topic areas before and after the frequency analysis. Given the challenges of our initial approach, we revised our methods and used a card sort technique. Card sorts are typically employed as a user-centered design approach for assessing web site structure (Maurer & Warfel, 2004). This process has participants sort a series of cards, each labeled with a piece of content or functionality into groups that make sense to them (Lamantia, 2003). This technique allows input from several experts, with the consensus between them resolving ambiguities in and across the review criteria.

In preparing the initial list of over 200 review criteria for sorting, we realized that some of the most granular criteria, especially those without definitions, would prove difficult to sort, appearing as so much noise to study participants. Therefore, we culled the list to include only criteria from the literature that included a definition and that would make sense when read outside the context of its original use. Our intention was not to represent criteria as they had been used within a particular review process, but to use the criteria as presented in the literature. The result was that 104 review criteria remained for use in the card sort exercise.

The card sort methodology recommends using seven to ten participants. Our sorting exercise included 10 participants who were graduate students, professors from instructional technology and education, and academic librarians. We presented the participants with a spreadsheet containing the review criteria, criteria definitions, and the source rubric or citation. We chose the "open sort" method and asked participants to sort the review criteria into groups of their own choosing within a spreadsheet and to provide their own titles for the groups. Participants were allowed to place criteria in more than one group as long as they indicated which criteria-group pairing represented their highest priority.

Each of the ten participants created an average of nearly 13 groups into which they individually sorted the 104 review criteria. One participant sorted criteria into multiple groups but did not indicate a top priority, so rather than guessing at the intention, the results were not included. Ultimately, we analyzed the nine result sets containing an average of 11 groups per participant.

A detailed analysis (Giersch, Leary, Palmer, Recker, 2008a; Giersch, Leary, Palmer, Recker, 2008b) yielded six elements from the 11 groups. These became the foundational set of criteria, which were standardized to the point where they could be used by any digital library with online education resources, thereby accomplishing our first goal. Table 2 shows the six elements, or standardized criteria, developed by study participants in the card sort exercise (e.g., Content). Corresponding definitions and the references for them are also displayed. The definitions (e.g., Resource content is accurate) are statements from the original 12 rubrics that participants associated with the standardized criteria.

Using these foundational criteria, we then began to address the second goal of creating a guide that could be used to assess the quality of materials in the Instructional Architect projects. Figure 2 shows the prototype of the foundational criteria and definitions in beta form before it was designed to be more user-friendly and visually appealing. This subsequently became the first version of the Instructional Architect Quality Guide, and included five Likert scale star ratings for each criterion, as these are widely used by rating systems, and less-detailed definitions of criteria.

Standardized criteria	*Definitions and references*
Interface Design & Accessibility	The resource is attractive (Liu & Ward, 2007) The resource is easy to navigate (Ohio Resource Center) The resource contains no advertising (Custard & Sumner, 2005; Sumner, Khoo, Recker, Marlino, 2003) The resource contains links that work (Liu & Ward, 2007) The resource is designed to accommodate disabled and mobile learners (Nesbit, Belfer, Leacock, 2003)
Technical Reliability (Muramatsu & Agogino, 1999)	The resource uses multimedia (Flash, sound clips, videos, or applets) that work (Custard & Sumner, 2005) The resource clearly identifies the supporting technical resources required (Knox et al., 1999) The resource contains help features (Nesbit, Belfer, Leacock, 2003)
Content	Resource content is accurate (Muramatsu & Agogino, 1999; Kastens et al., 2005; Nesbit, Belfer, Leacock, 2003; Recker, Walker, Lawless, 2003; Ohio Resource Center) Resource content is complete (Fitzgerald, Loving, & Branch, 2003) Resource content is impartial (Fitzgerald, Loving, & Branch, 2003) Resource content is clearly written (Ohio Resource Center) Resources content is maintained (Custard & Sumner, 2005; Liu & Ward, 2007)
Pedagogy	The resource is engaging (Liu & Ward, 2007) The reource is motivating (Fitzgerald, Lovoing, & Branch, 2003) The resource is interactive (Muramatsu & Agogino, 1999) The resources includes assessment(s) (Ohio Resource Center) The resource provides feedback (Nesbit, Belfer, & Leacock, 2003) The resource supports learners proceeding at their own pace (Muramatsu & Agogino, 1999) The resource supports introductory, reinforcing, or summative activities
Administrative	The resource contains direct and explicit links to state or national educational teaching standards (Custard & Sumner, 2005; Ohio Resources Center) The resource contains information about ist author or creator, email (Recker, Walker, Lawless, 2003), site domain (Custard & Sumner, 2005), role (Custard & Sumner, 2005) The resource is described by current metadata (Custard & Sumner, 2005)
Other	The resource requires a fee for access (Custard & Sumner, 2005) The resources overall rating/confidence level (Recker, Walker, Lawless, 2003)

Table 2. Standardized set of criteria with definitions.

Quality Guide

While viewing an IA project, rate the following six items as found in the project.

☆☆☆☆☆	**Interface design** Definition: dynamic, visually pleasing aesthetics, standards, accessibility, navigation, good user interface
☆☆☆☆☆	**Accessibility** Definition: technical reliability, reusability, usability design, reliability, adaptability, ADA
☆☆☆☆☆	**Content** Definition: accuracy, organization, quality, completeness, currency, value, interdisciplinary
☆☆☆☆☆	**Pedagogy** Definition: instruction methods, design methods, learning goals, anticipated outcomes, motivation, engagement
☆☆☆☆☆	**Administrative** Definition: authority, authorship, metadata, advertising, credibility
☆☆☆☆☆	**Overall rating**

Fig. 2. Prototype of foundational criteria and definitions

IA project ID:_________ **Reviewer Name:**_________________________

Circle the star you feel best describes the IA project, and provide any comments about your rating.

Number	Criteria	Rating
1	Content accuracy	☆ Very Inaccurate ☆ Somewhat Inaccurate ☆ Not enough Information ☆ Somewhat Accurate ☆ Very Accurate Comments:
2	Text clarity	☆ Very Unclear ☆ Somewhat Unclear ☆ Not enough Information ☆ Somewhat Clear ☆ Very Clear Comments:
3.	Links in project	☆ No links work ☆ Some links don't work ☆ Not enough Information ☆ Some links work ☆ All links work Comments:
4	Project completeness: includes the state standard learning goal, assessment, etc.	☆ Very Incomplete ☆ Somewhat incomplete ☆ Not enough Information ☆ Somewhat complete ☆ Very complete Comments:
5	The project: (circle one)	a. Provides a resorce list b. Teaches a concept c. Reinforces a concept d. Provides a summary of content with a learning activity e. Don't Know f. Does something else (describe below)
6	Overall rating of the project	☆ Meets no criteria ☆ Meets very little criteria ☆ Meets some criteria ☆ Meets criteria ☆ Exceed criteria Comments:

Fig. 3. First version of the Instructional Architect Quality Guide.

5.2 Testing the Instructional Architect Quality Guide

Twenty-eight participants were recruited to test the first version of the Instructional Architect Quality Guide. They were part of a cohort of U.S. K-12 teachers in an online graduate program, and they completed required activities as part of an online course. Complete data were received from 17 participants. Testing the Quality Guide was directed by the following research questions:

1. What is the student's view of using technology in a classroom?
2. How do teachers assess an online educational resource before and after using the Quality Guide?
3. Using the Quality Guide, how helpful are conducting and receiving peer reviews for the student?
4. What changes should be made to the Instructional Architect Quality Guide based on student use and feedback?

5.3 Data sources

The participants took part in an online learning module in the context of learning how to use the Instructional Architect and the Quality Guide. They completed pre-and post-online surveys, which used a combination of open-ended and Likert-scale questions. Surveys measured the extent of participants' experience and classroom practice in using online educational resources; their attitudes about online educational resources and technology in general and their use in a classroom; and, strategies for evaluating an online educational resource. Within the learning module, participants were placed in small groups of 4-5 participants, and they evaluated one another's Instructional Architect projects using the Quality Guide. Conversations about these evaluations were posted in a BlackBoard discussion forum and collected for analysis by the researchers. Lastly, participants wrote a reflection paper describing their experience using the Instructional Architect, how they used online educational resources in an instructional situation, difficulties and successes in designing and implementing their project, what they learned by reviewing their peers' Instructional Architect projects and by using the Quality Guide, and how they could improve their Instructional Architect project.

6. Results

Research question one used data from the pre-and post-survey Likert items. Effect sizes were calculated on questions relating to participants' attitude, experience with and use of online educational resources and technology in their classrooms in order to understand changes in participants' pedagogical choices and activities in their classrooms. An effect size (d_w) shows a magnitude of change and is considered small at 0.2 detectable by an expert looking closely at the phenomenon, medium at 0.5, and large at 0.8 detectable by an untrained observer (Cohen, 1988). Larger effect sizes equate to larger impacts due to the intervention. Small, but positive changes, statistically significant at $p < 0.05$, were shown from the pre-test to the post-test as teachers reported that they knew how to effectively teach with technology in the classroom ($d_w = 0.28$, $p < 0.05$), and they knew how to effectively use technology in their classroom ($d_w = 0.42$, $p < 0.05$). From this we know that after participating in the learning module, teachers began to overcome initial barriers of using technology in the classroom and could now focus on making better pedagogical decisions about the type of learning resources they could create.

We then used a qualitative analysis to address research question two with the understanding that participants had learned how to use online educational resources. Using a constant comparative analysis (Glaser & Strauss, 1967), data from the reflection papers, discussion boards, and one question in the pre-and post-survey were mapped into themes and analyzed. Participants reported in the pre-survey that when evaluating online educational resources they looked for fit with the curriculum, accuracy, ease of use, currency, text readability, and recommendations by others. After completing this course module, participants added in their post-survey comments that they looked for: content quality, distractions on the resource pages, credibility of the site, and engagement. Many of the criteria they added were items listed in the Quality Guide. Thus, it appeared that use of the Quality Guide helped refine participants' approach to designing online learning resources, in the form of Instructional Architect projects.

To answer research question three, the comments from the discussion boards in Blackboard where participants posted their evaluations of their peers' Instructional Architect projects were used. Some participants commented on the readability and text clarity of the Instructional Architect project, and many caught spelling errors. One participant commented after receiving some feedback, "I have learned that having a peer read through my projects can be very valuable. They catch mistakes that I do not see." Overall, 53% of the participants reported that providing and receiving feedback from their peers via reviews was valuable.

Two additional themes surfaced from analyses of the discussion boards during the process of peer evaluation that related to re-use of other teachers' Instructional Architect projects and ideas. First, participants asked if they could use an Instructional Architect project they reviewed, or said they planned to use it in their classroom. The second theme was that participants learned what others had done and wanted to implement the same idea in their project. A participant commented that, "Completing a peer review gives us an opportunity to see other creations and improve our programs as we see fit."

The final data collection point included participants' reflection papers. Participants were asked to report on their instructional situation, successes and difficulties, what they learned from their peers and using the Quality Guide, and how they could improve their Instructional Architect project. Three areas of learning were repeatedly reported in the reflection papers: what they learned by reviewing peer work; what they learned for their own work; and, the value of re-using Instructional Architect projects. Similar ideas were also expressed throughout the discussion boards and survey answers.

6.1 Reliability and improvements

Version one (see Figure 3) of the Quality Guide was tested for reliability in order to answer research question four. Peer ratings of Instructional Architect projects using the Guide, provided by the students in the online graduate course, were used for this analysis. The Quality Guide criteria (5 stars) were scored on a scale of 0-4, where zero or one star is low (e.g., very unclear) and four or five stars is high (e.g., very clear). See Figure 3 above. Means and standard deviations were run for each question.

Criteria one through four and six of the Quality Guide were analyzed using an intra-class correlation (scale of -1 to 1, high agreement is found as it approaches 1, with less agreement as it approaches -1). Criteria five was not analyzed as it asks for a classification on what the Instructional Architect project is doing (e.g., teaching a new concept, reinforcing a concept, etc). Table 4 shows the intraclass correlation values for each question analyzed.

A close look at the data (see Table 3) shows that the teachers generally rated their peers at an average of 2 or more (3 or more stars on the Quality Guide) for any of the criteria on the Guide. This could possibly be attributed to the fact that educators as a whole tend to provide high ratings for their peer, a phenomenon observed in prior work (Walker, Recker, Lawless, & Wiley, 2004). As a result of the high ratings, the full range of the scale was not used, and slight departures were magnified in the intraclass correlation. The negative values indicate that there was more variation between projects than there was between raters. As is shown in the low intraclass correlation (Table 4), agreement on those ratings was never high, and in most cases was non-existent.

Criteria	*Mean*	*Standard Deviation*
1 - Content accuracy	2.50	1.13
2 - Text clarity	2.34	0.98
3 - Links in project	3.30	0.83
4 - Project completeness	2.14	1.50
6 - Overall rating	3.22	1.84

Table 3. Means and standard deviations for criteria 1-4, 6 of the Instructional Architect Quality Guide.

Criteria	*Intraclass Correlation*
1 - Content accuracy	0
2 - Text clarity	-0.129
3 - Links in project	0.031
4 - Project completeness	-0.89
6 - Overall rating	-0.129

Table 4. Intraclass correlation (ICC) values for criteria 1-4, 6 of the Instructional Architect Quality Guide.

The reliability analysis suggests that the scale needs more explanation for each item and that the scale should encompass either a broader range or a dichotomous rating (yes or no). Improvements made to the Quality Guide as a result of this testing included adding more detailed definitions of the review criteria, re-arranging the order of criteria, and modifying scoring instructions. As a result of this testing, improvements were made to create the final version of the Quality Guide (see Figure 4), which is currently used to inform and support individual teachers as they create Instructional Architect projects.

INSTRUCTIONAL
ARCHITECT™

Use the following indicators to inform your choices when designing or reviewing IA projects.

Accuracy

Information is credible, truthful, reliable, current

Very inaccurate	*Inaccurate*	*Accurate*	*Very accurate*
Comments:			

Text Clarity

Appropriate grade level, length, and amount (as concise as needed)

Very unclear	*Unclear*	*Clear*	*Very clear*
Comments:			

Links in Project

Work and go to the correct page

All links fail	*Most links fail*	*Most links work*	*All links work*
Comments:			

Project Completeness

Includes the state standard, objectives, learning goal, assessment, or an example

Very Incomplete	*Incomplete*	*Complete*	*Very complete*
Comments:			

The Project

Provides a resource list	*Teaches a concept*	*Reinforces a concept*	*Provides a summary of content*	*Other*
Comments:				

Overall

Meets no criteria	*Meets some criteria*	*Meets all criteria*	*Exceeds criteria*
Comments:			

Fig. 4. Final version of the Instructional Architect Quality guide.

7. Conclusion

The foundational list of criteria (see Table 2), which was derived from rubrics of 12 different education digital libraries, can be used by other digital library developers to evaluate the quality of online learning resources, or it can be modified to fit the need of local contexts, such as the Instructional Architect. We created the Instructional Architect Quality Guide to encourage change in teachers' perspective and behaviors around designing and using online educational resources. The results of our evaluation indicate that participants found value in the Quality Guide as a means to improve their own projects through completing and receiving reviews. Unfortunately, we found that the Instructional Architect Quality Guide does not scale well when it is used to determine which of the 11,500 Instructional Architect projects are of sufficient quality to be ingested by the National Science Digital Library.

8. Future research

Future work is focused on addressing these scalability issues through using an already-developed and -tested automated and scalable quality assessment method, which will better support and facilitate teacher co-creation of online content. Similar to the work described in this chapter, this approach relies upon distilling the elusive notion of quality into a set of concrete indicators. We are also testing a previously developed machine learning algorithm, called Opera (Bethard et al., 2009), to assess whether its quality ratings along these indicators match teacher assessments (Recker et al., 2011). Results from these ongoing studies will help determine if Opera can serve as a proxy for the laborious and expensive task of having teachers or peer reviewers assess the quality of online resources and IA projects. We are still motivated by having online learning resources and Instructional Architect projects reviewed so that quality content can be ingested by educational digital libraries, such as the National Science Digital Library and ultimately included in the education cyberinfrastructure.

9. Acknowledgements

The authors would like to thank the study participants for their time and assistance, as well as members of the Instructional Architect research group. This material is based upon work supported by the National Science Foundation under Grant No. 0554440, and Utah State University. Any opinions, findings, and conclusions or recommendations expressed in this material are those of the authors and do not necessarily reflect the views of the National Science Foundation.

10. References

Anderson, C. (2006). *The Long Tail: Why the future of business is selling less of more.* Hyperion, New York.

Bethard, S., Wetzler, P., Butcher, K., Martin, J. H., Sumner, T. (2009). Automatically Characterizing Resource Quality for Educational Digital Libraries. In *Proceedings of the 9th ACM/IEEE-CS Joint Conference on Digital Libraries.* New York: ACM.

Cohen, J. (1988). *Statistical power analysis for the behavioral sciences* (Vol. 2). Hillsdale, NJ: Lawrence Earlbaum Associates.

Computing Research Association. (2005). *Cyber-infrastructure for Education and Learning for the Future: A vision and research agenda*. Washington, D.C.

Custard, M., & Sumner, T. (2005). Using Machine Learning to Support Quality Judgments. D-Lib Magazine, 11, 11.

Fitzgerald, M.A., Lovin, V., & Branch, R.M. (2003). A Gateway to Educational Materials: An Evaluation of an Online Resource for Teachers and an Exploration of User Behaviors. *Journal of Technology and Teacher Education*, 11, 1, 21-51.

Glaser, B. G. and A. L. Strauss (1967). *The discovery of grounded theory: Strategies for qualitative research*. Chicago, Aldine Publishing Company.

Giersch, S., Leary, H., Palmer, B., Recker, M. (2008)a. Supporting Meaningful Learning with Online Resources: Developing a Review Process. In *Proceedings of the Annual Open Education Conference*, Logan, Utah, September 24-26.

Giersch, S. Leary, H., Palmer, B., & M., Recker (2008)b. Developing a Review Process for Online Resources. In *Proceedings of the Joint Conference on Digital Libraries*, Pittsburgh, PA, June 15-20.

Hanson, K. & Carlson, B. (2005). *Effective Access Report*. Education Development Center Instructional Architect Quality Guide, latest version: http://digitalcommons.usu.edu/itls_research/5/

Kastens, K., DeFelice, B., Devaul, H., DiLeonardo, C., Ginger, K., Larsen, S., et al. (2005). Questions & Challenges Arising in Building the Collection of a Digital Library for Education: Lessons from Five Years of DLESE. *D-Lib Magazine*, 11, 11.

Knox, D., et al (1999). The Peer Review Process of Teaching Materials: Report of the ITiCSE'99 Working Group on Validation of the quality of teaching materials. *Annual Joint Conference Integrating Technology into Computer Science Education*, Cracow, Poland.

Lamantia, J. (2003). *Analyzing Card Sort Results with a Spreadsheet Template*. Retrieved January 18, 2008, from Boxes and Arrows Web site: http://www.boxesandarrows.com/view/analyzing_card_sort_ results_with_a_spreadsheet_template

Leary, H., Giersch, S., Walker, A., Recker, M. (2009). Developing a Review Rubric for Learning Resources in Digital Libraries. *ITLS Faculty Publications*. Paper 17. http://digitalcommons.usu.edu/itls_facpub/17

Liu, K. & Ward, V. (2007). Access Excellence @ the National Health Museum. *D-Lib Magazine*, 13, 11/12.

Maurer, D. & Warfel, T. (2004). *Card Sorting: a definitive guide*. Retrieved January 18, 2008, from Boxes and Arrows Web site: http://www.boxesandarrows.com/view/card_sorting_a_defini tive_guide

McMartin, F. (2004). MERLOT: A Model for User Involvement in Digital Library Design and Implementation. *Journal of Digital Information*, 5, 3.

Muramatsu, B. & Agogino, A. (1999). The National Engineering Education Delivery System: A Digital Library for Engineering Education. *D-Lib Magazine*, 4, 5.

Nesbit, J., Belfer, K., Leacock, T. (2003). *Learning Object Review Instrument (LORI 1.5)*, User Manual. Retrieved January 15, 2008.

Ohio Resources Center (ORC): http://ohiorc.org

Pea, R., with Christine L. Borgman (Chair), Hal Abelson, Lee Dirks, Roberta Johnson, Kenneth R. Koedinger, Marcia C. Linn, Clifford A. Lynch, Diana G. Oblinger, Katie

Salen, Marshall S. Smith, Alex Szalay (2008). *Fostering learning in the networked world – the cyberlearning opportunity and challenge: A 21st century agenda for the National Science Foundation (Report of the NSF Task Force on Cyberlearning).* Arlington, VA: National Science Foundation.

Recker, M., Leary, H., Walker, A., Diekema, A. R., Wetzler, P., Sumner, T., Martin, J. (2011, April). Modeling Teacher Ratings of Online Resources: A Human-Machine Approach to Quality. Paper *presentation at the American Educational Research Association,* New Orleans.

Recker, M., Walker, A., Giersch, S., Mao, X., Halioris, S., Palmer, B., Johnson, D., Leary, H., Robertshaw, M.B. (2007). A study of teachers' use of online learning resources to design classroom activities. *New Review of Hypermedia and Multimedia,* 13, 2, 117-134.

Recker, M. (2006). Perspectives on teachers as digital library users: Consumers, contributors, and designers. *D-Lib Magazine, 12,* 9.

Recker, M., Walker, A,. & Lawless, K. (2003). What do you recommend? Implementation and analyses of collaborative information filtering of web resources for education. *Instructional Science,* 31, 299–316.

Robertshaw, M. B., Leary, H., Walker, A., Bloxham, K., Recker, M. (2009). Reciprocal mentoring "in the wild": A retrospective, comparative case study of ICT teacher professional development. In E. Stacey (Ed.) *Effective Blended Learning Practices: Evidence-Based Perspectives in ICT-Facilitated Education,* Melbourne: IGI Global Press.

Sumner, T., Khoo, M., Recker, M., & Marlino, M. (2003). Understanding educator perceptions of "quality" in digital libraries. In *Proceedings of the Joint Conference on Digital Libraries,* Houston, Texas, May 27-31.

Walker, A., Recker, M., Lawless, K., & Wiley, D. (2004). Collaborative information filtering: A review and an educational application. *International Journal of Artifical Intelligence and Education,* 14, 1-26.

11

Multitasking Made Easy: Supporting Academic Writing in Digital Libraries with an Ambient Search System

Anatoliy Gruzd[1] and Michael B Twidale[2]
[1]*Dalhousie University*
[2]*University of Illinois at Urbana-Champaign*
[1]*Canada*
[2]*USA*

1. Introduction

When personal computers first arrived, many predicted that by the end of the century our desktops would become free from clutter as we moved to the paperless office. However, if we look at desktops of current researchers, we can see that this has definitely not happened (see Figure 1). But it is not only researchers' physical desktops that are cluttered; their computer desktops (and file systems) are just as cluttered. This should not come as a surprise. Because the process of writing is such a complex process, people need this space to lay out their notes, readings, drafts, printouts, etc. As a result, the desktop is literally disappearing under piles of paper, just not in the way predicted.

Fig. 1. Example of a cluttered desktop and office of a person (one of the authors) engaged in research and academic writing.

Writing is an extremely complex process, consisting of multiple components that can occur in many different combinations. With respect to academic writing, these components include planning and organization, presentation of facts, marshalling of arguments, preparing tables, figures, diagrams and references, searching for references, reading, annotating related and possibly related work, citation chaining, countering argument threads in related work, searching for inspiration, and searching for supporting and refuting evidence in the literature (Brockman et al., 2001; Fister, 1992; Kuhlthau, 2004; Palmer, 2005; Torrance et al., 1994; Wolber et al., 2002). At times it can help to consider these activities, some of which are very different, as a special kind of multitasking, raising the question of how best to support it.

Before personal computers, writing involved the accumulation of resources from books, journals, preprints, the authors' prior work, notebooks, outlines and previous drafts. These paper sources might be laid out on available flat surfaces (desks, tables, often the floor) in order to be easily available during writing, not only for immediate reference, but to serve as passive reminders and awareness agents of other activities to do and issues to consider. Working in an office means that even vertical surfaces can be recruited - whiteboards containing the results of discussions with co-authors, and bookshelves serving as reminders of other resources that might be considered, or as sources of inspiration when writing meets an impasse.

What is so noticeable is that since the arrival of personal computers in the mid 1980s, and despite the enormous improvements in processing power, memory capacity and screen size, as well at the dramatic improvements in online access to digital libraries, web pages, scholarly repositories etc., the paper-strewn scenario of the previous paragraph is still all too familiar. If anything, access to more resources more quickly just means that it is easier to print out and strew more documents around one's office while writing. Additionally, the access to online full text versions of papers means that researchers can also accumulate substantial personal digital collections of papers on their hard drives. If poorly organized, these collections themselves are difficult to navigate, and are in need of a context-aware retrieval system (Kljun & Carr, 2005).

The issue in interface design is that in the context of writing the desktop metaphor is *not* necessarily bad or obsolete. Rather the problem is that it has never really been tried. Desktop computers have limited screen real estate and so must employ various tricks of overlapping, iconization, listing of files, links and other tricks to manage the quantity and diversity of materials needed to support writing. Even with 24" screens and double, even triple monitors, the available space is small compared to most people's actual desktops (let alone their floors and walls that can be employed in the more intense periods of writing). If anything, current screens resemble the tiny individual desktops used by examination candidates (typically less than 3' by 3'), with just enough room for a question paper and an answer booklet (see Figure 2). That is fine for a test of memory, but is wildly unsuitable for rich, contextualized writing, let alone thinking and searching while writing.

The growing availability of academic literature on the Internet makes it possible for authors to multitask by switching between writing and information searching; as easy as switching between two windows on their computer monitors. However, this poses a new challenge to writers. The complexity of information searching (generating query, browsing, assessing results, etc) makes it very hard to stay focused on writing. Furthermore, an overwhelming diversity of poorly connected online research tools (search engines, digital libraries, bookmarking sites, etc) often leads to information fragmentation among their users (Boardman & Sasse, 2003).

Retrieved from
http://www.flickr.com/photos/comedynose/3571102858

Fig. 2. The existing manifestation of the desktop metaphor implies a very tiny desktop, more like that used for examinations involving writing from memory than larger office desktops (plus floors and walls) used for writing from resources.

We are exploring the design of an online context-aware retrieval system that allows users to multitask by writing while still actively engaged in research activities online. We have developed a web-based prototype called PIRA (Personal Information Research Assistant) available at http://writeNcite.com. PIRA relies on external digital libraries and search engines to produce a list of academic references related to what a user is writing at the moment; thus, allowing authors to stay focused on their writing.

PIRA attempts to support many of the awareness features provided by a papers strewn desktop and floor, but with a more active approach, providing an ambient awareness of work that *may* be relevant and inspirational. In its current form, PIRA remains locked into a single screen, although attempting to use it in a more integrated manner for supporting writing.

This paper focuses on the methodological aspects of user-centric evaluations of PIRA. More specifically, we investigate influences of multitasking as supported by PIRA on users' writing.

2. Related work

Previous research in this area produced a number of interesting design solutions for context-aware retrieval systems that can support writing and reading. Some examples of earlier work in this area include: Watson to support desktop-based writing/reading activities (Budzik et al., 2002), Implicit Queries (IQ) to support composing/reading e-mails (Dumais et al., 2004), Phrasier to support interactive document retrieval using keyphrases (Jones & Staveley, 1999), and systems like Letizia and PowerScout (Lieberman et al, 2001) and WebTop (Wolber et al., 2002) to support browsing and reading of web pages. There are also some context-aware desktop search engines for local files like Remembrance Agent, Margin Notes, and Jimminy (Rhodes, 2003). And more recently, there are also the Context Creation Tool which is designed to support interactive reference gathering, academic note taking and writing (Berendt et al, 2010) , CONTEXT - a context-aware information retrieval system for bloggers (Gruzd & Wong, 2010), and the Context Awareness Tool (CAT) - a general-purpose "writing for the web" tool (Powell et al., 2009).

The existence of these tools show that there is both interest and progress being made to develop a truly context-aware retrieval system that can better support users' information behavior. However, there is still a lot more work that needs to be done to address all of the challenges associated with writing (especially, academic writing) in the context of using digital libraries. Some of the challenges include designing interfaces that are more context-aware (e.g., Ruthven, 2008) and interfaces that enable users to serendipitously discover new ideas (e.g., Toms & McCay-Peet, 2009). One system that has been designed to address some of these challenges is PIRA.

3. PIRA's user interface

In this section, we provide a brief overview of PIRA. A more detailed description of PIRA and review of the related work can be found elsewhere (Gruzd & Twidale, 2006; Twidale et al., 2008).

PIRA is a web-based writing tool with two main interface components. On the left is a basic text editor. On the right is an area for searching and managing references. As the user writes (or pastes) new content in the editor, PIRA automatically extracts significant search keywords, displays them in the "Suggested Search Terms" pane, and retrieves and presents suggested references in the "Auto References" pane (see Figure 3). These can be simply ignored if the user is focusing on writing, or glances at them and deems them irrelevant. They are gradually replaced by alternate suggestions based on the current area of writing activity in the text editor. Mousing over a reference provides more details including the paper's abstract. If a user sees a potentially useful citation among the sources suggested by PIRA, they can temporarily lock the citation by clicking on the Pin icon in the front of the suggested reference. Along with temporarily locking the citation, a user can also open the full-text of an article in a new window (if provided by the digital library) or save the citation for use in future sessions using the Disc icon. If a user decides to save a citation for later use, he or she will have the option of associating the suggested reference with the current document or with any other (previously saved) documents. This is done to help users avoid situations when they "often don't remember that they've already saved potentially useful or meaningful material" (Fister, 1992). Once a citation is saved, it can be later accessed using a built-in bibliographic management interface (see Figure 4).

PIRA automatically and continuously suggests new reference sources related to the content of users' writing. Reference sources are suggested from various open-access digital libraries and search engines. By default, Google.com and CiteUlike.org are automatically selected. Users can leave the default selection or build their own personal list. For example, depending on their research topic, users may prefer to only use specialized data sources like CiteSeer.IST (Information and Computer Science - oriented), or they might choose to use only general sources like the Directory of Open Access Journals (DOAJ) (http://www.doaj.org). To select or deselect an external data source, users just simply need to click the "USE" or "DON'T USE" button accordingly (see Figure 5).

PIRA has been built as a web mashup, using a variety of different web services (different text editors, text and concept extraction services, and different user-specifiable digital libraries) enabling us to undertake a systematic exploration of the design space of variants on writing support and ambient search.

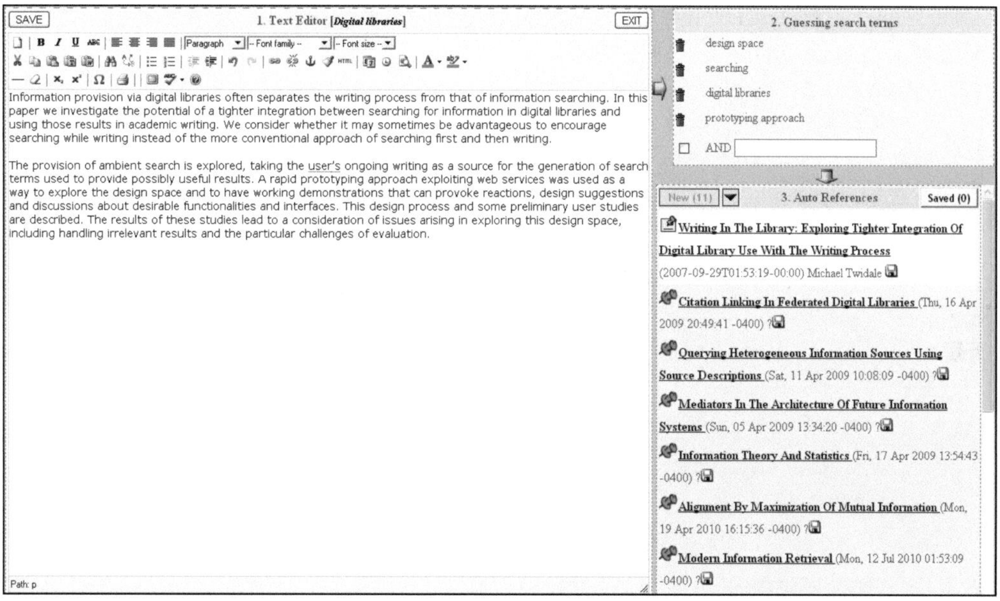

Fig. 3. PIRA's main display showing integration of writing and ambient searching.

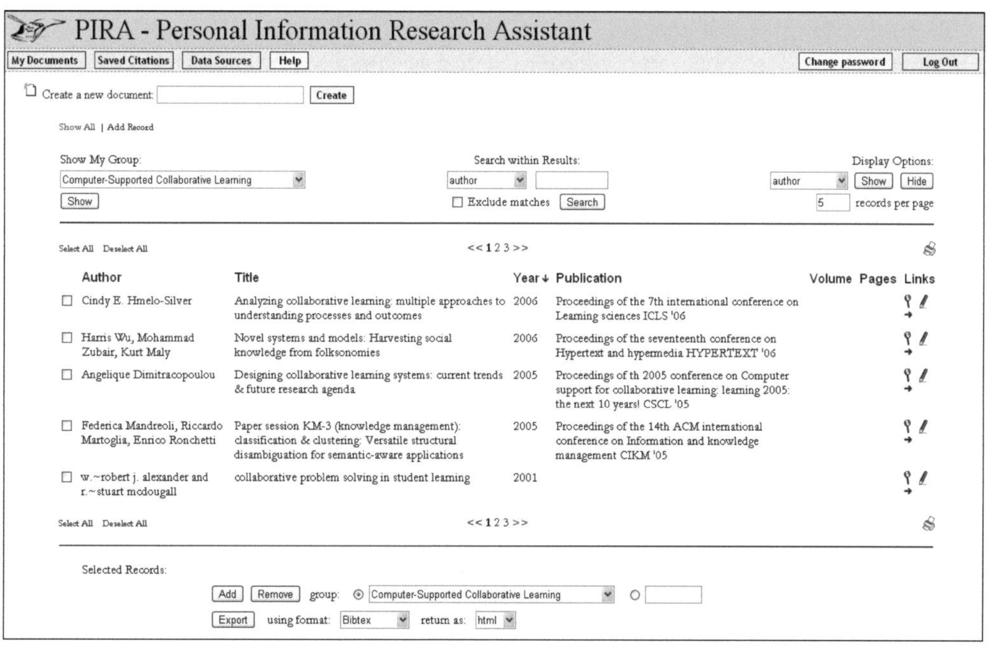

Fig. 4. Built-in bibliographic management interface based on RefBase, open source software.

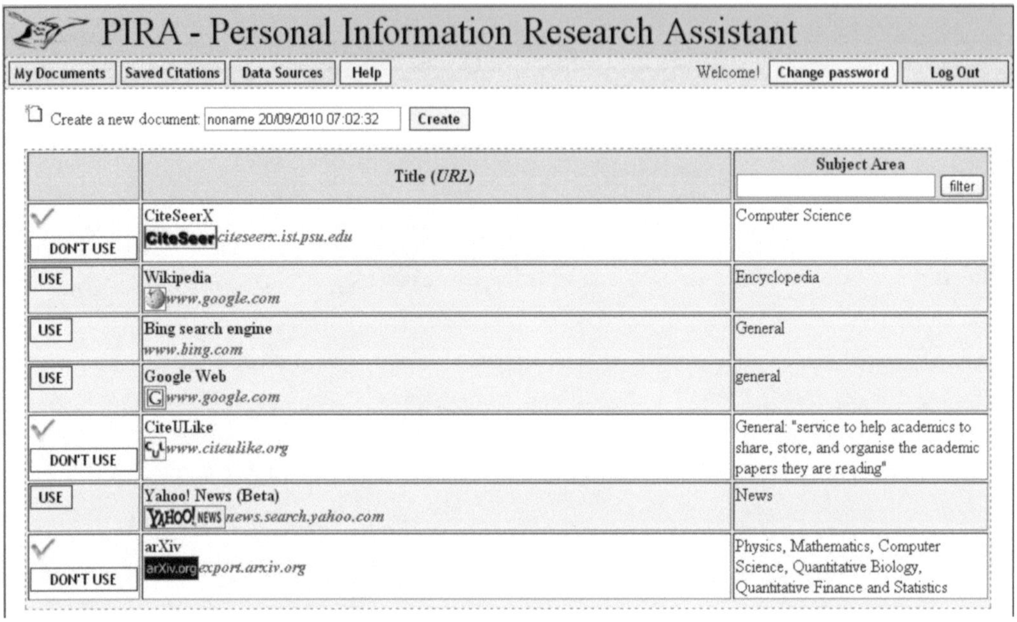

Fig. 5. Reference sources that are available in PIRA.

4. User study design

4.1 Research questions and method

In this chapter we try to address two research questions:

- Is multitasking in the context of writing and searching (as supported by PIRA) a manageable process that might be adopted and accepted by the average user?
- Is multitasking (as supported by PIRA) more effective than the more traditional approach to academic writing (first searching and then writing)?

To answer the first question, we need to identify whether users were actually engaged in the process of writing and searching in a sequential manner (one activity followed by the other) or in a more parallel manner (working on both simultaneously or frequently switching between the two). We will refer to the parallel manner as multitasking or a Write While You Search (WWYS) approach. In our analysis, we look for instances when a user was switching back and forth between writing and searching activities. We note that a user applied the WWYS approach whenever he or she consulted (e.g. accessed or saved) references suggested by PIRA in between making any changes to the text. Or, better yet, when a user actually cited any of references suggested by PIRA.

To answer the second question, we need to operationalize the effectiveness of PIRA usage. One way to do this is to conduct an assessment of reference gathering productivity. There are two parameters that can be used for this purpose: the number of references accessed by the user and the number of references saved by the user. The higher value of either of these parameters per user per session may be characterized as evidence of a higher level of effectiveness of PIRA usage. The reason we need to examine both parameters is because a user may access a relevant reference without saving it into his or her online account, or vice versa. Finally, we compare average effectiveness between users using the WWYS approach and those using the sequential model.

To answer both questions, we rely on content analysis of each user's drafts, quantitative analysis of users' interaction logs and users' responses to an online questionnaire.

4.2 Users and data collection

All participants in our study were volunteers invited at our demo sessions or by their colleagues or professors who attended our demo sessions. To become a user, a person has to create an online account with PIRA and agree to the terms of the informed consent. Participants were asked to use PIRA for their research-related writing tasks. Users could create and modify any text documents and reference collections. They could discontinue their participation at any time for any reason.

PIRA recorded users' writing, what it recommended, and what if anything users chose to do with those recommendations. After the user has used PIRA for three times, the user was asked some questions via an online questionnaire about what he or she thought about the use of PIRA, and how it might be improved. Completing this questionnaire was optional.

The log data was collected for the period of four months. During this period, our users consisted of two main groups: 11 undergraduate students in the English program and 14 graduate students in the Library and Information Science (LIS) program. On average, users in each group visited PIRA a similar number of times; 7 and 5 for undergraduate and graduate users respectively.

4.3 Data analysis

We began the analysis by identifying common approaches to writing used in PIRA by examining the content of papers and how that content changed over time. We distinguished four main writing approaches:

- **Keywords**. This approach is very similar to the way people search on the Internet. The user starts with a list of main keywords/concepts to describe a problem domain, and then modifies this list depending on the retrieved results.
- **Freewriting**. The user writes down full sentences about issues they want to address and/or statements about their prior knowledge of these issues.
- **Copy & Paste**. The user copies a chunk of pre-written text to PIRA's text editor. The chunk may range from a short paragraph to several pages.
- **Think by Writing**. The user writes down his or her thoughts when assessing the relevance of suggested references.

In addition to four common writing approaches described above, we added one new approach for the graduate students - *Proof Reading*. This approach involves only minor changes to the text, mostly to make one's writing sound better.

Tables 1 & 2 below show which approaches and in what order were used by each user. To indicate whether or not the user switches between writing and searching activities (the WWYS approach) or only was focusing on one activity at the time, we use an additional category: *Monitoring References*. If the user is engaged in *Monitoring References* this means that he or she completely stopped writing (at some point) and exclusively began interacting with some suggested search keywords and references.

Although *Copy & Paste* can be conducted in parallel with searching, we will not consider it as an indicator of the WWYS approach. This is primary because the copied text was already written prior to the session with PIRA. Similarly, we will not consider the use of the *Keywords* only approach as WWYS because this approach does not produce any coherent

Approach \ User ID	Keywrods	Freewriting	Copy & Paste	Think by Writing	Monitor References
49	#1	#2			
50		#1			
51		#1			
52		#1			
53	#2			#1	
54		#1			
58		#1			
59		#1			#2
60		#1			
67		#2	#1		
71			#1		#2

Table 1. Common writing approaches in PIRA for **undergraduate** students (each cell value indicates the order in which the particular approach occurred).

Approach \ User ID	Keywords	Freewriting	Copy & Paste	Think by Writing	Proof Reading	Monitor References
28			#1		#2	
31			#1			#2
32		#1				
33		#1				
37*	#1					#2
41		#1	#2			#2
44*		#1				#2
55	#1					#2
57*			#1			#2
62*			#1			#2
65	#1	#3		#2		
69*	#1					#2
84*		#1				#2
92			#1			#2

Table 2. Common writing approaches in PIRA for **graduate** students (each cell value indicates the order in which the particular approach occurred).

text that can be used in the future paper. However, if a user started with *Copy & Paste* or *Keywords*, but then switched to *Freewriting*, and he or she was not engaged in *Monitoring References*, then the overall user's approach can be considered as WWYS.
The following section presents results for each group separately. To ensure confidentiality, we refer to each user by a code number.

5. Results

5.1 Undergraduate students

Q1. Is multitasking in the context of writing and searching (as supported by PIRA) a manageable process that might be adopted and accepted by the average undergraduate user?
Based on the content analysis, we can conclude that the majority of undergraduate students in the study preferred to use *Freewriting* as their primary writing approach. This preference may be influenced by the fact that they are all English majors. The log data shows that as they wrote, the users were also interacting with various search features of the system such as accessing and saving relevant references. Different users were more or less involved in the use of these features. Although the majority of users accessed and read potentially relevant references as soon as they noticed them; there were two users (ID# 58 and 60) who preferred not to stop writing when they saw something interesting. Instead, they simply saved any potential relevant references to read later. (Such behavior is characterized by the much higher number of saved references than those that were accessed while in the midst of writing.) Despite these differences in reactions to potential relevant references, we can consider both types of behaviors as multitasking to some degree since both involved writing and reference assessment/gathering.
Additional evidence that multitasking as supported by PIRA was manageable can be found in the responses to the online survey. Many undergraduates expressed their support of the idea of multitasking and switching between writing and searching. As one student noticed, nowadays multitasking is part of their normal behavior on the Internet. They often do instant messaging with their online friends, browser websites, work on a class assignment, search for information, etc, simultaneously. This is a more extreme form of multitasking than the one we are referring to in this chapter - the switching between different components of the overall single goal of writing.
In general, our analysis of the current data suggests that the majority of the undergraduate users were able to successfully adopt the WWYS approach.
Q2. Is multitasking (as supported by PIRA) more effective than the more traditional approach to the academic writing (searching and then writing)?
The fact that two users, who were not engaged in the WWYS approach, accessed and saved a significantly smaller number of references compared to the group's average, may suggest that the WWYS approach is *likely* to be more productive than a more traditional approach. Unfortunately, since the majority of users preferred the WWYS approach over the other, we do not have enough data to draw a conclusion as to which of two approaches is more productive. Further testing is necessary to answer this question.

5.2 Graduate students

Q1. Is multitasking in the context of writing and searching (as supported by PIRA) a manageable process that might be adopted and accepted by the average graduate student user?

Graduate students did not multitask much (except 4 users). About half of all graduate students in the study re-used parts of their papers written elsewhere and simply pasted them into PIRA. Many other users either wrote one or two sentences stating their research topic or simply typed a few search keywords into the text editor. After this, they were mostly monitoring references. This type of behavior suggests that graduate students in our study perceived PIRA primary as a searching tool rather than a writing tool. This does not necessarily mean that multitasking was not manageable, but rather that users adopted other ways of using PIRA (to our pleasant surprise) which will be one of the subjects of our future evaluations. As with other context-aware interfaces, it is important that developers be reminded that a measure of success is not merely that the application is adopted by those users who work in the way that the developers intend, but that the application is flexible enough that alternate, even novel uses are facilitated or at least not impeded.

Q2. Is multitasking (as supported by PIRA) more effective than the more traditional approach to the academic writing (searching and then writing)?

To conduct a reliable comparison, we decided to exclude the 6 "spectators"-users from this analysis (marked with an asterisk * in Table 2). This is due to the fact that their interactions with PIRA were limited to only few minutes. As a result, it is hard to say which approach they really followed or would follow. (After a close examination of the log data and documents created by these 6 users, we came to the conclusion that these users were just checking out PIRA's functionalities.)

Among the 8 remaining users, there were 4 users (ID# 28, 32, 33, 65) who were engaged in multitasking (further referred to as Group A) and 4 users (ID# 31, 41, 55, 92) who were not (Group B). Group A accessed an average of 20 and saved an average of 13 references per user. Group B accessed an average of 8 and saved an average of only 4 references per user. In sum, users who were engaged in multitasking accessed about 2 times more and saved 3 times more references per user than those who were not. Therefore, although based on our very small sample, we would claim that in general, multitasking seems to be a more productive approach, despite the risks of distraction.

6. Conclusions and future consideration

The results from our small scale user study suggest that undergraduate users are more likely to multitask between writing and search-related activities than graduate users. The difference between two groups may be due to the difference in their tasks. Most graduate users were focusing on finding relevant references (Keywords approach) or making sure that they had already cited all relevant references (Copy & Paste approach); whereas undergraduate users were more concerned with producing coherent text. This, in turn, may be explained by many different factors such as specific requirements of the assignment, students' major and/or upcoming deadlines. However, this matter requires further investigation.

Our second conclusion is that in general those users from both groups who did use the multitasking approach demonstrated a more productive reference gathering behavior than those who did not. This can be explained from the system's point of view. Users who multitasked were often modifying their drafts. As a result, PIRA was able to suggest references that are related to newly emerged themes in the text. Furthermore, users who multitasked also interacted with suggested search keywords and references more frequently than those who did not. Since every such interaction provided PIRA with user's relevance feedback, the system was able to significantly improve the relevance of its suggestions.

PIRA enabled users to manage the information that could inform their evolving thinking, supporting that fine line between an overly narrow focus just on the resources currently on the users' mind, and the insights and balance that come from a larger perspective, but one that can lead to endless distraction.

In our future work on PIRA, we are planning to increase the size of our user sample as well as diversify its population by including students and faculty members from disciplines other than English and LIS. Also we are planning to explore other ways to measure the effectiveness of PIRA usage to consider the quality of gathered references as well as their impact on the completion of the user-specific tasks (for example, to complete a literature review versus prepare a paper outline versus come up with creative ideas).

The challenge of context-aware retrieval for supporting the web-based writing process is similar to that of the more conventional issues of planning, coordinating appointments and organizing and accessing personal files. However, it has rather different emphases. The fluid, rapid multitasking nature of the different components of web-based writing means that it is important to support low-effort context-aware information retrieval. There is also a need to support both awareness of the familiar (papers already read, issues that must be considered), as well as the unfamiliar (new papers not yet considered, possibly relevant related work, interesting inspirational insights etc.). As with much research on Digital Libraries, there is a recurrent need to help people handle complexity and diversity, and to exploit context and visibility as a way of supporting ambient rather than distractingly intrusive awareness. Finally the diversity of ways in which people accomplish complex tasks such as writing reminds us that digital libraries must accommodate a wide range of use patterns rather than forcing users to conform to an idealized mode of acting. Such diversity typically means allowing for a range of appropriation activities including combination with other resources and tailoring to fit both long term user preferences and the particular needs of the current task at hand.

7. Acknowledgements

This work was partially supported by the Social Sciences and Humanities Research Council (SSHRC) grant.

8. References

Berendt, B., Krause, B., Kolbe-Nusser, S. (2010). Intelligent scientific authoring tools: Interactive data mining for constructive uses of citation networks. *Information Processing & Management*, 46(1), 1-10.

Boardman, R. and Sasse, M.A. (2003). Too Many Hierarchies? The Daily Struggle for Control of the Work-space. *HCI International'03 International Conference on Human-Computer Interaction*, Crete, Greece.

Brockman, W.S., Newmann, L., Palmer, C.L., and Tidline, T.J., (2001). *Scholarly Work in the Humanities and the Evolving Information Environment*, Washington, DC: Digital Library Federation and Council on Library and Information Resources.

Budzik, J., Bradshaw, S., Fu, X. and Hammond, K. (2002). Supporting online resource discovery in the context of ongoing tasks with proactive software assistants. *International Journal of Human–Computer Studies*, 56 (1), 47–74.

Dumais, S., Cutrell, E., Sarin, R. and Horvitz, E. (2004). Implicit queries (IQ) for contextualized search. *Proceedings of the 27th Annual International Conference on Research and Development in Information Retrieval,* ACM Press, New York, NY, pp. 594-594.

Fister, B. (1992). The Research Processes of Undergraduate Students. *Journal of Academic Librarianship,* 18 (3), 163-169.

Gruzd, A.A. & Twidale, M.B. (2006). Write While You Search:Ambient Searching of a Digital Library in the Context of Writing. *Proceedings of the 1st International Workshop on Digital Libraries in the Context of Users' Broader Activities (DL-CUBA) at the Joint Conference on Digital Libraries(JCDL'06),* Chapel Hill, NC, USA, pp. 13-16.

Gruzd, A. and Wong, J. (2010). Blogging with CONTEXT: A context-aware information retrieval system for bloggers. *Proceedings of the 3rd Information Interaction in Context Symposium,* ACM Press, New York, NY, pp 289-292.

Jones, S. and Staveley, M.S. (1999). Phrasier: a system for interactive document retrieval using keyphrases. *Proceedings of the 22nd Annual International Conference on Research and Development in Information Retrieval,* ACM Press, New York, NY, pp. 160–167.

Kljun, M. and Carr, D. (2005). Piles of Thumbnails - Visualizing Document Management. *Proceedings of the 27th International Conference on Information Technology Interfaces (ITI2005),* Cavtat, Croatia.

Kuhlthau, C.C. (2004). *Seeking Meaning: A Process Approach to Library and Information Services.* 2nd ed., Westport, CT: Libraries Unlimited.

Lieberman, H., Fry C. and Weitzman, L. (2001). Exploring the web with reconnaissance agents. *Communications of the ACM,* 44 (8), 69–75.

Marshall, C.C. and Jones, W., (2006). Keeping Encountered Information. Commun. ACM. *Communications of the ACM,* 49(1), 66-67.

Palmer, C.L. (2005). Scholarly Work and the Shaping of Digital Access. *Journal of the American Society for Information Science and Technology,* 56(11), 1140-1153.

Powell, J.E., Collins, L.M., Martinez, M.L.B. (2009). The Fierce Urgency of Now: A Proactive, Pervasive Content Awareness Tool. *D-Lib Magazine,* 15 (5/6).

Rhodes, B. (2003). Using physical context for just-in-time information retrieval. *IEEE Transactions on Computers,* 52 (8), 1011–1014.

Ruthven, I. (2008). The context of the interface. *Proceedings of the Second International Symposium on Information Interaction in Context,* London, United Kingdom, pp. 3-5.

Toms, E.G. and McCay-Peet, L. (2009). Chance Encounters in the Digital Library. In Agosti, M., Borbinha, J., Kapidakis, S., Papatheodorou, C., Tsakonas, G. (Eds.). *Research and Advanced Technology for Digital Libraries,* Springer: Berlin / Heidelberg, 192-202.

Torrance, M., Thomas, G. V., & Robinson, E. J. (1994). The Writing Strategies of Graduate Research Students in the Social Sciences. *Higher Education,* 27 (3), 379-392.

Torrance, M., Thomas, G.V., and Robinson, E.J. (1994). The Writing Strategies of Graduate Research Students in the Social Sciences. *Higher Education,* 27 (3), 379-392.

Twidale, M.B., Gruzd, A.A. & Nichols, D.M. (2008). Writing in the Library: exploring tighter integration of digital library use with the writing process. *Information Processing & Management,* 44(2), 558-580.

Valentine, B. (1993). Undergraduate Research Behavior: Using Focus Groups to Generate Theory. *Journal of Academic Librarianship,* 19(5), 300.

Wolber, D., Kepe, M. and Ranitovic, I. (2002). Exposing document context in the personal web. *Proceedings of the 7th International Conference on Intelligent User Interfaces,* ACM Press, New York, NY, pp. 151–158.

12

Integrating Digital Libraries with Instruction: Design and Promotion of Educational Applications

Kuo Hung Huang
National Chiayi University
Taiwan

1. Introduction

Digital libraries are collections of information represented as digital text, images, audio files, video files and other media, and are gaining increasing importance in people's everyday activities due to their continuously updated contents and services. Digital libraries store great amounts of a variety of information and deliver associated services to user communities using a variety of technologies (Frias-Martinez, Magoulas, Chen, & Macredie, 2006). Although many websites provide a great deal of media including text, pictures, animation and maps, a rich assortment of media does not necessarily guarantee the valid delivery of information. In fact, most websites are structured for navigation according to the classification of materials, rather than the cognitive abilities of learners. Previous studies have reported that multimedia contents for navigation do nothing to help in the comprehension of knowledge (Eveland & Dunwoody, 2000; Nilsson & Mayer, 2002; Schwartz, Verdi, Morris, Lee, & Larson, 2007). On the contrary, learners actively organize what they read to develop their own cognitive models to maintain the internal structure of the knowledge (Ausubel, 1978). Therefore, the content structured according to users' conceptual models will be appropriate for learners of diverse backgrounds. This chapter described the experiences of designing and promoting web-based learning environments with integrated digital libraries through a sequence of projects across a number of years.

2. Digital archives project

2.1 Background

The National Digital Archives Program (NDAP), sponsored by the National Science Council of Taiwan, was launched in 2002 (NDAP, 2003). The purpose of this program is to promote and coordinate content digitization and preservation at leading museums, archives, universities, research institutes and other content holders in Taiwan.

Since 2002, the program has being digitizing Taiwan's natural treasures and cultural heritage in order to be preserved and utilized in the digital era. However, another goal of the NDAP is to promote the utilization of the digital archives. Its missions are to popularize knowledge, improve information sharing, enhance education and life-long learning, as well as to improve literacy, creativity and quality. To achieve these goals, the training and promotion division under the NDAP has started projects to integrate NDAP resources with the curriculum in elementary and high schools.

The author, also a researcher of the above projects, designed a sequence of activities to promote the application of digital archives in the educational community. In doing so, the researcher first formed teams consisting of college and graduate students and in-service teachers, as well as scholars, and then provided basic training on the topic. When handling these projects, team members were asked to browse the available resources and interact with potential users in order to implement system and determine its usefulness. The information that emerged from the interaction with people in the educational community and from the process of solving various problems made the project more complete.

2.2 Integrating GIS with digital libraries

In the information age, activities in the real world are recorded in digital forms. People tend to use space, either physical or cyber, as a framework for understanding information (National Research Council, 2006). According to geography researchers, Geographic Information System (GIS) supports contextually rich student learning by extending the ability to perform inquiries, promoting in-depth data explorations, and by giving meaning to their works. Particularly for projects in the school community, GIS can facilitate the data-to-information transition by providing the essential interpretive context that gives meaning to the data (National Research Council, 2006).

Social studies and geography are subjects that involve concepts of time and space, which must be integrated to understand the historical implications of land and culture, as well as changes in nature and humanity. Using space as a framework to understand domestic affairs helps students synthesize complex information regarding history and geography during instruction. According to Bunch and Lloyd (2006), the constructive use of maps in classrooms can promote the communication of information that is often too complex to easily express with words. With the ability to efficiently provide large amounts of visual information, mapping tools such as GIS offer new ways to present spatial information and deliver an engaging learning experience. As a tool for the presentation of location-based subject matter, GIS has helped social scientists to search for patterns and order in society and discover knowledge in cyberspace (Slocum, 1999; Sui, 2004).

Based on the aforementioned rationale, this study designed websites with GIS interfaces covering geography and digital libraries to help students interact and learn through the use of digital archives. After evaluating the available resources of digital archives and the feasibility of the projects, this study decided to use web-based GIS technologies and Flash animations to produce works useful for young students. The project was implemented in three stages: the implementation stage, the promotion stage and the enhancement stage.

3. Implementation stage: Integrating with electronic maps

3.1 Contents

Chiayi, a historical city in Taiwan, has played an important role in the past hundred years of Taiwan history. Thematic information about Chiayi includes language, history, geography, nature and arts. Data related to Chiayi City is identified in some of the archives, which consists of different types of data including images, texts, maps, drawings and sound collections. To reduce the waiting time for visualization, a client-server architecture was implemented. The front-end interface used Flash technology and the web server stored the archive data.

3.2 Design

GIS provides the users with intuitive perception through information visualization. Atlases and photos describe the landscape created by either natural processes or human activities during a period of time, annotate what happened during specific space-time conditions, and reflect the culture of a place (Summerby-Murray, 2001). Reviewing maps of the same place from different periods can assist users to rehabilitate history and understand changes in the environment, society and culture. In order to correlate unstructured information such as images, sounds, drawings and textual descriptions with spatial information, the system designed three levels of interaction to represent the complex associations: an interactive map, a time map and a hyperlinked map. There were two main user interface designs to facilitate learning.

The first component was an interactive map. Layers of maps, which are similar to GIS, were used as the information visualization technology to organize and display various kinds of information for every point on a computerized map. This involved powerful, complex computer databases that organized information around a specific location (see Fig. 1). Users could select a thematic representation or an automatic combination of layers of maps. The thematic representation was selected and tested as a better view to comprehend the information about a specific topic about Chiayi (see Fig. 2).

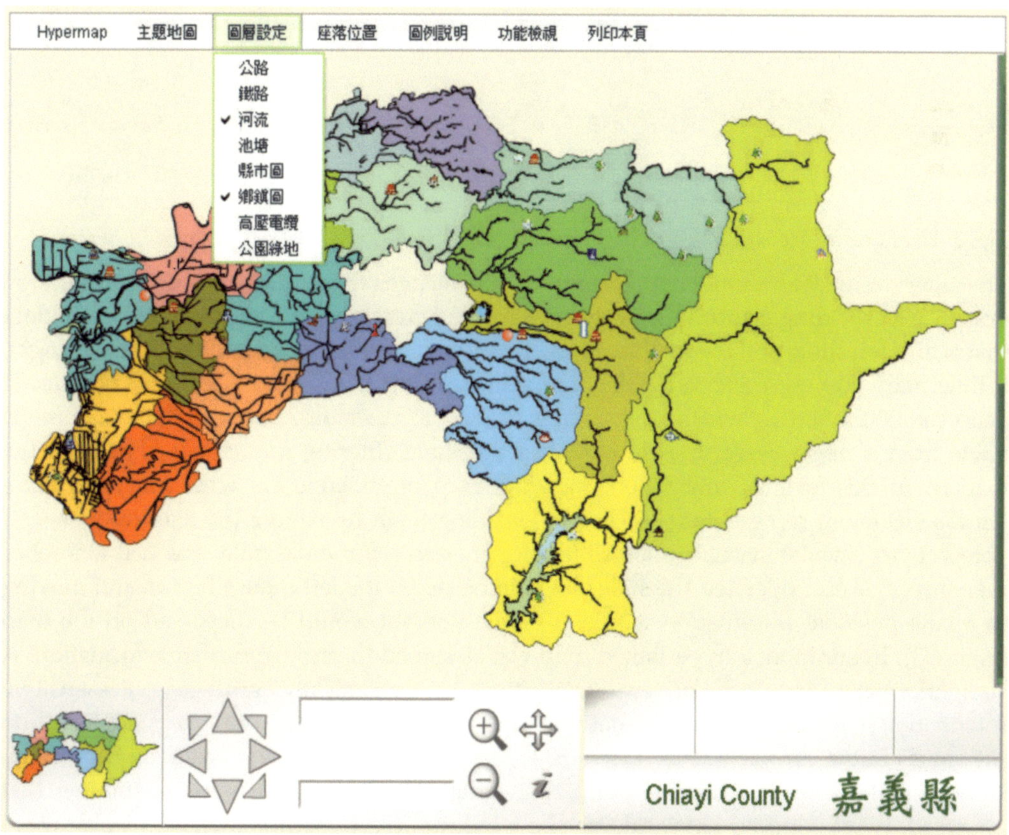

Fig. 1. Users can zoom, move and select different map layers

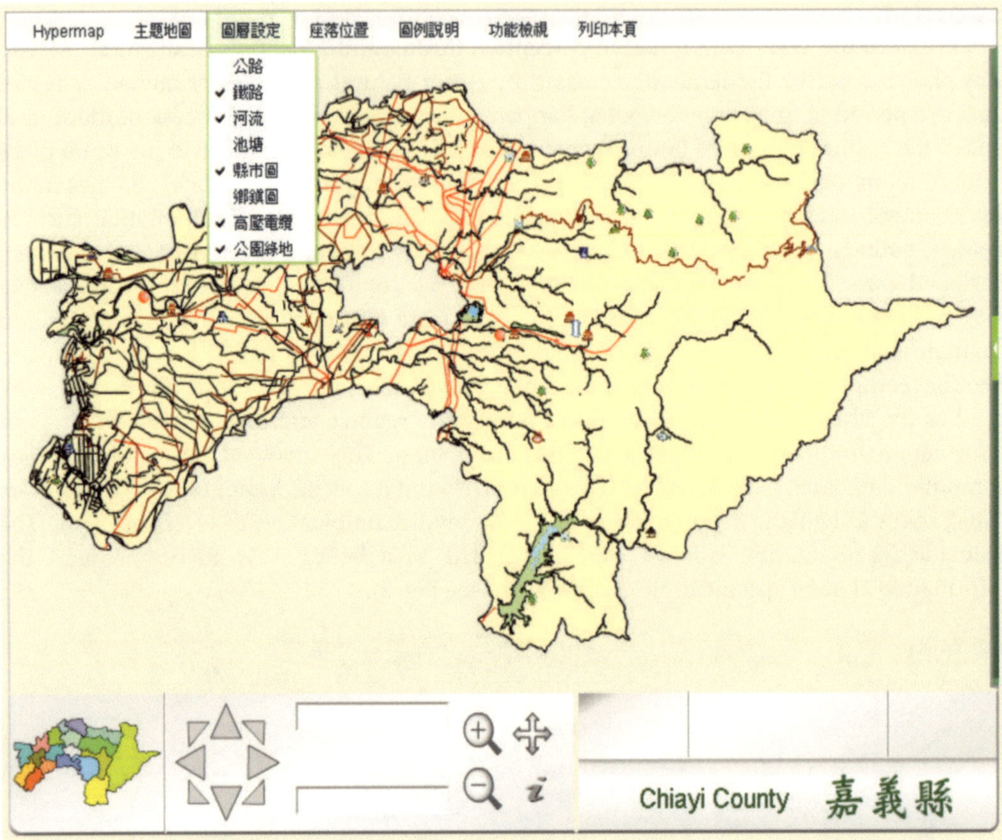

Fig. 2. Users can select map layers to obtain a better view about a specific topic

The other design was a time map. Three major challenges for a time-series data exploration system are providing algorithms for the analysis and creation of metadata, filtering out data that is uninteresting, and the interactive exploration of the regions of interest. In this project, a time map was used a tool to filter out uninteresting data (Grady, Flanery, Donato, & Schryver, 2002). Sliders, which are a generic user input mechanism for specifying a numeric value from a range, were used to control a threshold filtering the entities shown on the display. In this level of interaction, the time map provided users with a tool to move between different representations, thereby enabling them to explore the data from several perspectives. The data visualization slider, designed as a chronicle scale, was tied to a set of map layers. A user operated the slider by holding down the left mouse button and moving to a new position. Information within the time interval would be displayed on the map (Figure 3). In addition, a hyperlinked map was designed to retrieve further information. A straightforward approach of enabling users to dynamically retrieve time-sensitive information is to link further information to the entities distributed over the map, based on the values in the chronicle field (Risch, et al., 1997). Users were able to click on each entity shown on the map and retrieve additional information through a pop-up window that appeared. By clicking on keywords on the windows, the hyperlinks would display more information stored in the original archives (Figure 4).

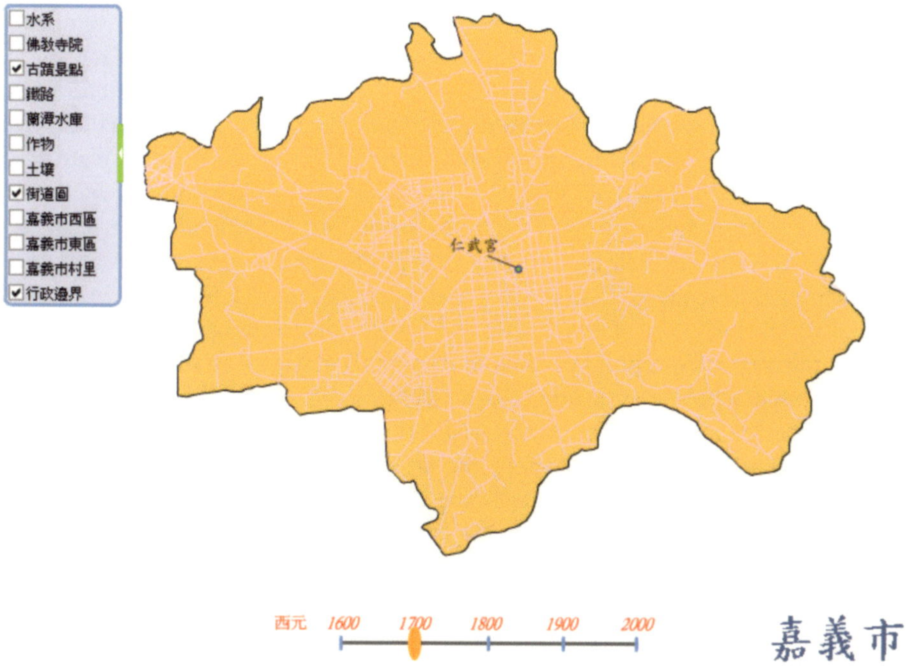

Fig. 3. The slider sets the calendar year and related information is shown.

Fig. 4. A pop-up window and hyperlinks retrieve information.

3.3 Instruction and evaluation

To evaluate the effects of these learning environments, two empirical studies were conducted in two elementary schools respectively (see Figure 5). In the first study, the subjects were 32 fourth-grade students. The teacher integrated the electronic map and digital archives with classroom instruction. The achievement test after instruction showed that the students performed significantly better than those under traditional instruction. In the second study, project-based learning activities were arranged to collect qualitative data for assessment. After becoming familiar with the resources, the students were divided into several groups to complete their own project. The project for each group was to construct a thematic map based on the electronic map and digital resources. Students in each group participated in the activities of discussing the theme, distributing tasks, collecting data, constructing the map and preparing a slide to present their works. Analysis showed that the students possessed a positive attitude toward using digital libraries for constructing their own presentation. In addition, the teacher was convinced of the educational advantages of using digital archives. Through watching the students working together as a team, she realized that the digital archives were playing the role of mediating the students' active learning. In addition to factual knowledge, the students also learned by doing.

Fig. 5. Two teachers using digital libraries in classroom instruction

4. Promotion stage: Additional media and workshops

4.1 Extension and promotion

The successful experience encouraged the research team to promote additional learning resources. Resources on Chiayi City and Chiayi County were developed in the previous stage. However, there are 16 cities or counties in Taiwan. The research team utilized the same design pattern to create resources on the other 14 cities or counties (see Figure 6). Later, several training workshops were held to train teachers how to use the digital libraries. These teachers were first introduced to the concept of digital libraries and their educational applications. Then, the speaker demonstrated how to use a web-based interactive map to retrieve resources related to the curriculum. At the end of the workshops, questionnaires were dispatched to assess their impressions and intention to use these materials. Table 1 shows the workshop attendants' positive attitude toward these materials.

Fig. 6. Users can choose specific cities in Taiwan when accessing the digital library.

Items	Strongly agree	agree	neutral	disagree	Strongly disagree
This web-site is well designed	12	26	3	0	0
This website will help to comprehend the contents	22	15	4	0	0
You will use this website in your instruction	13	23	4	1	0

Table 1. Workshop attendants' attitude toward the developed materials (N=41)

4.2 Follow-up evaluation

Six months after the workshops, the research team interviewed the attendants on the phone to understand the status of their digital library utilization. Surprisingly, none of the interviewees actually used these resources in the classroom. The major reason for not using these media was a lack of time. Since the textbooks used in the classroom were not city-oriented, teachers had to spend time retrieving related information for certain cities. Teachers were too busy to re-organize these materials for instruction. If the resources could be designed as independent components according to the concepts in the textbooks, teachers could easily select related media and assemble them as teaching resources.

5. Enhancement stage: Revision for teachers' needs

In light of the importance of providing easy access to media for instruction, the research team selected themes on domestic geography in the social studies curriculum as the teaching content and designed computer animations as the instructional media to foster teachers' interests in integrating technology with classroom instruction. There were two major enhancements: one was to organize the resources into the structure of the textbooks, and the other was to organize the resources into themes.

5.1 Resources in textbook structure

The goal at this stage was to bridge the gap of expected usability between the instruction material developers and the practicing teachers. From the perspective of the teachers, integrating the GIS and digital archives with the existing curriculum as packages would help teachers to use these instruction materials. The tasks of this project included selecting related units in the textbooks, searching for useful resources in the digital archives, and then designing instruction plans and digital resources. Table 2 shows the selected units and the associated media.

School year	Unit Name	Number of Lessons	Media
Grade Four	Name and location of hometown	3	Interactive maps
	Natural environment and living of hometown	2	animations
	Development of hometown	2	animations
	Festivals and folk cultural activities in hometown	2	Video clips
	Unique sights and products in hometown	2	pictures
	Tours around hometown	2	maps
Grade Five	Where is Taiwan	2	maps
	Natural environment of Taiwan	3	Satellite images
	Resources in Taiwan	2	pictures
	Population and change of towns	2	Interactive maps
	Area and traffic	3	Interactive maps
	Care for Taiwan	2	pictures
Grade Seven	Environment of Taiwan	6	pictures
	History of Taiwan	6	animations

Table 2. Textbook units selected for media development

5.2 Resources in theme structure

The themes related to geographic subject content in the elementary and junior high school social studies curriculum were associated with the topics of population, economy, settlement and traffic, as well as regional development and environmental protection. With the combination of texts, pictures, digital maps, simulated animations and games, these e-learning resources supported teachers in constructing a learning environment to engage students in learning and discussion. Animated simulations were used to illustrate abstract concepts. For example, an animation with different phases of urbanization aroused students' feelings towards various environments, and provided students with a context to share their experiences (see Fig. 7). This was helpful for teachers to explain the process of how a settlement develops in the suburbs. As Brookfield (1987) pointed out, the process of internally examining and exploring an issue of concern, when triggered by a relevant experience, creates and clarifies meaning in terms of self and results in a changed conceptual perspective.

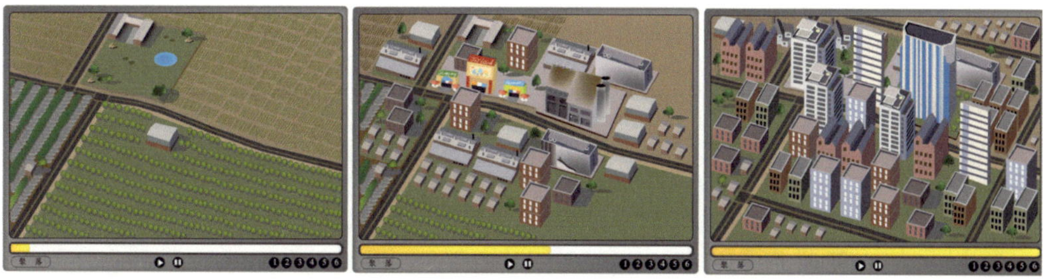

Fig. 7. Simulation of the urbanization process. From left to right: Phase 1, 3 and 6.

Thematic maps were used for cross-referencing to create meaningful learning. Animations provided cross references associated with a particular topic, to encourage students to reason and seek evidence for arguments. To develop their critical perspective, students need to reason within various points of view and use evidence in order to draw conclusions, make decisions or seek solutions. For example, to answer why the intensive construction of traffic infrastructure was needed on the west coast, a link to a population distribution map and a traffic network map provided evidence for reasoning (see Fig. 8). In addition, statistical data could be converted into a graphical form to facilitate comprehension (see Fig. 9).

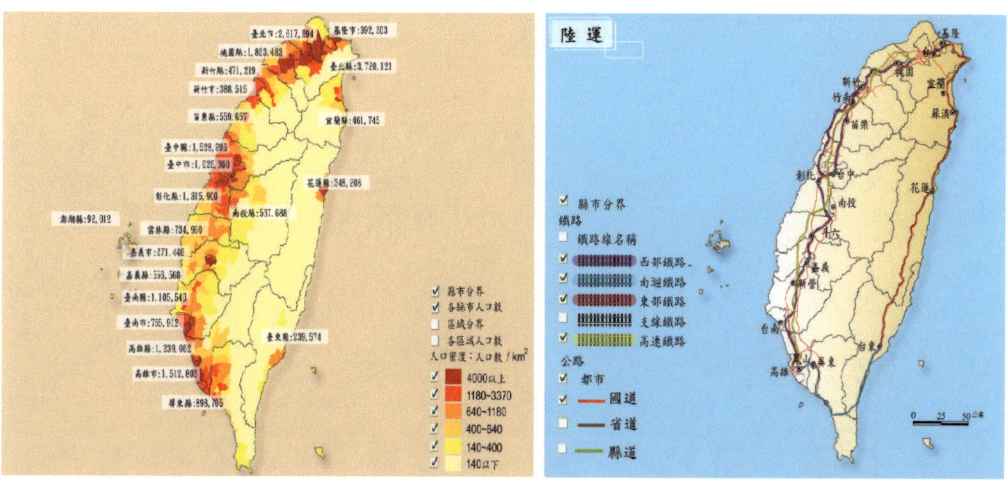

Fig. 8. Maps referencing traffic issues. The left is the population distribution and the right is the traffic network.

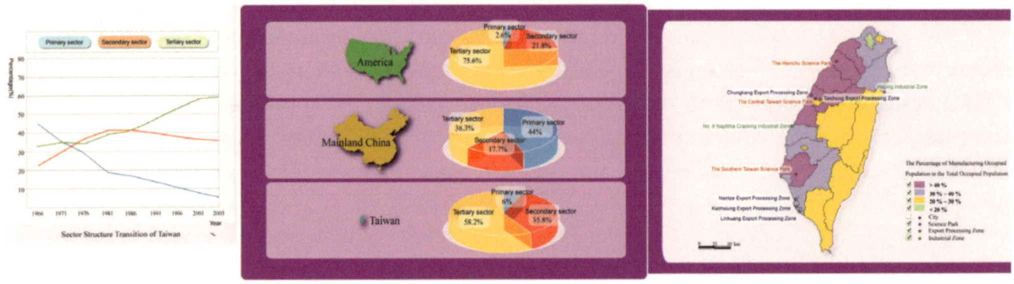

Fig. 9. Visualization of economic transition and distribution of industrial parks

6. Future works

The future work is to develop digital media and activities on interactive whiteboards based on the digital archive resources. The research team will first search and organize the resources in the digital archive project, and then integrate in a spatial concept with touch-control operations to design efficient instructional activities and media. For example, as shown in Fig. 10, an interactive tool for settlement planning was developed for students to practice their urban design. Using drag and drop operations, students arranged constructions such as buildings or airports according to their ideal locations to build a village or city. Students' works were then be presented and evaluated by classmates. Students with diversified backgrounds and values designed cities with a variety of features and functionalities. The teacher used challenging questions to inspire students to respond, expand and develop the topics during critical-talk lessons. In addition, an interactive quiz to compare traffic infrastructure was used to attract students' attention and efforts on reaching consensus (see Fig. 11). According to Moon (2008), peer assessment provides practice in making judgments on the basis of evidence. The act of assessing the work of another is a matter of making a judgment. It more deeply involves learners in the process of meta-cognitive critical thinking skills.

Fig. 10. Settlement designs by two students.

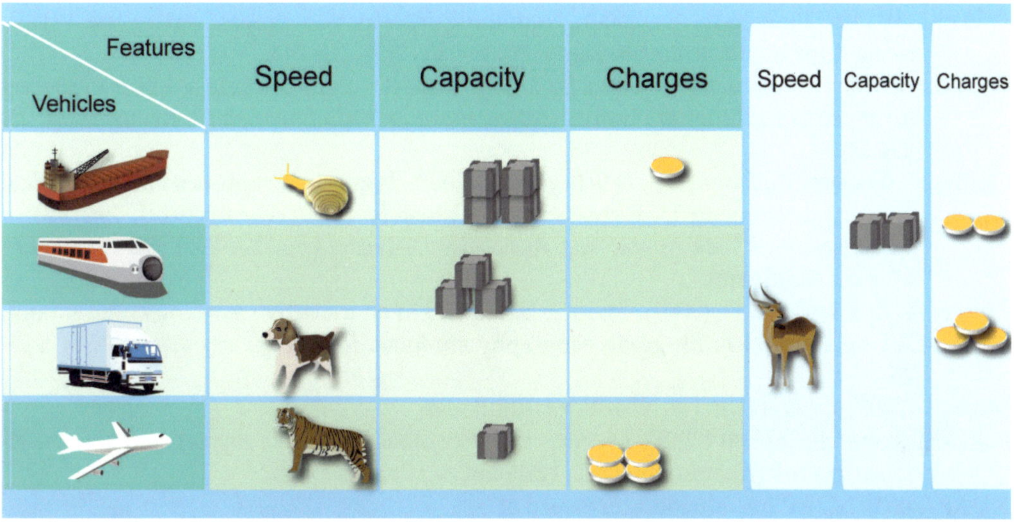

Fig. 11. Interactive matching quiz partly completed by a student

7. Conclusions

Web-based instruction is known for its media-rich online environment, providing users access to remote resources for self-paced learning. Although a number of schools have designed educational websites to integrate in-classroom learning activities with the school curriculum, designing effective learning resources based on sound educational theory will encourage students and teachers to use them more often.

Constructivist educational models are based on the theory that instead of being passive receivers of information, learners should be active explorers of their own understandings. Teachers and technology merely serve as mediators or guides to support the development of learners. Several researchers have treated technology as a vehicle to foster active learning and believe that such learning environments motivate and facilitate the acquisition of knowledge by providing an intuitively comprehensible context (Milson & Earle, 2007; Papert, 1980; Piburn, Reynolds, MacAuliffe, Leedy, & Birk, 2005).

The prevalence of computer usage in schools is driving the need to understand its effects on learning when technology is integrated within instruction. The experiences of this project addressed the needs of teachers to enhance students' geographical knowledge through the use of GIS-based resources. Such knowledge is a useful reference when examining issues related to educational practices using digital libraries.

8. References

Ausubel, D. P. (1978). *Educational Psychology: A Cognitive View*. New York: Holt McDougal.

Brookfield, S. (1987). *Developing critical thinkers: Challenging adults to explore alternative ways of thinking and acting*. San Francisco: Jossey-Bass.

Bunch, R. L., & Lloyd, R. E. (2006). The cognitive load of geographic information. *The Professional Geographer, 58*(2), 209-220.

Eveland, W., & Dunwoody, S. (2000). Examining information processing on the WWW using think aloud protocols. *Media Psychology, 2*(3), 219-244.

Frias-Martinez, E., Magoulas, G., Chen, S., & Macredie, R. (2006). Automated user modeling for personalized digital libraries. *International Journal of Information Management, 26*, 234-248.

Grady, N., Flanery, R., Donato, J., & Schryver, J. (2002). Issues in time-series and categorical data exploration. In U. Fayyad, G. G. Grinstein & A. Wierse (Eds.), *Information Visualization in Data Mining and Knowledge Discovery* (pp. 229-235). San Francisco: Morgan Kaufmann.

Milson, A. J., & Earle, B. D. (2007). Internet-based GIS in an inductive learning environment: A case study of ninth-grade geography students. *Journal of Geography, 106*(6), 227-237.

Moon, J. (2008). *Critical thinking*. New York: Routledge.

National Research Council (2006). *Learning to think spatially: GIS as a support system in the K-12 curriculum*. Washington D.C.: National Academies Press.

NDAP (2003). NDAP Introduction, Accessed at http://www.ndap.org.tw/1_org_en/introduction.php

Nilsson, R. M., & Mayer, R. E. (2002). The effects of graphics organizers giving cues to the structure of a hypertext document on users' navigation strategies and performance. *International Journal of Human-Computer Studies, 57*, 1-26.

Papert, S. (1980). *Mindstorms*. London: Harvester Wheatsheaf.

Piburn, M. D., Reynolds, S. J., MacAuliffe, C., Leedy, D. E., & Birk, J., P. (2005). The role of visualization in learning from computer-based images. *International Journal of Science Education, 27*(5), 513-527.

Risch, S., Rex, D. B., Dowson, S. T., Walters, T. B., May, R. A., & Moon, B. D. (1997). The STARLIGHT information visualization on system. *Proceedings of the IEEE Conference on Information Visualization*, 42-49.

Schwartz, N. H., Verdi, M. P., Morris, T. D., Lee, T. R., & Larson, N. K. (2007). Navigating web-based environments: Differentiating internal spatial representations from external spatial displays. *Contemporary Educational Psychology, 32*(4), 551-568.

Slocum, T. (1999). *Thematic Cartography and Visualization*. Upper Saddle River, NJ: Prentice Hall.

Sui, D. Z. (2004). GIS, Cartography, and the ?黴hird Culture?? Geographic Imaginations in the Computer Age. *Professional Geographer, 56*(1), 62-72.

Summerby-Murray, R. (2001). Analysing heritage landscapes with historical GIS: Contributions from problem-based inquiry and constructivist pedagogy. *Journal of Geography in Higher Education, 25*(1), 37-52.